THE NATIONAL BANK OF COMMERCE of Seattle,

1889-1969

THE NATIONAL BANK OF COMMERCE of Seattle, 1889-1969

Territorial to Worldwide Banking in Eighty Years, Including the Story of the Marine Bancorporation

ELLIOT MARPLE & BRUCE H. OLSON

PACIFIC BOOKS, PUBLISHERS/PALO ALTO, CALIFORNIA

International Standard Book Number 0–87015–189–4

Library of Congress Catalog Card Number 72–134228

Printed and bound in the United States of America

Designed and illustrated by Nicholas T. Kritikos

PACIFIC BOOKS, PUBLISHERS / P. O. BOX 558, PALO ALTO, CALIFORNIA 94302

FOREWORD

As the years go by, the events that are the fabric of corporate history are easily forgotten. This book has been written in an effort to record some of those events as they relate to the early years of the National Bank of Commerce of Seattle and of the Marine Bancorporation. The book also records the particular contributions to those organizations of four men—the first four leaders of the Bank. The story of the Bank and the Bancorporation is told against the background of the economic development of the area they serve—the Puget Sound country and the Pacific Northwest.

In 1969, the bank celebrated its 80th anniversary. Many interviews were conducted during the book's preparation with people who were among the bank's very early customers or were directly related to or well acquainted with the early officers of the bank. Documents written by the founder of the bank and his associates during its formative years, and articles and advertisements of the time provided further substance from which the authors were able to reconstruct much of the thinking that led to the founding and growth of the bank.

When the National Bank of Commerce was 38 years old, it became the cornerstone of Marine Bancorporation, one of the earliest bank holding companies. Founded and headquartered in Seattle and controlled by citizens of the Pacific Northwest, Marine Bancorporation has grown at a rate that has paralleled that of the bank. Very recently the corporate structure of the parent company was reorganized and a step toward diversification was taken. That begins a new story, which may be written some years hence.

We were pleased that Elliot Marple and Bruce H. Olson were willing to undertake the challenge of chronicling the growth of a financial enterprise from the frontier economy of 1889 to the jet age economy of 1969. Mr. Marple concentrated his efforts on the bank's history while Professor Olson did the research into the founding and growth of the Marine Bancorporation. Both men had free access to the people and documents they needed for their work. They have not been asked to eliminate or change any material of substance. The result is intended to be an objective story of what has become one of the major financial organizations of the Pacific Coast. The narrative and related statistical detail carry through 1969, the bank's eightieth year.

The book will appeal to a broad group of readers, and it is hoped, it will lead to a better understanding of the role of a large and strong commercial bank in our region's economy. Perhaps it will even encourage some young men and women to pursue banking as a career as did Robert R. Spencer, founder of the National Bank of Commerce, and his successors, Manson Backus, Andrew Price, and Maxwell Carlson, each of whom has left his mark on the organization.

ANDREW PRICE, JR.

CONTENTS

ILLUSTRATIONS

THE NATIONAL BANK OF COMMERCE of Seattle,

1889-1969

"I *want an institution*

that will ride any financial storm, no matter how hard

it blows and it is the only kind I would have

anything to do with"—Robert R. Spencer, founder of the

National Bank of Commerce of Seattle, in a letter

November 29, 1888, detailing his plans.

P A R T   I

ROBERT R. SPENCER/ A State and a Bank Are Born

On a mild autumn day in October 1888, a quiet, intensive man of 34, a little more than a week out of Iowa, arrived in Seattle on a tour of inspection to learn for himself what the business prospects were in the bubbling young city.

He looked into the stores and talked with merchants. He called on every bank. He tramped the waterfront, studied the ships of sail and steam, and watched their loading to learn what cargoes they carried. He climbed the steep hill back of the city to look over the construction of new residences. He visited the rival city of Tacoma.

Everywhere he went he sought answers to the central questions: What of the future of this city? How do its prospects compare with those of other new cities in the West? How are the banks doing? And most important of all, is there room for another?

His name was Robert R. Spencer. A banker from Iowa City on his first trip to the West Coast, he was a tightly knit man with dark hair, black eyebrows, and moustache. His inquisitive mind was more given to asking questions than expressing his own views. Henry Broderick, who first met him several years later, recalled some sixty years afterward: "Once you saw him you would remember him." [1]

Spencer came from a prominent family. His father, Oliver M. Spencer, was the third president of the State University of Iowa and later served as U.S. consul at Genoa, Italy, and consul-general at Melbourne, Australia. Robert returned from Genoa at the age of 17 to enter the State University of Iowa. To help support himself he got part-time work at the Johnson County Savings Bank in Iowa City. After three years at the university, Spencer left to take full-time work at the bank and to marry. At the age of 23 he became cashier and as such, manager of the bank.

After eleven years as cashier Spencer grew restless. He had built a solid reputation among bankers in the area but he did not see much chance to grow. His mind turned to the Pacific Northwest, then being opened by the new transcontinental railroads.

"I want to get away from this little place," he told his wife. "It's not going to progress. I want to go out West." [2]

To a friend in Iowa City Spencer said, "Here everything is overdone and there is apparently but little chance for profitable enterprise and investment which I hope to meet in a newer country." [3]

With characteristic thoroughness Spencer prepared months ahead for the tour of inspection, as he called his western trip. He combed through the magazine *West Shore* and wrote to advertisers in Tacoma and Seattle who offered descriptive material. He asked the postmasters in Spokane Falls (as Spokane was then known), Tacoma, and Seattle to send him "the name of some gentleman of known standing and having the confidence of the citizens and not engaged in the banking business." [4] To the contacts thus established he wrote asking "as to the advisability of starting another bank in your city."

Of each letter, written in a clear, strong hand, he kept a copy by pressing the letter with a moist cloth in a book of tissue sheets. Enough of the ink was transferred from the original to leave a legible reproduction on tissue bound in a single, convenient volume.

By coincidence Spencer's younger brother, Oliver Ames Spencer, was visiting in Denver in the summer of 1888 before returning to Melbourne, where he ran an export business. Robert used Oliver, on his trip back to Melbourne, as an advance man to look over various cities of the West. If a new bank was formed, Ollie agreed to join the project.

In June Robert sent Ollie $120 for expenses, together with the names of contacts Robert had developed, and a torrent of directions:

Tacoma, Seattle and Spokane Falls seem to present the most attractions. If possible, ascertain the amount of deposit in the different towns mentioned, the amount of interest paid on time (demand, if any) deposits and the amount of profits made by the banks . . . Notice particularly the condition of the farmers and whether their numbers are considerable. Ascertain the rate of interest paid on 30, 60 and 90 day paper secured by collateral, chattel mortgage or personal indorsement and rate on real estate loans, long time . . . *keep me posted.*[5]

How much detail Ollie was able to ferret out and what conclusion he reached as to the cities of greatest opportunity are matters now lost. But Robert wanted more information before he would risk his own career and the capital of others in a new banking venture. Early in October 1888, Spencer set out on the Northern Pacific Railroad. His first stopover was at Spokane Falls, which was renamed Spokane in 1890. He called this "our first resting place," a phrase that suggests something of the hardship of early-day transcontinental transportation. He was impressed with Spokane Falls as "a very live pushing city and one that is bound to grow, a place where the banks are coining money." [6]

Then he turned south through the rich Palouse Valley and thought "it everything claimed for it." Farther south in Walla Walla, Spencer had hoped to talk to two men with whom he had been in touch by mail, Philip Ritz, for whom Ritzville, Washington, was named, and Levi Ankeny, president of the First National Bank of Walla Walla, but he missed both men.

Spencer continued by steamer and portage down the Columbia River to Portland, a section of the trip that he had laid out well in advance, apparently so that he might let his Iowa eyes delight in the majesty of the already famous Columbia Gorge. Then he turned north, traveled by train as far as Tacoma, and took a steamer 35 miles farther to Seattle.

Most of the latter half of October Spencer spent at Seattle. He

Spencer kept a book of tissue copies of his letters. Here in 1888, in a characteristically firm hand, he wrote of "going west on a tour of inspection."

also looked over Tacoma, booming as the terminus of the Northern
Pacific. His earlier correspondence, however, had brought out
that Tacoma already had six banks, a seventh was being organized,
an eighth was in the talking stage, and he felt the opportunities
there were pretty well taken up. From Seattle he also made an
excursion north to Victoria, B.C.

In the Puget Sound country, and particularly at Seattle, Spencer
obviously liked what he saw—the harvesting and shipping of
products of forests, mines, farms, and fisheries; the horizons of a
busy world port; and the hustle and drive of the new settlers. A
little later he was to quote from the report of a Seattle resident:
"The fourteen mills run night and day and cannot supply the demand for lumber right here in the city. Blacksmiths work by electric light away into the night. A new cable line is being constructed
and work never stops. The electric line is being constructed in
the same way."

The weekly summary of ocean vessels loading on Puget Sound
—sailing ships with great masts towering over the waterfront and
steamships with dirty plumes of coal smoke—whispered of distant
markets. The October 28th report, for example, listed 8 vessels in
the coal fleet, 32 in the lumber fleet, 4 hauling wheat, and 4 in
miscellaneous offshore service. The lumber fleet was loading for
San Francisco, Hong Kong, Melbourne, Montevideo, Valparaiso, and
sometimes even for Boston via the Straits of Magellan. Coal
moved in shiploads every week to California, where oil was yet to
be discovered.

The harvest pouring in from farms of the territory told of
wealth waiting to be drawn from rich virgin soils. Wheat from the
interior moved over the Northern Pacific to Tacoma and thence to
world markets. Dairying supplied local markets. Late in October
the first complete trainload of hops rumbled east routed direct to
New York. The first train had 16 cars, the next 21.[7] By present
standards the trains were short and the cars small, but who in
1888 could miss the point that buyers in New York, and even
London, were reaching for the products of this new country?

Spencer's eyes were on the prospects for growth. His reports
said nothing of the irritations inevitable in a booming pioneer
town. One of those irritations at the start of the fall rains was mud.

October 1888 was mild but wet. Temperatures recorded at Port
Blakely, the bustling lumber center on Bainbridge Island within

Seattle in 1882. Henry Yesler's first sawmill appears at extreme left on the waterfront at the foot of the present Yesler Way. Just right of the mill lies the business district. (Photo from Thomas W. Prosch Albums, University of Washington.)

view of Seattle, and the only weather station on Puget Sound, averaged the warmest in ten years. Rainfall was heavier than normal. By the end of October the daily *Post-Intelligencer* reported: "The mud on Washington Street is becoming a serious impediment to travel and property owners are criticizing the City Council for not ordering the street planked from Commercial Street to South Fourth. South Second and South Third Streets also need planking for their full length." [8]

Rain or no, the town was bursting with construction of houses, stores, and business blocks. Land prices were increasing rapidly. Typical of the news when Spencer was visiting Seattle was the report in the *Post-Intelligencer*, under the heading, "Doubled in Value," that Captain David Gilmore had been offered $100,000 for two lots on Front Street (now First Avenue) at the foot of University Street, which he had bought a short time before from A. A. Denny for $50,000. Wood & Osborne's monthly report on real estate transactions placed total sales during the first ten months of 1888 at $22,872,000, almost nine times the volume in the same period a year earlier.

Spencer was fascinated with the city and stayed so long that he had to hurry the rest of his trip. He took a steamer from Portland to San Francisco, spent a day there—undoubtedly getting fresh perspective on the cities to the north—made a quick visit to a cousin in San Diego who might put capital into a new bank, and returned home "safe and sound with a bad cold." [9]

The first day back Spencer had his hands full catching up at the savings bank, but the second day he began working on his plans. Two weeks later in a letter headed "Turkey Day, November 29, 1888," he took time to write a long report to his brother in Australia and to apologize for the delay because, he said, "I have been working like a horse since my return."

On the choice of a city for a bank, Spencer explained:

After carefully looking over the situation in the various cities along my route I had no difficulty in arriving at the conclusion that for a large corporation, Seattle is the place. With its large resources of iron, coal and lumber, splendid harbor and intelligent wide-awake citizens it is bound in my judgment to double in population and triple in wealth in the next five years. Already there is a stream of immigration flowing in that promises in spring to become a flood.

The center of downtown Seattle as Robert Spencer saw it in 1888, looking north on Front Street (now First Avenue) at the intersection of Main Street. The large wooden building at the left is the New England Hotel; at right, Squire Opera House. (Prosch Albums.)

The same feeling was expressed to H. S. Garretson, a banker in Sioux City: "Seattle, I think, from the amount of attention it is now receiving from the general public and backed as it is by wonderful resources, is bound to enjoy a very large portion of the prosperity which it is evident to me is in store for the Territory." [10]

There was room, too, for a bank. Spencer told his brother that Seattle had a total of only $750,000 in bank capital, "really not one half what it would in my judgment support." He had obtained financial statements from 13 banks in the Territory. Only one, he said, "was paying less than 20 per cent on its capital stock, some as high as 40 per cent, and one had made $508,000 on $100,000 of capital in 10 years." Spencer was satisfied that "a bank conservatively managed will pay 15 to 18 per cent, and without taking any risks."

Spencer knew that in a new section opening up as fast as Washington Territory he would have to move fast. He had remarked earlier that once he had selected the city he would be "compelled to act promptly as an opening today is occupied tomorrow." The task now was to raise the capital, to find men in Iowa and in Washington who would buy enough stock to start a new bank. The task would be made easier by the burst of growth that had caught Seattle up and by the attention that this corner of the country was capturing in older and wealthier parts of the nation.

Seattle in 1888 and 1889 was well along in the transition that changed it from a frontier settlement to a world port, a base for manufacturing, and a financial and trading center for a wide area.

The coming of railroads was a major factor in this transition. For several years transcontinental trains had been running into Portland, an older and much larger city. But the shortest connection to Seattle was by boat from Portland to Kalama, Washington, on the Columbia River, then by Northern Pacific to Tacoma, and finally by boat to Seattle—a cumbersome route that made all of Puget Sound secondary to Portland.

The Northern Pacific opened the 110 miles between Tacoma and Kalama in 1873. Ten years later, driving westward from St. Paul, the Northern Pacific completed its line across the Rockies. In 1888 it punched the Stampede Tunnel through the Cascade Mountains and extended its ribbon of steel from St. Paul to Tacoma, and in 1890 picked up a connecting line that eager Seattle leaders had started.

15

The Canadian Pacific in 1885 completed the difficult route across the Rockies to Vancouver, British Columbia. In 1891 a line was completed from Seattle north to Bellingham and Vancouver, British Columbia. Other lines ran to coal mines east of Seattle and Tacoma, and a branch was soon to extend to Grays Harbor. When Washington became a state in 1889, it boasted 1,475 miles of track. In 1893 the Great Northern brought its transcontinental line into Seattle.

Restless steamers hustled passengers and freight between new cities on Puget Sound and connected with the railroads. R. L. Polk's *Seattle Directory* of 1889 reported a Puget Sound fleet of 87 steamboats. Daily schedules linked Seattle, Tacoma, and Olympia, and the two-hour boat run between Seattle and Tacoma was for many years one of the pleasantest excursions on the Sound. Other boats offered services to Everett, Stanwood, Mount Vernon, Port Blakely, Port Gamble, Port Townsend, and numerous lesser communities. Puget Sound became a fast, broad highway that linked every settlement on its shores.

The opening of transcontinental rail connections turned the nation's eyes to the new lands of the Far West. W. H. Ruffner, Virginia educator and consulting geologist, commissioned by the Seattle, Lake Shore & Eastern Railway to present in book form an account of the resources and means of transportation in Washington Territory, wrote in 1889: "The fact seems suddenly to have burst upon the country at large that here, in this neglected corner, is a wide region offering perhaps the richest inducements to immigration of any part of the United States." [1]

As soon as the transcontinental railroads extended their tracks into new and unpopulated sections, they began advertising in older parts of the country and in Europe to attract settlers. By this means, the lines built agriculture and industry, whose products, in time, would move by rail. For a number of years both the Northern Pacific and the Great Northern operated colonization offices in Europe.

The fame of the Puget Sound country spread, and sometimes took on extra luster in the telling. The renowned Massachusetts senator, George Frisbie Hoar, recognizing that many who settled in Puget Sound carried a New England heritage, said in a speech in Boston in 1889:

It is difficult to imagine what must be the destiny of that wonderful region, unsurpassed on this earth for the fertility of its soil, and with a climate where it seems impossible that human life should come to an end, if the ordinary laws of health should be observed, and with a stimulating atmosphere where brain and body are at their best.[2]

The lush forests, the abundant fisheries, the outcropping of minerals, and the mild climate combined to give this region great prospects. The virgin soil, particularly in the valley bottoms, yielded big crops. It would take time to learn the limitations—of some soils best left to raising timber and of minerals that lacked sufficient reserves or quality for commercial development.

Even prosaic government reports picked up the fever of the new country. Along with heavy statistical detail, for example, the U.S. Treasury Department's *Report of the Internal Commerce of the United States* for 1890, in a section by Clarence M. Barton, "U.S. Treasury expert at Olympia," set out:

The average yield per acre of wheat, oats, barley, rye, and vegetables can not be surpassed in any portion of the United States . . . . Farmers are wanted badly to furnish Tacoma as well as Seattle with farm products. While the soil is enormously productive, there are not yet farmers enough to furnish the food products for the markets.[3]

The Treasury Report listed the Port Blakely mill, rebuilt after a fire, as "the largest mill on the Pacific Coast." Plants cutting lumber at Port Blakely, Port Gamble, and Port Madison "were all small affairs at first, but are now the great mills of Puget Sound, and the owners among the wealthiest men on the Pacific Coast." [4]

The five principal exports, the report noted, were lumber, coal, fish, hops, and wheat.

Lumber was the cornerstone of the new economy. In 1889 Washington sawmills cut almost 1.2 billion board feet of lumber, equal to more than one-fourth of today's output. Some of the lumber, of course, was used within sound of the sawmill whistle to build houses, stores, and other structures for a fast-expanding population. A substantial volume went to California, where San Francisco was a big market, and to the Orient. Cyrus Walker of Puget Mill Co., Port Ludlow, wrote at this time: "It is safe to say that the lumber market of the Sound may be considered to be all countries and ports on the Pacific Ocean." [5] Later, as the mills of the upper

Midwest began to run out of timber, the new transcontinental railroads carried increasing quantities of Washington lumber eastward.

The *Seattle Directory* of 1890 called lumber "the most important of Seattle's interests." In just two years the number of mills increased from 8 to 20 and the number of lumber millhands tripled from 504 to 1,571. Many a settler on moving West carried only hand luggage, and it was no surprise that Seattle had six furniture plants.

Minerals provided a great—and exaggerated—hope at the time when statehood was attained. "Gold, silver, copper, iron, lead, and other minerals exist in nearly all parts of the state," Clarence Barton reported in 1890. "Iron," he said, ". . . abounds in mines yet undeveloped." [6] Barton also quoted a letter from the state geologist, George A. Bethune:

There is no section of the country where there is such promising indication of mineral wealth. There are a number of gold, silver, and lead districts throughout the State which are in every sense flourishing mining camps in spite of the lack of transportation facilities. I am fully convinced that as soon as railroads are extended to the heart of those districts the output of ore bearing these metals will be enormous.

But it takes time to establish the size and quality of ore bodies. Time was to show that these early reports had greatly overstated the extent of mineral resources.

Coal, which was sold primarily in San Francisco, did become important. First shipments were made from Bellingham Bay in 1860, but the big expansion did not come until twenty-five years later in the Newcastle mines east of Seattle. The mines were developed by the Oregon Improvement Company, which was organized by Henry Villard of the Northern Pacific. Coal from Newcastle, and later from Roslyn, near Cle Elum, moved by rail to Seattle for loading aboard schooner and steamship. By 1888 output topped one million tons. Spencer took a special train to see the coal mines of the Oregon Improvement Company a few miles southeast of Seattle and exclaimed: "Biggest thing I ever saw! Their income is over $4,000 a day." [7]

The combination of coal and iron ore led to the hope that Puget Sound would become a center for steel mills. In 1889 the Puget Sound Iron Company brought into operation a blast furnace at

Irondale on Port Townsend Bay; the ores were low grade, however, and the company failed.

Part of the same early enthusiasm over iron is reflected in the *Seattle Directory* of 1889, which reported the Moss Iron & Steel Company of America was building at Kirkland; "the plant will cost $2-million, and the works will employ 1,500 to 2,000 men." That was a heady prospect for a frontier town, but the mill was never built.

By the late 1880's, salmon canneries had become well established, first on the lower Columbia River, then on Puget Sound, and finally in Alaska. George T. Meyers, identified in the *Post-Intelligencer* simply as "the cannery man," reported that 15 new canneries being set up in Alaska would bring the total there to 29, compared with 21 on the Columbia River.[8]

Agriculture continued to expand as timber was taken off the lower valleys and the land was laboriously cleared of massive stumps of cedar and fir. Wheat production in 1888 topped nine million bushels to rank Washington third in the West, after California and Oregon. The wheat harvest in Washington averaged 23 to 24 bushels an acre, the highest of any state, then as now. In the upper Yakima Valley the first soil was coming under irrigation.

Hops became an extraordinary but not a lasting bonanza. Train-load shipments had begun during Spencer's visit in 1888. The crop from the first planting on the Meeker farm in 1866 brought the fantastic price of 85 cents a pound—roughly double today's cash market. As hop culture spread rapidly through the Puyallup and Snoqualmie Valleys, Indians traveling in canoes from all parts of Puget Sound came by the hundreds to pick the crop.

Yields were so great on the virgin bottom lands that Washington growers took the leadership from New York in production of hops. Buyers for London firms bid for Puget Sound hops, and quotations for this crop led the daily report on agricultural markets in Seattle. The *Post-Intelligencer* devoted 5½ tightly packed columns to a report on hop culture and markets by Ezra Meeker, the famed Puyallup pioneer, who in time came to symbolize the days of the covered wagon.[9] But over-production gradually took the profit out of hops, and aphids and mildew in the moist Puget Sound climate wrought havoc with the crop. The center of production moved to the irrigated lands of the Yakima Valley where it remains to this day. Indeed, two-thirds of the na-

tion's hops now come from Washington and most of the rest
from Oregon and Idaho.

Growth of communities at the time of statehood was nowhere
more evident than in Seattle. Land from which virgin timber had
just been cut was a tangle of brush and stumps, soon to be divided
into city lots. Construction of houses, hotels, stores, and mills became in itself an important part of the economy. In the business
directories of those early days the largest classification was real
estate, where listings ran for nearly three columns. Next largest
was that under the heading of carpenters and builders. Saloons
outnumbered grocery stores.

The sale of city lots to newcomers required something of the
talent of a circus barker. Samuel L. Crawford and Charles T. Conover, who had just formed the real estate firm of Crawford &
Conover, put on the market in 1889 an addition owned by Captain William Renton of Port Blakely Mill Company. Advertising
described the site as "the plateau on the summit of the second hill
on Madison Street, one of the most high, sightly points about the
city," roughly between what is now 15th Avenue East and 19th
Avenue East and between East Howell and East Marion Street.
On April 2, Crawford & Conover announced in the *Post-
Intelligencer:*

> Our instructions from Captain Renton are to sell one-third of the 320
> lots distributed throughout the addition. From present indications these
> will all be sold the first week and when they are gone no more can be ob-
> tained at any price. Captain Renton will positively sell only one-third of
> the lots at this time. He may possibly sell another third later on, but it
> will be at largely increased prices, and he intends to keep a large holding
> there for permanent investment.

Twice the sale was postponed: an advertisement explained that
owing "to more or less wet weather the clearing of the addition
has been somewhat retarded," which probably meant the mud was
too deep for horses. Postponement gave Crawford & Conover an
opportunity to tout the tract by quoting Captain Renton's instruc-
tions: "I particularly desire that the clearing shall be entirely
finished. I take some pride in that piece of land and would much
rather have it look well when I offer it than have it covered with
stumps and debris." [10] When the tract was finally put on the market
June 5, the sale was advertised as the only one until next year

"when the cable road will be completed out Madison Street and the electric road out Filbert Street." Captain Renton ran into bad luck in the timing of the sale, just one day before the famed Seattle fire.

In the downtown area Richard Holyoke, who later joined Spencer's bank, let a contract for a six-story building on Front Street, now First Avenue and Spring. The Holyoke Building would be one of the largest in town. Design would be the most modern; ceilings on the first floor, it was announced with pride, would be 10 feet high, the next four stories each 13 feet. That project proved a blessing for the city on the day of the great fire; the excavation for the foundation helped establish the northern limit of the flames. The building stands today, empty above street-level stores but with its red brick exterior newly cleaned.

Along the waterfront, busy locomotives belching smoke and cinders were looked upon as a happy sign of industrial might. Grant's *History of Seattle* drew this grimy picture of the area just south of Yesler Way:

It is here that Railroad Avenue also begins, and near it all the principal railroad depots and docks are located. The locality itself is not enrapturing, being the sootiest, most crowded and most unpretentious angle or radiating point in the city, but to the business man who gloats over long trains of coal, or freight cars crowded with bales of produce, hops, or cattle, or flat cars laden with stone and brick, the grime and stench are no objection. It savors of enterprise.

In a broader look over Seattle, this chronicle continues:

It will be no disrespect to the city to say that one finds the mean and the magnificent, the finished and the crude, in very close juxtaposition—strikingly so, even for a western city. This is because the place has been growing so rapidly.[11]

Such was the bubble and excitement that caught hold of Spencer as he set about the task of founding a new bank.

A BANK IS BORN

On returning to Iowa City, Spencer had hardly hung up his hat and coat before he started to raise capital for the new bank. He wanted $100,000 on the day the bank opened, a sum equivalent to perhaps five times that amount today. He had saved some money from his salary as cashier and had made a few investments, but most of the capital had to come from others, mainly associates in business and banking. He wanted to raise $75,000 in Iowa and the balance in Seattle. He tried an advertisement with Investors Directory Company, New York, and inquired about the same approach in the *American Bank Reporter,* New York, but there is no evidence that these efforts were productive.

Spencer had had ample time on the long trip back from the West Coast to lay out in some detail the kind of institution he wanted to form. His plan of action, he wrote Ollie,

. . . may seem very conservative compared to what you expect in plans outlined by you but it is the only way I should feel satisfied to go in. I have always been connected with solid conservative institutions and am getting a little too old and stiff in the knees to go kiting . . . I would much rather have an institution paying 15 to 20 per cent on a solid base, than paying 50 per cent that was liable in troubled and stormy water to go up in thin smoke.

I want an institution that will ride any financial storm, no matter how hard it blows and it is the only kind I would have anything to do with . . .

As to salaries, your ideas are rather high. I expect to run the institution at a total expense not exceeding $5,000 for salaries, etc. In an institution of this kind, the shareholders are entitled to the profits.[12]

Garretson of the Sioux National Bank liked the project and sent word right back: "Put me down for 1/10th of the stock." Highly pleased, Spencer remarked: "This coming from him has encouraged me greatly."

Early in December, Spencer wrote his uncle, Eugene de Steiguer, in Denver, that the "banking scheme is moving along as well, if not better, than I had expected." He hoped that De Steiguer would take $10,000 in stock "as I am more than ever convinced it is going to be a good thing." [13] He cited an investment by P. M. Musser of Muscatine, Iowa, who had bought $4,000 in stock in a Seattle bank a few months earlier at $100 a share and recently refused an offer of $140.

Spencer wrote Philip Ritz at Walla Walla that because Seattle was growing so fast, a new bank could be profitable almost from the start without taking business away from established banks. Ritz said he could take $10,000 to $15,000 in the bank himself and could raise $40,000 to $50,000 from "some of the best men in Seattle," [14] but he died unexpectedly before participating in the bank.

Some who had said they would buy stock dropped out. At one point in December, Spencer wrote his brother that he was becoming discouraged.[15] But by late January, Spencer had $72,500 in subscriptions and asked a supply house to quote "on a full supply of books for a new bank." [16] Now at last had come the time to cut his ties with Iowa. On February 9 he set out for Seattle. Until he found a house for his family some weeks later, he stayed at the businessman's headquarters, the Occidental Hotel, located where a parking garage at Second and Yesler stands today.

Spencer plunged at once into the three major tasks remaining. He had to raise the rest of the capital and formally organize the bank; he had to find quarters that would be suitable yet not too costly; and he had to line up customers in advance of the opening.

This was work Spencer enjoyed. He liked to get out and meet people and he was more than ever convinced of the opportunities that lay ahead in Seattle. On March 4 he called resident stockholders to a meeting in the offices of Eshelman, Llewellyn & Co., investment brokers, to complete the board of directors. Those chosen were E. H. Alvord, M. D. Ballard, Richard Holyoke, and W. H. Llewellyn. The other five directors were the incorporators of the bank: R. R. Spencer, W. C. Hill of Washington, D.C., D. F. Sawyer of Iowa, and J. H. Elder and T. W. Prosch of Seattle. The directors then elected Holyoke president; Sawyer vice president; and Spencer cashier.

The board included several men prominent in Seattle. Holyoke, about whom little is now known, was an investor putting up a new business block. The city directory listed his occupation as farmer, but he lived in town on Eighth Avenue. Elder was a lawyer. Ballard had worked in a hardware store in Iowa about forty miles from Spencer's home, crossed the plains at the age of 23, drove pack trains in the Northwest and built a flour mill at Albany, Oregon. He traveled widely as a salesman, liked the looks of Seattle, and settled there late in 1882. The next year he founded Seattle Hardware Company and served as president. In 1893 he succeeded Holyoke as president of the bank, a largely honorary position that carried no salary then.

Spencer intended originally to establish a national bank rather than a state bank. But he ran into a hitch—the requirement that

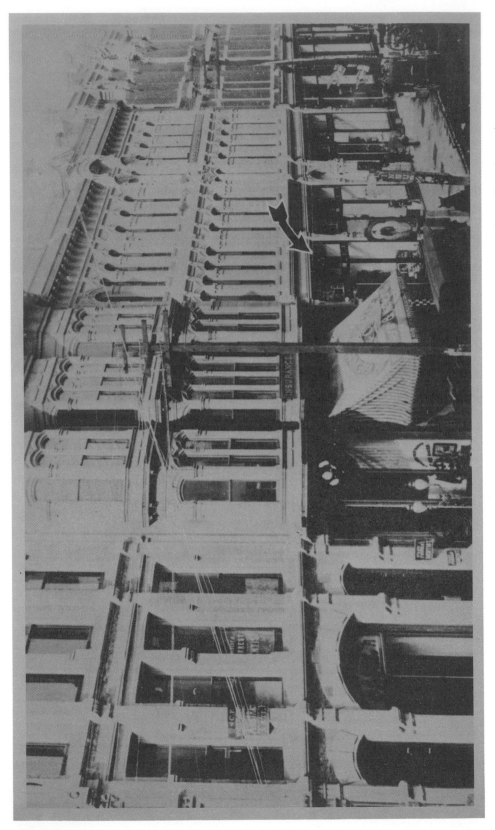

The bank's first office (indicated by arrow) was in the Griffith Davies bookstore on Front Street (now First Avenue) near Cherry Street.

three-fourths of the directors of a national bank be residents of the state or territory where the bank was located for the year preceding its founding. In Spencer's bank a majority of the capital came from out of state, primarily Iowa, and Spencer felt that these shareholders should be adequately represented on the board.

In early planning Spencer used the name Seattle Banking Company, but this did not satisfy him. His daughter, Mrs. George de Steiguer, recalled many years later that Spencer told his wife: "I want a good name for the bank. I think Commerce—Bank of Commerce—is a good name." [17] Such the name became, and a year after the opening, when the institution was changed to a national charter, the name became the National Bank of Commerce. Almost two decades later Spencer doggedly held to this name in a merger that doubled the size of the bank.

In April Spencer lined up several strong accounts. With great relief he wrote his wife: "Am much pleased with the turn affairs have taken. For a while was afraid the whole thing was going to pieces, in which case we might have had to scratch pretty hard. We got the a/c of the Farmers Insurance Company . . . and think it is going to be a good one as they have even now a considerable sum of money on hand and it is increasing right along." [18] Spencer said he also got the account of a new clothing firm.

A little later he wrote: "Secured the largest retail grocery business in the city yesterday—business averages $15,000 monthly." The owner "took $3,000 in stock—wanted $5,000." [19] The owner was J. H. Glenn, the grocery, Haley-Glenn, which was soon to provide a haven for the bank after the devastation of the Seattle fire.

Spencer found a ready welcome in the new city. In mid-April, he wrote to Sawyer, the bank's vice president, in Iowa City: "I am pleased to discover one thing, and that is that the newcomers seem generally disposed to discriminate in favor of a new institution as against the older ones." He went on: "I am making new and some very pleasant acquaintances every day, some of whom will be of great benefit in business as well as in a social way. There is much more and better society here than I had imagined."

A few days later, in describing Seattle and Tacoma, he wrote to another associate in Iowa: "At present there is no real comparison. . . . Tacoma as a residence city would be slightly preferred

DR. **BANK OF COMMERCE**, *In Account*   *with* G. Davies   CR.

1889						
				aug By Cash	75	
May 16	To Cash		421		215	65
20	" "	280			44	57
22	" "	194			1000	
25	" "	102			178	11
June 4	" "	100			400	
18	" "	201	50		100	
"	" "	244	10		80	
19	" "	150			420	
22	" "	150		3	680	
26	" "	1000			49	60
5	" "	7000			300	
27	" "	140			517	50
29	" "	1600			145	
July 15	" "	200			38	65
aug 30	" "	1002	22		1000	
31	" "	16610			12	
July 15	" "	60			5074	08
22	" "	50			500	
aug 14	" "	600			324	
21	" "	348		Balance	651	15
		9917	92		9917	92

20 Vouchers rec'd

as such by eastern people on account of that element being in greater numbers than here. In business the advantages appear entirely the other way—the wholesale houses in Seattle are located right on the waterfront with the R.R. facilities at their door. In Tacoma the Northern Pacific owns every bit of the waterfront and have in no way improved it to an extent worth mentioning."

Quarters for the bank were not easy to obtain. Mrs. De Steiguer recounted in 1964 that her father played chess with Griffith Davies and remarked one day, "I don't believe I can stay here, Mr. Davies, because I haven't got my bank started." To this Davies returned: "I have a bookstore on Front Street. I'll move the books over to one side of the room and you can have the north side to open the bank." Subsequently, Davies became a stockholder in the bank that opened its first office in his bookstore. On April 27, Spencer with delight wrote his brother in Australia: "The Bank of Commerce today is an assured fact, born after much labor, many trials and tribulations. Our room is in one of the series of brick blocks of which the 1st National has the corner room." The quarters, he added, "are by odds the finest in the city and are really handsome."

The opening was held back by delay in construction of the counters, but already Spencer found business coming his way. On May 1 he wrote: "A friend of mine dropped in this morning and said he had a little money he didn't want to use for a couple and possibly not for 6 mos. and handed me $20,300. Quite a starter, wasn't it—and he wasn't a stockholder, either."

A few days before the bank opened, Spencer put some of the capital to work by discounting a 27-day draft for $1,000 issued against a raft of logs. He was pleased that the discount of one per cent gave him a profit of $10. But Spencer did not want to tie up too much money until he knew more fully what the needs of the bank's customers would be. Ballard, a director, brought in a man with two notes that Ballard strongly recommended. Spencer turned the man down and wrote on May 3: "I do not care, however, until I know the ropes better, to take any paper running over 3 or 4 months." [20]

Spencer repeatedly expressed admiration for the people of the city. He wrote his father May 8: "Citizens here raised $130,000 yesterday and will increase it to $250,000 toward completing a

The Seattle fire of 1889, at its place of origin on Front Street (now First Avenue) and Madison. This picture looks south from Front and Spring.

connection with the Canadian Pacific. I tell you they are dandies when they start anything."

On May 15, 1889, almost seven months to the day after Spencer first set foot in Seattle, the bank officially opened for business on Front Street (now First Avenue) at the foot of Cherry Street. "Counters are very handsome," Spencer noted, "and have attracted a great deal of notice and comment and will prove a good advertisement . . . . Everything is starting as favorably as I expected."

The first depositor was Griffith Davies, founder of the firm known today as Davies Coffee, Inc. The second was G. O. Guy, founder of the drug chain operating today under that name.

Business built up rapidly. On June 3 Spencer reported, "Deposits would have exceeded $50,000 today but one dep. drew $5,000 which kind of knocked our eye out. We only dropped back $3,000. Loans $40,000."

Three days later, however, business was interrupted with the chilling cry of "Fire!" Flames had broken out in a paint shop at Madison and Front, three blocks north of the Bank of Commerce. At first it looked like not much more than a routine fire, but then as the water gave out, a north wind set the flames roaring southward into the main business district, and disaster was imminent. Spencer just had time to gather up the bank records before a policeman came along and warned: "Get out of here! You'll be burned to death!" [21]

This was the famed Seattle fire of 1889. It tore through stores and hotels, warehouses and flophouses, houses and shanties, wharves and livery stables; it fed on wooden sidewalks and the planked surfacing of streets. Some 50 blocks that included most of the business district were reduced to ashes and rubble. The loss, Spencer reported, was $15 million, only $3 million insured.

The catastrophe seemed overwhelming; yet without hesitation the city set about rebuilding, with wider streets, sounder construction, more brick and steel, larger wharves, and the pattern for a greater city.

Spencer, a man of restrained statement, bubbled with admiration for the spirit of the city: "This is the nerviest body of businessmen it was ever my good fortune to run against. All are preparing to build on a better scale. A large majority are already doing business in tents waiting for the brick to go up." [22] Land in the burned district, Spencer reported, "is more valuable than before the fire."

Less than two years later the *History of Seattle*, edited by Frederic J. Grant, chronicled:

The great fire is . . . in a certain sense an assistance to the growth of a city and is not by any means an unmixed evil. As a matter of fact every growing city inevitably reaches the period of conflagration at some time. Wooden structures, shanties, heterogen[e]ous agglomerations of architectural misfits, and compromises between respectability and . . . profits, are certain to burn altogether, if once ignited, and the ignition is certain to come.[23]

The Bank of Commerce was burned out, but Spencer was undaunted. He recovered the safe and estimated that the loss in furniture, fixtures, and stationery amounted to less than $2,000. Just a week before the fire, Spencer, so proud of his counters and furnishings, had taken out $1,250 in insurance.

All banks in the city closed the day after the fire. On the second day, a Saturday, Spencer resumed business in a tiny space hardly six feet by eight feet just inside the Haley-Glenn Grocery. The grocery store was in the Boston Block at Second and Columbia, a building of brick that had helped frantic firefighters contain the holocaust.

A few days later the bank moved to a frame structure at Second and Cherry where the Alaska Building now stands. The quarters were cramped, only 12 feet by 14 feet, but Spencer was very pleased. He reassured an associate in Iowa: "The shell of the Bank of Commerce went up in smoke along with the rest of the business portion of the city, but the kernel was left and I am now satisfied that the fire will prove advantageous to us—we now have the best location in town for temporary quarters." [24]

The new location had one serious drawback: As a wooden building it afforded no protection against another fire. Morning and night Spencer and one or two of the staff lugged some 250 pounds of bank books, papers, gold, currency, and other valuables one block to a public safe deposit vault at the foot of Cherry Street, a vault unused in recent years and torn out in 1969 to make way for a ten-story parking garage. For Spencer the fire proved hardly more than a momentary break. On June 29, little more than three weeks later, Spencer wrote Garretson, "Business is growing rapidly. On the day of the fire our deposits were about $60,000, tonight they are $104,000." Already Spencer was talking about erecting a building for the bank, but he remained for two years more in makeshift quarters that became ever more cramped.

The vigor with which Seattle went about rebuilding after the fire added impetus to the efforts to attain a deeply cherished goal—statehood.

Congress in February 1889 authorized the formation of five states along the northern border from Minnesota to the Pacific Ocean. In June citizens of Washington elected delegates to a constitutional convention, which assembled on July 4 at Olympia. Delegates included leaders in law, medicine, business, farming, and other activities throughout the state. Several had served in the Territorial Legislature.

At the end of 52 days the convention had reconciled conflicting interests, save for two matters that it decided to refer to the people. The Constitution for the new state was ratified by the voters on October 1. Two articles submitted separately, one for women's suffrage and the other for prohibition, were rejected. In the competition for the location of the capital, the territorial seat of Olympia won easily over Ellensburg, North Yakima, and Vancouver. On

November 11, 1889, President Harrison issued a proclamation and
Washington proudly stepped forward as the 42nd state. The
population of the new state, estimated at the time at 257,000, was
very close to that of Alaska on its admission to the Union nearly
70 years later. The census a year later proved the estimate to be
low.

The granting of statehood focused new national attention on
Washington and brought fresh confidence to her citizens. Late in
1889 Spencer wrote, "We are going to have a city of 100,000 to
150,000 by 1895. This part of the letter, mark down in your hat." [1]
The panic of 1893 slowed the arrival of newcomers, but even so,
Spencer was only about seven years ahead in his forecast.

The year of statehood saw a number of companies in business
that have grown with the city and remain active today. Seattle
Hardware Company, founded in 1882, and Schwabacher Bros. &
Company (now Pacific Marine Schwabacher, Inc.), founded in
1888, were early-day retail hardware dealers; both later became
strictly wholesalers. Seattle Cedar Company, now Seattle Cedar
Lumber Manufacturing Company, was incorporated in 1889.
Other early manufacturers included such firms as Washington
Iron Works and Crescent Manufacturing Company.

The teams of Seattle Transfer Company were busy hauling
goods in the year of statehood. The city's two daily newspapers,
the *Seattle Post-Intelligencer* and the *Seattle Times,* were being
published before Washington was admitted to the Union. Seattle
Gas Light Company, forerunner of Washington Natural Gas, also
was serving the young city well before statehood.

Other familiar companies that date back at least to 1889 include
Bonney-Watson, Kroll Map, Manning Seed, and Sunde & d'Evers.

Among present-day financial institutions, Washington Mutual
Savings Bank traces back to the Washington National Building Loan
and Investment Association, founded in 1889. Seattle-First National
Bank grew out of the pioneer Phillips, Horton & Company,
founded in 1870.

The census of 1890 could hardly have been awaited more
eagerly anywhere than in the new state of Washington. An un-
disputed measure of growth, the census even put a conservative
cast on estimates made at the time of statehood.

Ten years earlier, in 1880, Seattle was a town of only 3,533,
scarcely larger than The Dalles, busy portage point on the Colum-

bia River. The largest city in Washington Territory was the wheat center of Walla Walla, with 3,588 residents. North of San Francisco, Portland was ranked first with 17,577 residents.

But the census of 1890 told quite another story. Seattle jumped to 43,914, almost catching up with Portland, then 47,294. Most of Seattle's increase had come in the last two years of the decade. Of all the cities in the West only San Francisco made a larger increase in number of residents. Tacoma soared in ten years from 1,098 to 35,858, and the combined increase of Seattle and Tacoma exceeded even that of San Francisco.

The surge of settlers throughout the state lifted Washington's population from 75,116 in 1880 to 357,232 in 1890. Excepting only the period from 1900 to 1910, this was the greatest net increase in population that Washington was to experience until the decade of the Second World War. The rate of growth was 14 times that of the nation as a whole.

The railroads, so essential for bringing in settlers and building industry and trade, continued to extend their lines. As the Northern Pacific pushed westward and trips grew longer, the railroad put on dining cars, starting in 1882. In Polk's *Seattle Directory* for 1889, the railroad described itself as "the only dining car line." For tourist and emigrant passengers, trains carried kitchen cars with coal stoves, sinks and ice boxes where passengers traveling emigrant and second-class could cook their own meals. Names of first-class passengers were telegraphed ahead for newspapers to carry before their trains arrived.

Transcontinental rail service helped build traffic through the ports of Puget Sound. Foreign trade via Puget Sound swelled in 1889 to 856,156 tons, and more than doubled in two years. Indeed, the total for Puget Sound came within challenging distance of San Francisco's foreign trade of 1,064,738 tons.

The Northern Pacific chartered five steamships in 1889 and sought to dominate the tea trade with the Orient. In 1892 the railroad inaugurated passenger and freight service between Tacoma and the ports of Japan and China.

In 1890 the Northern Pacific introduced its daily flyers—the Pacific Express westbound and the Atlantic Express eastbound. Seattle and Tacoma now were within five days of Chicago.

Fares ran somewhat higher than they do today and in terms of wages or buying power were several times higher. A one-way

The front window of the Haley-Glenn Grocery Company in the Boston Block, Second and Columbia, provided temporary haven for the bank after the fire of June 6, 1889.

ticket from St. Paul to Seattle, Tacoma, or Portland cost $101 first class, $80 second class or tourist, and $50 emigrant. The Pullman charge added $13.50 for a double berth in first-class cars, but only $3 in tourist cars.[2]

The emigrant-class provided settlers cheap yet reasonably comfortable accommodations for the journey to a new life. Their coach seats were upholstered in leather rather than the plush mohair used in higher-class cars. Curiously, values today are turned about, and leather-finished seats in automobiles are a status symbol. If a settler who traveled emigrant-class bought land from the Northern Pacific, his full fare went toward the purchase of land. Low emigrant freight rates applied to personal and household goods.

The expansion of trade and continued influx of settlers meant more business for the young financial institution, and under Spencer's management, the bank continued to grow. He drove himself hard. His hours at the bank were from 8:30 or 9:00 A.M. to 7:00 P.M. He had lunch at the bank and got home to supper around 7:30. All entries in the bank books were made by hand. Accounts were balanced without an adding machine. Spencer and his two assistants— the entire staff—found themselves on the jump just to keep even with the work.

When a suggestion reached Spencer that D. F. Sawyer, one of the larger Midwest stockholders, might come out to join the bank, Spencer protested: "I have no objection to his coming, but not to take any official position in the bank. I have stood the brunt of the work and slaved early and late to make the thing go. Now that the thing is an assured success, I purpose to run it myself until the stockholders think he [Sawyer] can do it better." [3] Sawyer did not come out.

Later, when more staff was needed, Oliver Spencer closed out his export business in Australia and came to Seattle. In February 1890, the directors elected Oliver assistant cashier. This freed Robert to spend more time outside the bank to work on new business. Directors set Robert's annual salary at $3,000; Oliver's at $1,200; a bookkeeper's at $1,000; and a messenger's at $300.

Oliver's boyhood years in Italy and his fluency in Italian turned into a plus value for the bank. He was appointed Italian consul in Seattle, and at the bank he handled remittances of Italian immigrants sending money back to their families. When the Pike

For two years the bank shared space in this wooden building at the corner of Second and Cherry. In the background are tents erected as temporary shelter after the great fire of June 6, 1889.

Place Market opened in 1907 he became a favorite with Italian farmers, who brought their produce in from nearby farms.

By March 1890 deposits had reached $192,000. The bank had suffered no losses other than to its own quarters in the fire, but it was clear that further growth required more capital. To C. P. Lovelace, his father-in-law and a stockholder, Robert Spencer wrote: "We are very much handicapped in our efforts to secure heavy customers by the smallness of our capital and our inability to make loans to them, as we are loaned up to our neck." [4]

In the early years the total that the bank placed in loans was substantially greater than the amount of its deposits. Where today loans generally range between 60 and 65 per cent of deposits, the ratio in Spencer's bank in 1890 exceeded 125 per cent and in 1891 topped 180 per cent. This meant that the bank had to have proportionally much more capital than it would today, and if Spencer wanted growth in loans, he would first have to increase the bank's capital through sale of additional stock.

Money seemed available for new stock. Garretson, the Iowa banker and shareholder, proposed to push the capital up from $100,000 to $500,000, but a committee of Seattle directors favored going only to $300,000, which would require the bank to sell $200,000 in new stock.

The stockholders approved the increase to $300,000 and also approved a change to a national charter. Thus, in the first year, Spencer's institution stepped out as the National Bank of Commerce with increased capital, now one of the larger banks of the state.

When the bank was organized, 715 of 1,000 shares were held by out-of-state residents, primarily in Iowa. The 100 shares of Robert Spencer were included in this number. In the succeeding months, some of the Midwestern stock was bought by Seattle residents. Just prior to the time the bank converted to a national charter, 505 shares were Seattle-owned, including the 100 held by Spencer. Sale of additional shares to boost the capital to $300,000 further increased the proportion held in Seattle.

THE PANIC OF '93

Spencer had plenty of competition. During the boom years of 1888 to 1892 more banks were created in Seattle than at any time in the city's history.

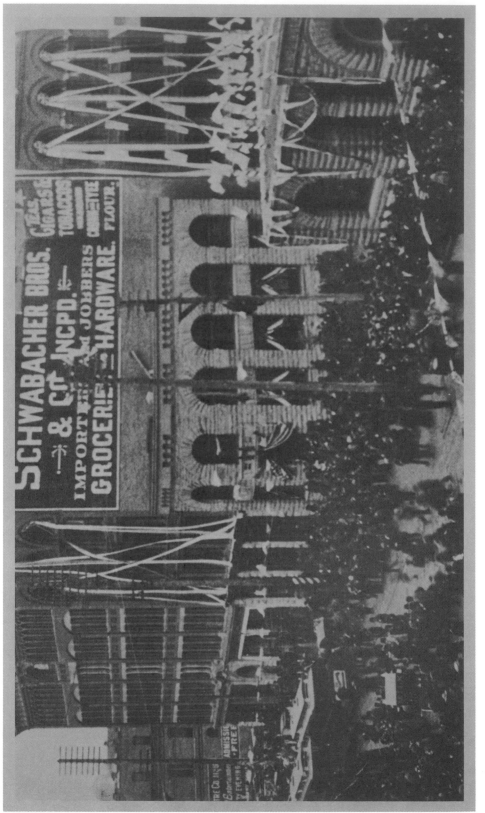

The bank's fourth location was in a gray, stone building (beneath the Schwabacher sign) at First and Yesler, now a tavern.

Washington Savings Bank (no connection with the present Washington Mutual Savings Bank) was launched in June 1888 with capital of $50,000. In the following January the Bank of North Seattle was formed, to be reorganized a year later as Commercial National Bank with capital of $100,000. It was located at First Avenue and Battery Street in the area known as Belltown.

A few weeks after the Bank of Commerce began business, Washington National Bank opened its doors with capital of $100,000. In the same year Boston National Bank began with capital of $300,-000; some years later it was to merge with Seattle National Bank, which was formed in 1890 with capital of $250,000. Toward the end of 1889, Peoples Savings Bank was chartered with capital of $100,000; many years later Joshua Green resigned as a director of National Bank of Commerce to buy Peoples Savings Bank and built the present Peoples National Bank of Washington.

Private banks—firms not under national or state charter, but accepting deposits and making loans—also sprang up. George E. Miller & Company entered the banking business in 1889; a year later the firm increased its capital to $100,000 and was chartered as the King County Bank. L. H. Griffith Realty & Banking Company, another private banker, began in March 1890 with capital of $300,000. Filkins Banking Company also opened that year. About this time the Bank of British Columbia, an institution with home office in London, established a branch in Seattle that later became a part of the Canadian Imperial Bank of Commerce. A little later one of the prominent private banks was Wm. D. Perkins & Co.

In 1892 the Scandinavian American Bank was launched, its name attesting to the tide of migration flowing in from Scandinavia and Minnesota. The following year Marine Savings Bank, which opened in Port Townsend in 1889, moved to Ballard for a more favorable location; it continued operations there for three years until it was placed in voluntary liquidation.

In the four years from 1889 through 1892 the number of banks in Seattle tripled, and the paid-in capital swelled from $700,000 to $2,270,000. The same proliferation of banks was occurring throughout the state, not just in the larger cities but in smaller lumbering and farming towns that were springing to life.

For two years in a row—through October 31, 1890—the Comptroller of the Currency reported that Washington stood first in the

The bunkhouse at the end of a hard day, about 1891. (Darius Kinsey photo from University of Washington.)

West and fifth in the nation in the number of national banks organized.

The Rand McNally Bank Directory for 1892 listed 138 banks in Washington, but even this very substantial total was not complete. For these 138 banks, paid-in capital came to $12,680,250; the addition of surplus and undivided profits brought the total of capital funds to $15,908,660. Tacoma, then the second city in Washington in population, led the state with 19 banks; their capital funds totaled $4,196,580. Seattle followed with 18 banks with $3,395,060 in capital funds. Spokane had 10 banks, the Bellingham Bay area 9, and Port Townsend 6. On the basis of population alone, if Seattle had as many banks today as in 1892, the total would exceed 200.

Optimism over the growth that was sure to come tomorrow ran through most businesses and was shared by many bankers, though not all. In the mid-eighties, four years before Spencer passed Tacoma up in favor of Seattle, N. B. Coffman withdrew to Chehalis and there founded the Bank of N. B. Coffman, which he was to head for almost half a century. Later Coffman was to speak of the times leading to the panic of 1893 as "an era of adventure and wildcat speculation on the Pacific Coast such as can never again be witnessed. In its early history it passed through a speculative period of townsite promotion, during which mushroom cities of vast proportions were platted and sold at fabulous prices to credulous investors throughout the United States. This period was succeeded by one of broken fortunes, depression and disaster." [5]

Tacoma, already the busy western terminus of the Northern Pacific, counted also on becoming the northwestern terminus for the Union Pacific. The Tacoma Real Estate and Stock Exchange, the Chamber of Commerce, and various individuals raised $415 for a series of articles about the city in the *Chicago Times*. Herbert Hunt's *Tacoma, Its History and Its Builders* sets out that Tacoma "had the ablest band of real estate salesmen on American soil" and along with them "a full share of the gullibles." Eighteen trains arrived and departed daily, and "every train brought to the city a load of enthusiasts." [6] Hotels were crowded beyond capacity. Eastern money poured in.

During 1889 Tacoma established the first bank clearing house north of San Francisco. Two years later the real estate boom was

Oxen and a steam donkey engine move logs along a skid road on Bainbridge Island. (*Seattle Historical Society Collection.*)

tempered by disclosure of frauds in which easterners were the victims. Some prospective investors left, still holding tightly to their money. When land could no longer be bought with the expectation that it would sell on the morrow for a profit, the boom was over. Real estate transfers in Tacoma tumbled from $8,541,565 in February, 1892, to $101,894 in July.

Earlier signs of trouble had been ignored. One was the closing of Spokane National Bank in 1891. Here, as in many bank failures of the time, funds had been placed in ventures which, by present-day standards, simply could not qualify for bank loans. Spokane National had made heavy loans to officers and directors, but its chief asset lay in the Morning Mine in the Coeur d'Alene District of Idaho. The receiver for the bank finally sold the mine for $400,-000 to a syndicate of Milwaukee and New York bankers, and as a result depositors got almost 94 cents on the dollar. No one realized it at the time, but depositors were lucky that the bank failure came early while there was still a market for the mines.

Another Spokane bank, which closed two years later, had tied its money up in a banking house with a marble interior and in coal mines, a coking plant, and a portage road around Celilo Falls on the Columbia River. When depositors lined up to take out their money, the till quickly emptied.

The panic of '93 began in the East. In June the stock market collapsed. This was followed by heavy withdrawals of New York deposits in the West and South. Fear spread that the United States might go off the gold standard. Money suddenly became tight. Worried depositors queued up to get their funds, and when one bank had exhausted its cash and closed its doors, the run often spread to another in the same city.

Banks found that what had once been regarded as good loans now were frozen. In cities where soaring land prices had tumbled, the loan on a piece of property might far exceed the deflated value, assuming that a buyer could be found at all.

Tacoma was hard hit. A run developed at Merchants National Bank in the spring of 1893. The Clearing House Association, representing all the banks of the city, advanced $50,000, then, in return for a mortgage on the bank building, another $50,000. Other funds were sought, but there was no let-up from depositors, and on June 1 the bank closed. The failure, the Comptroller of the Currency reported later, was due to "general stringency of the money

market, shrinkage in values, and imprudent methods of banking." [7]
Depositors whose funds remained in the bank when it closed ultimately received 18 cents on the dollar.

Panic spread. Depositors of other Tacoma banks demanded their
money. Some hoarded their cash, some put it into postal money
orders, some into local branches of British-owned banks.

On July 21 the Traders' Bank, a substantial institution with
$500,000 in capital, closed temporarily. Its deposits had been
pulled from $800,000 in the previous October to $150,000. The bank
obtained new funds from New York and reopened. But the runs
continued and some months later, with deposits only $55,000, the
bank closed for the last time. Three stockholders—Col. C. W.
Griggs, Henry Hewitt, and H. A. Strong—had personally endorsed
the bank's paper, and ultimately depositors were paid in full, something rare in a bank panic.

On July 24 the Comptroller of the Currency took over Tacoma
National Bank. The president raised $70,000 on his own securi-
ties and the bank was reopened, but the pressure for money
continued and in December a receiver was appointed. Depositors
received only 21 cents on the dollar.

Two other banks closed, one ultimately returning depositors 84
cents on the dollar, the other 75 cents. Four state-chartered banks
went under, two amidst charges of fraud.

The panic struck all businesses, not just banking. Herbert Hunt
recalls in *Tacoma, Its History and Its Builders:*

Crash followed crash. The country was in the throes of hysteria . . . .
Gigantic liquidation was in progress and it paralyzed every sinew. The
Northwest suffered most. Rich men sawed wood, picked blackberries and
dug clams for a livelihood. Men who had ridden in carriages walked,
though the empty street cars, rattling in their own poverty, would carry
them for five cents . . . . Those who had been rich, and especially the
bankers, were held responsible.[8]

Another area where speculation gave way to panic and disaster
embraced the settlements on Bellingham Bay, where in later
years consolidation of New Whatcom and Fairhaven created the
city of Bellingham. First gold, then coal, and finally lumber built
these settlements. Then speculation took hold, compounded of
railroad construction and the dream that the Great Northern

would make Fairhaven its western terminus. Neil Roy Knight in a doctoral thesis, *History of Banking in Washington,* said that the collapse of the boom on Bellingham Bay, "combined with the nationwide panic and depression then impending, resulted in one of the worst conditions in the entire state." [9]

A run ascribed by Bellingham Bay residents to the failure of Merchants National in Tacoma hit in June 1803. On June 22 the First National Bank of New Whatcom went under. The next day the run spread to the larger Columbia National Bank, and by nightfall its days were ended. Those who had money in the First National Bank ultimately received 26 cents on the dollar; at the Columbia National, 18 cents on the dollar.

On July 29, Puget Sound Loan, Trust and Banking Company went into receivership, and on July 31, the last bank in New Whatcom, Bellingham Bay National, suspended operations. Later, with voluntary restrictions on withdrawals and with new capital funds, the bank reopened, but it lasted less than two years more.

Runs spread to other institutions on Bellingham Bay. Some banks closed, reorganized, and reopened. Some liquidated voluntarily. Two new institutions came into business, then gave up. By 1897, nine banks on Bellingham Bay had gone under; only one survived.

Seattle fared much better. It had built a broader economic base than other cities in the new state, and speculation in land had not run to the excesses it had in Tacoma and Bellingham.

Not until 1895 did the first Seattle bank fail. On June 19, 1895, the end came to Merchants National Bank, which had been one of the largest in the city. At the time of closing it still held $231,000 in deposits on which it ultimately returned 77 cents on the dollar. Merchants National earlier had cut a wide swath. During its twelve-year life it had paid stockholders a total of 220 per cent on their investment, an average of 18 per cent a year. The Comptroller of the Currency laid the closing to injudicious banking and depreciation of securities.

Four small institutions later failed in Seattle, two in 1895 and one in each of the next two years. Other banks suffered sharp reduction in deposits but survived.

Across the state the picture was equally grim. In 1892, the peak year before the panic, 173 banks were doing business in Washing-

Seattle waterfront at the west end of the present Broad, Cedar, and Vine Streets. This was a camping place for Indians as they came from their settlements on Puget Sound to harvest hops in the valleys south of Seattle. (Prosch Albums.)

ton. Four years later the number was cut to 91.[10] Of 10 banks in
Spokane, 7 failed. Of 21 banks in Tacoma, 14 failed. Disaster fell
on depositors and stockholders alike.

Tightness in the money market was recognized at the National
Bank of Commerce as early as March 1891. At that time the
directors required the board's approval of any loan over $5,000 and
instructed Spencer to call in a portion of any loan made to a
director where a long line of credit existed.

Spencer continued to control costs carefully. In the second half
of 1891 the bank's entire operating expenses came to only $6,635,
of which salaries accounted for $3,000 and rent $2,100. Meantime,
the bank earned well; it paid stockholders their first dividend in
1890 at 6 per cent. In 1891 the dividend was raised to 8 per cent
a year and remained there until the panic of '93, when dividends
were abruptly discontinued.

By the end of 1893, with the toll of the panic and tightness of
money increasing, the Comptroller of the Currency wrote the bank
that it had $75,696 in overdue loans, of which $25,604 were classed
as bad debts. Spencer's reply gives a picture of the worried times:

Speaking generally of the conditions on the Coast, would say that they
are such, at present, as to make it very difficult to follow strictly the requirements and spirit of the National Banking Law. We have a great
many loans fully secured, which, were we to press, would result in a
needless loss to the maker, and no practical good to ourselves.

Money is excessively scarce, and a great many are unable, while per-
fectly good, to raise money even to meet their interest payments
promptly. Should we renew [the loans] at maturity, we should be compelled to take their notes for the interest, which we do not like to do,
except in extreme cases. We, therefore, prefer to let the notes run overdue until such time as they can raise the money to pay the interest.

Conditions seem to be changing for the better and we hope soon to get
back to our old style of doing business, which means prompt payment or
renewal of notes and a small line of suspended or overdue paper.[11]

Meantime, Spencer added, the bank "intends to charge off all
paper which we consider bad." During the next three months
alone, the bank wrote off $35,500 in questionable loans.

The National Bank of Commerce continued to serve its customers
and to make new loans. In April 1893, just prior to the panic, it
had loans outstanding of $621,000. Of these loans, the minutes show
that almost half, or $308,000, were repaid or charged off by the

The new banking office at First and Yesler in the early 1890's. Robert Spencer at the left and his brother Oliver.

state, Washington stepped up to rank first in 1905, a position it was to hold for nearly four decades before it yielded the crown to Oregon. Weyerhaeuser interests, working westward to replace the dwindling timber resources of the Midwest, bought 900,000 acres of timberland from the Northern Pacific at $6 an acre, described by the Weyerhaeuser historians as "one of the largest single land transfers in American annals." [12] The Great Northern Railway put a fleet of steamers to work on the Great Lakes to carry Pacific Northwest lumber from rail cars at Duluth to Cleveland, Detroit, and Buffalo.

Each year new land went under the plow and was seeded to wheat. Irrigation opened up farm lands near Spokane, Okanogan, Wenatchee, Ellensburg, and Yakima. In 1901 the first carload of apples rolled eastward out of Wenatchee.

But the greatest lift of all came from an event as dramatic as it was unexpected—the discovery of gold in Alaska. On July 15, 1897, the steamship *Excelsior* sailed into San Francisco with a load of prospectors out of the Yukon and the story of an unbelievably rich strike on Klondike Creek.

Two days later, with the nation on edge to hear more, the steamship *Portland* docked at Seattle with 68 excited miners who confirmed the story of the *Excelsior* and told of even greater finds. As proof, the *Portland* carried almost a ton and a half of gold, worth close to $700,000. A Tacoma boxer brought out $6,000 in nuggets. A man from Michigan, one of the original discoverers of gold in the El Dorado district, worked his claim for three months and brought out $96,000. A Fresno miner counted his hoard at $130,000.

The news swept across the nation and lifted the spirits of people worn by four years of depression. Thousands responding to the challenge of adventure and wealth streamed to Seattle, where, heeding the common advice, they stocked up on tents, blankets, clothes, tools, and food. Some took 500 pounds, some half a ton. They crowded every ship that could be pressed into service. Much of the gear would later be abandoned on the tortuous trail over mountain passes and ice, and uncounted numbers of adventurers would never return. But their surge northward gave Seattle a gold rush all its own. Hotels were so crowded that cots were set up in hallways. Some gold-seekers were happy to sleep in the hay of a livery stable. Stores hummed with business.

Gold! The Seattle waterfront throbbed with excitement as the S.S. Victoria prepared to sail for the north in 1898. (Seattle Historical Society Collection.)

Gold lifted Seattle to a new era of prosperity and gave the city its place, never relinquished, as the supply point for Alaska, whether for gold, salmon and halibut, or later crab, pulp, and timber. The Klondike brought into being new shops to outfit men heading for the north country. It turned the waterfront into activity such as no city north of San Francisco had ever seen. It set Moran Bros. shipyards humming to build a dozen stern-wheelers for the Yukon River.

Gold made the name Seattle known throughout the country and helped draw new residents, not for precious metals in Alaska but for the steadier life in young communities on Puget Sound.

The tide of migration pushed westward again in ever greater numbers. During the 1890's hard times had slowed this movement so much that growth in Washington did not even match that of the previous decade. But the turn of the century opened a decade that brought an average of 1,000 new residents to Washington every week. In those ten years the population of the state more than doubled, reaching a total of 1,142,000.

Seattle's population in 1910 reached 237,200, up almost threefold in a decade. Seattle passed Portland in size, and as Spencer had forecast twenty years before, ranked as the largest city north of San Francisco. The job of building houses, stores, schools, churches, streets, and public buildings to serve this swelling number required the labor of thousands of construction men.

The flood of migrants into Washington State and the emergence of Seattle as the largest commercial and financial center north of San Francisco put pressure on the city's banks to expand, too. The need was not for more banks but for larger banks.

The rising requirements in financing were obvious. A sawmill that doubled its output would have to start the winter season with a substantially larger supply of logs in the millpond. For this the mill would borrow to pay the logger as he made deliveries into the pond. A flour mill expanding to serve the new trade in the Orient would carry more wheat in its elevators and more flour ready to load into the next ship. A wholesale supply house reaching out to serve retail stores in the growing towns of Washington and Alaska would need more help in financing its inventory, and perhaps, also in carrying the accounts of its customers.

The challenge to a bank was to grow at least as fast as its customers. A national bank was permitted to lend no more than 10 per cent of its capital and surplus to any one customer. When the customer needed a loan larger than this limit, the bank had to share the business with another institution, sometimes one as far east as New York or Boston. For young western banks seeking recognition elsewhere in the country, as well as in their own community, size was more than just a matter of prestige, and the quickest way to gain size was through acquisition or merger.

Other forces tended to bring rival banks together. Sometimes pressure for merger came from a bank in trouble, a situation in which a sound bank moved with care lest it be pulled under. Toward the close of 1894, Merchants National, one of the largest Seattle banks, proposed consolidation with the National Bank of Commerce. Two weeks later Boston National approached Commerce for the same purpose, and a negotiating committee sought a three-way consolidation.

The committee, working cautiously in the aftermath of the panic of '93, segregated loans into categories.[1] Those called "good paper" included loans that were "unquestionably good, active, and on which the interest was being paid." Each bank was to put up good paper, cash, and exchange to cover its direct liabilities, and remaining good paper would be accepted for stock in the new bank. Other loans, classed as "slow paper," would be accepted only in limited amount. However, efforts to find a basis for consolidation broke down. Merchants National survived for fifteen months, then closed its doors. Boston National merged in 1903 into Seattle National Bank.

The first decade in this century saw the consolidation of a number of banks in the Puget Sound area, but far more proposals went into negotiation than ever reached completion. Sometimes a proposed sale fell apart over the amount of premium to be paid for the stock. Sometimes the problem centered on titles and positions for the top officers.

Early-day banks generally were headed by strong individuals accustomed to leadership and sensitive to their position. The founder, whether under the title of president or cashier, ran the bank and stood as the symbol of his institution in the community. Banking was on a much more personal basis than it is today. Loans were based on the character of the borrower and on the banker's personal appraisal and hunch about a man.

Henry Broderick, whose career spans more than six decades in Seattle and includes many years as a bank director, recalled:

"Banking was very different in the early days. A banker looked then more to character than to collateral. Today, collateral comes first; if you loaned just on character, you would soon have the bank examiner breathing down your neck and asking, 'Where is this man's financial statement?'" [2]

As a new bank grew and matured, the burden on the top official also grew, often at a time when he wanted to free himself from day-to-day detail. Perhaps a better balance in staff would come through consolidation. Recognition of the need to bring in an older man as cashier was reported to stockholders of one Seattle bank early in the century. The bank was highly profitable, but the president explained that it was "getting the reputation of being run by a lot of kids." [3]

Late in 1904 the National Bank of Commerce and a slightly larger institution, Seattle National Bank, announced a proposal to merge that was complete even to the titles for officers. Out of this was to come a bank that ranked first in the city in capital, surplus, and undivided profits and a close second to Dexter Horton, the oldest and largest bank in Seattle, in deposits. The newspaper announcement stated: "The object of consolidation is to give Seattle a bank where capital and resources will be commensurate with the commercial and financial importance of the city." [4] The merger was approved by directors of both banks, but because of difficulty in obtaining adequate quarters for the combined operation, the final step, that of asking approval of the stockholders, was delayed. Weeks passed by, and ultimately, the proposal was quietly dropped. [5]

It is hard to believe that a consolidation worked out in such detail should stumble over lack of space, but no other explanation remains. In those days banks were not allowed branches; when two banks merged they had to fit into one location. Even before the proposed merger with the National Bank of Commerce, the lack of space had become a serious handicap for Seattle National, which had consolidated with Boston National a year earlier.

Late in 1905 the National Bank of Commerce and a smaller institution, First National Bank, roughed out plans for merger. Spencer wrote of this in confidence to P. M. Musser of Muscatine, Iowa, his long-time business friend, who had been an associate of Frederick Weyerhaeuser in the Midwest lumber industry and became a director of Weyerhaeuser Timber Company on its found-

A pioneer's cabin in the Grays Harbor area just before the turn of the century. (University of Washington Collection.)

ing in 1900. With high hopes of making the bank acquisition a means toward building a larger institution more active in lumber and foreign trade, Spencer wrote Musser that if the proposal went through, he wanted "yourself, the Weyerhaeuser people and J. J. Hill interested in it." He continued: "We already represent a very considerable lumber interest in this section and are anxious to make this a lumberman's bank, as well as a large foreign exchange bank, which it has already become." [6]

Spencer reported that the board of directors had been strengthened through the addition of Moritz Thomsen, president of Centennial Mill Company and "one of the strongest men, both mentally and financially, in the city." He continued that for the National Bank of Commerce, the year was "very prosperous." He estimated that earnings would run between $80,000 and $90,000. With acquisition of First National he was sure he could make the combined institution earn $140,000 a year.

But First National's price was high. Its capital, surplus, and undivided profits totaled $258,000. First National's president, Lester Turner, wanted in addition a bonus or premium of $150,000 for his bank's stock. Spencer thought $75,000 would be liberal, but he was "willing to pay in the neighborhood of $100,000." The deal fell through. Two years later M. A. Arnold bought First National Bank, the beginning of what Arnold and his son Lawrence ultimately built into today's statewide Seattle-First National Bank.

Of the many reasons for the merger of two major banks, one of the strangest is the shopkeeper's cry: "We lost our lease!" Yet such was the essence of the announcement in March 1906 that the National Bank of Commerce and Washington National Bank were preparing to consolidate as a result of "the forcing of Washington National Bank from its present quarters in the New York Block," where the Dexter Horton Building now stands. [7]

A few months earlier the president of Washington National, Manson F. Backus, had discussed merger with N. H. Latimer, manager of Dexter Horton & Company. Dexter Horton needed more space, and consolidation apparently hinged on Dexter Horton's taking over Washington National's banking quarters. The matter did not go beyond informal discussion. [8]

In the spring of 1906 the Dexter Horton Estate, which owned the bank and also was the landlord of Washington National Bank, served notice on Washington National to vacate its premises July 1.

Dexter Horton and Company wanted this space for itself, and indeed, moved in soon afterward. But the notice to vacate put Washington National in a hard spot, and Backus wryly wrote a close associate: "In diplomatic language I suppose his [Latimer's] move would be termed an 'unfriendly act.'" [9]

Whether the act was unfriendly or not, Washington National plainly had reached a turning point in its history, and, it soon developed, so had the National Bank of Commerce.

PART II

MANSON BACKUS / Two Decades of Growth

Washington National Bank, like the institution Spencer had built, was the product essentially of one strong man—Manson F. Backus. A banker from upstate New York, Backus set up shop in Seattle in 1889, just a few weeks after Spencer. Through seventeen years of hard times and lush times the two men had been competitors. They differed in many respects, yet, they shared a common adherence to sound banking and must have formed a high professional regard for each other.

Backus was a year older than Spencer. At 19, Backus began as a clerk in the First National Bank of Union Springs, New York, of which his father was president. Three years later young Backus was elected cashier. Along with work at the bank he served from 1881 to 1885 as postmaster, a position which gave him recognition in the community and some extra income. He was also the part-time manager of a gypsum company. To broaden his training he studied law with books borrowed from a law office in the bank building. Early in 1889 he passed the New York Bar examination, but he never took up the practice of law.

Like Spencer, Backus felt the challenge of the opening of new lands in the West and wanted to move out and found a bank. He talked of this with Edward O. Graves, Chief of the Bureau of Engraving and Printing at Washington, D.C., and a summer visitor at Union Springs.

Graves had been west on various government assignments and served for a time as a bank examiner on the Pacific Coast. With the change in the national administration in 1885, Graves thought he would be out of office, and he and Backus set up their plans to go west at that time. Graves was retained in office, however, and Backus turned to other ventures. With all the money he could scrape up, including money borrowed from his father, he bought into First National Bank of Auburn, New York, late in 1887.

Backus purchased his interest from a long-time friend, Charles O'Brien. However, Backus had no more than been elected president when O'Brien, knowing that his handling of the bank would not stand the scrutiny of new management, absconded and the bank closed. Stockholders not only lost their entire investment but also were called upon for a 100 per cent assessment to help pay off the depositors. The disaster wiped out Manson Backus's savings and left him dependent in any new bank venture on funds he could raise from others.

Backus continued at his old position in the Union Springs Bank and also as general manager of the gypsum company. When the company refused to raise his pay to $150 a month, Backus was ready to go west. So was Graves, who, with the change in administration and inauguration of President Harrison in March 1889, was out of office.

The two men stopped off at Omaha to check on the business outlook and prospects for a new bank. They went on through the Rocky Mountain states, where the mining industry was opening up, and stopped at Denver, Pueblo, Ogden, Salt Lake City, Helena, and Butte. They liked Butte but continued to Spokane Falls, Tacoma, and Seattle.[1]

Graves and Backus were immediately impressed with the Puget Sound country. Less than two weeks after reaching Seattle, they had settled on this city for their bank, lined up a blue-ribbon board of directors, obtained subscriptions for $100,000 in stock, and named the directors and officers. Then they took the train east to close up their affairs and move west with their families.

Word of the new bank, to be called the Washington National, appeared in the *Post-Intelligencer* Saturday morning, April 27, 1889, two days after Backus and Graves had held their organization meeting. The detailed newspaper account made the most of the inclusion of top names on the list of directors.

Washington National stock, the paper reported, had been oversubscribed in less than five days. Directors included W. C. Hill of Washington, D.C., "a leading capitalist of that city and a large holder of real estate in Seattle"; Watson C. Squire, former territorial governor and later United States senator; W. R. Forrest, county auditor; Robert Moran, mayor of Seattle and a shipbuilder; and three other prominent citizens: Alfred Holman, a member of the *Post-Intelligencer* staff; J. D. Lowman of the stationery and and printing firm, Lowman & Hanford; and Dr. H. B. Bagley. Graves also was a director. Backus did not come on the board until late the next year after Hill's death. Hill was also on the board of the Bank of Commerce at its founding.

The newspaper account noted that Graves, the president, "has had long experience in financial matters and thoroughly understands the national banking system." It added that Backus, elected cashier, "has served in a like capacity in the First National Bank of Union Springs, New York, for 20 years and is said to represent large capital as well as long experience."

The initial capital of 1,000 shares was subscribed largely in the East through Graves, the Backus family, and friends. Graves was the largest investor with 322 shares ($32,200). Clinton T. Backus, father of Manson, bought 200 shares and Hill 100; thus these three shareholders held majority control. In all, 10 investors from the East bought 765 shares and 9 from Seattle and Spokane Falls 235 shares.

Manson Backus, undoubtedly still suffering from his loss in First National Bank of Auburn, put no money into formation of Washington National. Later, however, as he built up his own wealth he became much the largest stockholder.

Backus and Graves were in the East when they learned of the devastating Seattle fire. By the time they reached Seattle, the burned-out downtown area had become a tent city and construction of permanent buildings was already under way. Catching the enthusiasm of the times, the two men went right ahead with plans for their bank.

A site was found at Second between James and Cherry. George J. Kilgen was putting up a cheap two-story building but had run out of money. Backus leased the building for a year and paid the rent in advance so that the building could be completed.

The Backus biography and a marginal notation in the minutes of Washington National both state that the bank opened for business on July 21, 1889.[2] That date is probably close enough to the fact, but the 21st was a Sunday and seems an unlikely day for a bank to open.

Deposits grew. In September, Watson Squire, one of the directors, came into the bank to ask Backus how much he had in deposits. Backus replied that he had $75,450. Thereupon Squire wrote a check for that exact amount and told Backus, "Deposit this to my account." Probably that was the only time in the bank's history that deposits doubled in a day. Squire had received the money from an insurance settlement after the fire.

Washington National earned a profit from the first year. By September 1891, at the end of its second year, the bank reported to the Comptroller of the Currency surplus and undivided profits totaling $29,592 built from earnings. The next year the return on capital reached almost 23 per cent and pushed the surplus and undivided profits to $52,277.

To the disappointment of some stockholders, the directors paid no dividends but insisted on retaining all earnings to provide capital for growth. This policy differed from that of the National Bank of Commerce directors, who between 1890 and 1893 paid dividends totaling 26 per cent on the stockholders' investment, then found after the panic of '93 that they had to draw down the bank's capital and surplus in order to write off losses on loans.

The panic proved the soundness of Washington National's conservative dividend policy. Like other banks, Washington National had heavy withdrawals, and in a single year deposits dropped from $385,767 to $179,275. For four years in succession the bank operated at a loss. At the bottom in 1896 its undivided profits, built out of earlier earnings, had shrunk from $37,567 to only $4,202, but capital and surplus remained unimpaired.

With the upturn of business in 1897, deposits more than doubled in a year and by September 1898 pushed past the $1 million mark, a year ahead of the National Bank of Commerce. In 1898 Washington National paid its patient stockholders a dividend of 4 per cent, the first return on their investment in almost ten years. In 1902 dividends were raised to 12 per cent.

Graves, partner of Backus from the outset, sold his interest in the bank and retired as president in 1900. Backus then took over the presidency with a salary of $5,000 a year, an increase from the $3,000 at which he and Graves had each begun. To strengthen the management, Backus persuaded C. J. Lord, founder of Capital National Bank in Olympia and one of the best-known bankers of the state, to come in as cashier. But this association lasted less than a year. Backus and Lord, sound bankers, were both strong individuals who found it hard to yield authority to others. Lord returned to Olympia, but the two remained life-long friends. Lord continued as a director in Washington National and decades later played a key part in development of statewide banking.

Growth in Seattle banking continued during the prosperous early years of the century. Washington National and the National Bank of Commerce, though not the largest in the city, each exceeded $2 million in deposits in 1901 and $3 million in 1903. By 1906 deposits at Commerce topped $4 million and those at Washington National $5 million.

Earnings rose, too. Washington National's capital remained at the original $100,000 which stockholders invested in 1889, but by 1905 the surplus and undivided profits, built from earnings, exceeded $500,000, and thus, shares that had sold originally for $100 each had grown in book value to more than $600 each.

The rise in earnings made bank stocks more attractive to investors. At the same time the increasing pressure of work found Backus giving serious consideration to selling out. He spoke of this in 1903 in offering the position of cashier to a banker in North Dakota:

I wish to tell you also that I have twice come near selling out my interest in the bank, but at this time no negotiations are pending. My chief motive in considering a proposition . . . has been the close confinement which the management of the bank entails upon me, and the difficulty I have experienced in finding the right kind of men to assist me.

I am getting very tired and nervous as a result of the constant work, and feel that I must secure someone to relieve me without delay.[3]

Six months later he wrote an associate in upstate New York that new competitors were taking away some of the bank's business:

The amount of our business is nearly as large as a year ago, but we are not making money quite so fast, as new competition has sprung up by the organization of two trust companies, which pay interest on deposits and cut into the exchange business as well. However, I hope if the city continues to grow in the future as in the past, that the new business coming in will make up for the loss arising from this source.[4]

Seattle banking, nevertheless, continued to expand and to draw wide attention. In correspondence with two officials of the Royal Bank of Canada in Montreal, Backus in 1905 offered to deliver 80 per cent of Washington National's stock—500 shares at $1,000 each and 300 at $700. Backus said he was sure the stock would bring at least $700 a share in liquidation.[5] The offer was made in a letter marked *Confidential* and written in his own hand rather than dictated to a secretary. He preserved a copy out of sequence in the back of a book of his personal letters. Apparently nothing further developed.

In the same year Backus brought in Ralph S. Stacy as cashier. Stacy had been one of the joint managers of the Seattle office of the London & San Francisco Bank, which the Bank of California had just bought to establish its entry into Seattle and its present-day branch. Later Stacy was to serve for many years as King County assessor. With Stacy as the strong No. 2 man, Backus left in November 1905 for a three-month vacation in the South Seas. He returned to face the landlord's notice from the Dexter Horton Estate for the bank to vacate its premises.

A FORCED CONSOLIDATION

The sudden necessity to find new quarters and to move the bank within four months gave a fresh and impelling reason for Washington National to buy, sell, or consolidate. Clearly there was not time to build. But neither was it easy to rent satisfactory quarters in the heart of the financial district already crowded by expanding firms.

Backus wrote almost at once to his old associate, E. O. Graves, in Santa Barbara:

. . . You can, of course, appreciate what a very serious matter this is, and so far I have been unable to hit upon any plan for the future which will be at all satisfactory. Of course, several have presented themselves to my mind, but none which I have felt willing to fully adopt. I think it would be a very bad policy to move far from our present location [Second and Cherry], but it seems impossible to get any satisfactory quarters nearby. A consolidation with some other institution, if it could be effected on satisfactory terms, would solve the problem, but I hardly know how to go at it yet. . . .[6]

Within two weeks, however, Backus had reached a solution which he detailed March 15, 1906, to Graves in a letter so confidential that Backus made a point of writing it in longhand rather than dictating it.[7]

"I had already been at work on the lines suggested in your recent letter when it came to hand—that is, to buy," Backus told Graves. Then he plunged at once into the proposal to merge Washington National Bank into the National Bank of Commerce. The evening before, the two top men at Commerce—Horace C. Henry and Robert Spencer—had met at the Backus home and the three had agreed on the exchange of stock, the sale of additional shares to bring the capital to $1 million, and the selection of top officers.

Henry, railroad builder and investor, who had succeeded M. D. Ballard as president of Commerce in 1900, ranked next to Spencer as the largest stockholder in the bank. Starting at $100 a month for part-time services, he was the first president of Commerce to receive any salary, but he was not a banker and left operations in Spencer's hands. The Henry Building in the White-Henry-Stuart block of downtown Seattle was named for him and also the Henry Art Museum, which along with his collection of art, he donated later to the University of Washington.

The plan that Backus, Henry, and Spencer agreed upon deftly divided top positions among the leaders in the two constituent banks. H. C. Henry would move up to the new honorary position of chairman, and Backus would become president. Robert Spencer and J. W. Maxwell, both from the National Bank of Commerce, would become vice presidents. Stacy from Washington National would become cashier, and Robert Spencer's brother, Ollie, from Commerce, and R. S. Walker from Washington National would become assistant cashiers. The structure was carefully balanced from the beginning, though before actual consolidation there would be some minor changes.

Backus wrote Graves:

Now tell me sincerely and frankly if you care the least about the vice-presidency and, if so, the whole scheme may go to pot unless they yield this point. Spencer's objection is that he does not want to be buried in a

The strategic fifth location of the bank, 1897–1909, which saw consolidation of the Washington National Bank and the National Bank of Commerce. This building at Second and Cherry now is headquarters of Henry Broderick, Inc.

mass of vice-presidents. Both Maxwell and Stacy must necessarily be provided for and neither would accept any place ranking lower than cashier.

The proposal for merger, Backus continued, "is far from satisfactory to me, but I could do no better." The valuation of the stock in the two banks "I think pretty fair . . . the name [continuation of the National Bank of Commerce and disappearance of Washington National Bank] I regard a mistake, but I could not induce the other side to yield the point. It may be that we will have a little larger official force than necessary but that cannot be helped either."

THE CHOICE OF NAME

A week later directors of Washington National also expressed disappointment over the name, but Backus said that Spencer had made continuance of the National Bank of Commerce "an essential point." [8]

Curiously, the proposal to merge came in the first instance not from Backus but from the National Bank of Commerce, and specifically, from Maxwell, a former national bank examiner who had just been appointed cashier of Commerce. Maxwell arranged a meeting between Backus and Spencer in the office of one of the directors. Maxwell, still young, was to become one of Seattle's best-known bankers. Spencer brought him in especially to work on "securing new business at regular rates," little knowing that within three months Maxwell would bag an entire bank.

An insight into the consolidation comes from the meeting of Washington National's directors on March 21. Backus explained, the minutes record, that the building that Dexter Horton & Company was leaving at First and Washington was for sale at $250,000, but he thought that was the wrong location because the city was moving north. By contrast he felt that Commerce's location at Second and Cherry in the offices now occupied by Henry Broderick, Inc., would remain for years the center of the financial district.

Backus told directors that it was certain the city would soon have some large banks and that Dexter Horton, after moving into the quarters Washington National was to vacate, might increase its capital to $1 million, as indeed it did two years later. The minutes add the Backus comment: "We may forestall the effect of this and become one of the largest banks in the city by consolidation with the National Bank of Commerce. The latter is a good bank, with a clean business, and a very strong directorate."

One of the directors, E. E. Ainsworth,

. . . raised the question whether or not consolidations, such as the above, are, as a rule, successful. The opinion, however, prevailed that they were, for the reason that large banks can handle large transactions, and there is a feeling prevalent among the public that they like to deal with large banks. Mr. Green [Joshua Green, Sr., then president of Puget Sound Navigation Co. and later president and today honorary chairman of the Peoples National Bank of Washington] was quite outspoken in his belief that the consolidation would prove beneficial.

The proposal was readily approved by directors and stockholders of both banks, and a week before the deadline Washington National moved its staff and business across the street to the now-crowded offices of the National Bank of Commerce.

New horizons opened. The National Bank of Commerce carried the largest capital and surplus in Seattle, and, Backus boasted, the largest deposits "west of Minneapolis in the northern tier of states," a bank "in shape to handle any business which is likely to be offered for some years to come." [9]

Leadership in the National Bank of Commerce passed from Spencer to Backus. For more than two decades that saw panic, world war, and then prosperity, Backus guided the institution—the longest presidency in the bank's history. Under him deposits tripled and profits exceeded anything the bank had yet known. He took a hand in launching the Federal Reserve System, and in time bore the proud title of "Dean of Seattle Bankers."

Robert Spencer, in the new position of first vice president, was second in command. He remained loyally with the bank until his unexpected death of stomach hemorrhage in 1916 at the age of 61. At that time, as though to point up that no officer ranked even close to the presidency, Backus left the title of first vice president vacant as a tribute to Spencer. The title did not reappear until a new leader from a new generation came into the bank in Backus's closing years.

Even before the consolidation of the Backus and Spencer banks in 1906 had been approved, Backus with obvious pride took over the task of seeing that new shares were sold where they would help the bank most, particularly in getting new business. To a number of top bankers in Washington and in the Midwest and East, Backus wrote of the forthcoming merger and urged them to take 10, 20, or 25 shares of the new stock. He did not offer much to any one person and obviously wanted to place the shares as widely as possible.

Backus and Spencer respected each other's judgment. Each could now take long absences for travel and leave the other in charge. In the year after the consolidation, Spencer sailed for the Orient on a business and pleasure trip. When Spencer returned, Backus set off around the world. But the harness that teamed up two such strong, independent men inevitably also brought some chafing. Backus was positive and dominant, short in build, and sometimes short in speech. Spencer, concerned more with the day-to-day operations, was equally firm. J. A. Swalwell, whom Spencer brought in as cashier from First National Bank of Everett in 1908, recalled with a touch of humor more than fifty years later: "Backus had his room on the north side of the bank, Spencer on the south side. I sat in the middle and was the go-between." [1]

Because Backus kept a tight rein on salaries, some ambitious junior officers such as Swalwell and J. W. Maxwell went to other banks, Swalwell to Dexter Horton and Maxwell to Seattle National and then to found and head National City. Backus could be brusque and sometimes drew a brusque response. Once when a note Swalwell had initialed for renewal went sour, Backus started to take him to task, but Swalwell snapped back: "You know that was *your* loan. My initials were just a matter of form."

The consolidation of Washington National into the National Bank of Commerce severely crowded the bank's quarters. George Bringolf, who came to work a month after the merger and retired in 1948, recalled that the bank's main room was about 40 feet wide with desks of officers along the Second Avenue side. Tellers' cages for foreign exchange and savings were placed in a back room, and alongside them a special cage was partitioned off with chicken wire for handling payrolls on Saturday. At that time it was common to put up about $40,000 each Saturday for customers who wanted cash to pay their help. The payrolls were made up mostly in gold with some silver coins in rolls of small denominations.

One Saturday Bringolf had a shipment of $60,000 in gold to get out as well as the payrolls. When he had finished counting out

$60,000 he found he was short $200. Half of that shortage Spencer insisted that Bringolf make up; the other half came from the bank. Bringolf made a stormy protest because he had no vault of his own, and when the money was delivered to him from the bank's vault in the morning, he had no place to count it. But he still had to pay $100 because of the shortage, an entire month's salary.[2]

Backus and Spencer were highly regarded among bankers. Swalwell, speaking in 1964 of the early years of the century, singled out Backus, Spencer, and Jacob Furth, president of Puget Sound National Bank of Seattle, as "sound men and excellent bankers." Joshua Green, Sr., long a close friend of Backus, spoke of him as "the keenest, best all-round banker I ever knew."[3]

The interests of Backus and Spencer outside the bank differed widely. The Backus family took a prominent part in social affairs. Backus became a regent of the University of Washington, and in later years he collected etchings and prints, which he subsequently donated to the Seattle Art Museum, and Northwest Americana, which he donated to the University of Washington. Spencer was more an outdoorsman. He was fond of duck hunting and fishing and at one time kept a launch on Lake Washington.

Both men were schooled in the hard times of the nineties. This produced a sense of caution, perhaps even greater than that which marks today's older generation of bankers and businessmen who came through the depression of 1932. Spencer's caution sometimes flashed with a touch of humor. He wrote Harry Welty, cashier of a Bellingham bank in which Spencer had an interest:

In regard to letting young Burke go, you will have to use your own judgement. I do not like to see the bank left with but one man in it, as it is an inducement for a hold-up in a quiet town like Fairhaven. Do not carry very much cash on the counter, as it is easier to replenish it from the safe than to get it back from some man on the outside.[4]

To another associate about the same time he remarked: "My experience has been that more money is lost by being in a hurry than going slow, and I would always rather lose a deal than lose money."

STORM OF 1907

Ten months before the panic of 1907, Spencer saw trouble ahead. To C. E. Bingham, a banker in Sedro Woolley, Spencer wrote:

There is another thing that personally I want to write you about, and that is this, future conditions do not look favorable to me. Interest rates are high everywhere, and I can see that even with us money is getting tighter as time progresses. I believe were I in your position that I would keep myself in a position for a possible storm at any time, with the least amount of liabilities outstanding possible.

This has absolutely no reference to the amount of your advances from this bank, to which you are, and have at all times been welcome. It is intended merely as a little note of warning. We are gradually shrinking our credits, have called practically all of our New York loans and are putting ourselves in just as strong a position as we possibly can.[5]

Backus too was disturbed by boom and inflation, and what might follow. Returning from a three-month trip early in 1906, he wrote his old associate, E. O. Graves:

I find the town has gone real estate mad. The existing conditions remind me vividly of those which we so well remember as prevailing the first year or two after our arrival in Seattle. To my mind there can be but one end to this craze.[6]

Speculation centered in tidelands south of the main wharves and business district. Backus related that purchases of land by the Milwaukee Railroad and Union Pacific for terminals "has set loose a large amount of extra funds which have not yet found investment and incidentally has had the effect of sending prices for property skyward." By April Backus suggested to an associate in Toledo, Ohio, that it was time to sell lands which they had jointly bought in Seattle.

In June 1907, four months before the panic, Backus wrote:

Business continues very good, but I think the edge is off from speculation all over the country, and I feel that it is a good thing to have it so. We were all going too fast and our chief trouble was too much prosperity. To slow up and get a fresh start will be beneficial everywhere.[7]

Backus, a seasoned banker, knew that any turnabout from a period of excess speculation would give all financial institutions a difficult time. His paramount responsibility lay with his depositors. He remarked to an associate: "Some persons may call me cold-hearted, but my depositors shall never have occasion to do so."

Banking, Backus felt, was a business where a man made his reputation and had to live with it. When asked to support legislation for insurance of deposits in national banks, Backus wrote:

I regret to say that I cannot see my way to endorse this measure. Under its provisions all deposits in national banks would seem to be equally protected. This would naturally cause a feeling of indifference among the depositors as to which bank their monies were lodged with and would thereby seem to me to work an injustice on the banks of known conservatism and strength, whose reputation, established perhaps by long years of patience and hard work and which is now a valuable asset, would be in great measure sacrificed. It would further tend, or at least it seems so to me, to make the bank officers themselves less careful than they are now.[8]

Ten years later Washington State tried, then abandoned, voluntary insurance of deposits in state-chartered banks. Not until after the wave of failures in 1933 was the present nationwide system of insurance of deposits adopted.

Panic in 1907 was triggered by the closing on October 22 of the Knickerbocker Trust Company in New York, and in that city alone ten banks failed. As the news of these failures spread across the country, uneasy depositors for whom the panic of '93 was still vivid lined up at their banks to withdraw and hoard their money.

As money disappeared from circulation, banks were squeezed for cash. Normally, they would hold back on making new loans or renewals, but such a policy would lead to hardship and deflation, and it could not begin to generate cash fast enough in a money panic.

Banks needed a central or wholesale institution to which they might take sound collateral and borrow against this to provide temporary funds. The Federal Reserve System, which later did perform such a function, had not been created. For common action in emergency, bankers turned to their local clearing house association, an interbank agency set up in each larger city for the return of checks and the settlement of balances.

Eastern cities were the first to use clearing house associations to perform the function of a central bank. Individual associations printed temporary paper money, called clearing house certificates, and allowed member banks to obtain these certificates in exchange for collateral.

Use of clearing house certificates spread quickly westward, and on Monday, November 4, 1907, after a feverish Sunday, bankers announced through the Seattle Clearing House Association that they would "cease cash payments except in small amounts for emergency purposes only," and clearing house certificates would be put into circulation as quickly as they could be printed.[9]

A steam-powered "traction train" moved big stems in 1907. (Darius Kinsey photo from University of Washington.)

Certificates were issued in denominations of $1, $2, $5, $10, and $20 for a total of $1,675,000; an almost equal amount was issued in denominations from $1,000 to $10,000 for interbank transactions. The sheer task of preparing the certificates for use almost overnight was immense. The certificates were too numerous for officers of the Clearing House to sign, so younger men were also authorized to sign them. George Bringolf, who began his career in banking only the year before, recalls that he alone signed 25,000.

Gold and silver were then the principal currency. Paper money, issued both by the United States Treasury and by individual banks, had relatively little circulation and was distrusted by many customers. Clearing house certificates were accepted only grudgingly. To ensure greater public acceptance, certificates carried the backing not only of collateral posted by individual banks but also the guarantee in full of every bank of the Clearing House Association.

The panic of 1907 spread into every corner of the nation. What happened in one area, Grays Harbor, was recounted a few years ago by Will France, who in 1907 was manager of the Montesano State Bank (later the Montesano branch of the National Bank of Commerce) and later for many years a director of Marine Bancorporation.

About 8 A.M. on November 7th I was informed by a Portland representative of the First National Bank of Portland that a national banking emergency would prevent that institution from shipping any more money to the Harbor until further notice. This money normally would flow back to the Harbor in payment for lumber and other goods which our mills shipped out. We were dependent on it for payrolls and the general business of the area.

A train bound from Aberdeen to Seattle was waiting for me at the Montesano station on the 7th. I hurried down, found W. J. (Billy) Patterson of the Hayes & Hayes Bank of Aberdeen and W. L. Adams of Hoquiam First National. They said to get right aboard and we were all going to Tacoma to print some temporary currency.

The printer ran off $300,000 in currency labeled "Certificate of the Associated Banks of Chehalis County" [Grays Harbor was then part of Chehalis County]. This was to be our local money. The three of us were in such a hurry that we had time to print only one side of the currency, but it served its purpose beautifully. All the banks on the Harbor used the certificates just like United States currency, and so did their customers.

The issuance of certificates to the banks was closely regulated. First the banks had to put up collateral, and a committee consisting of Patterson, Adams and myself had to approve the collateral before authorizing Superior Court Judge C. W. Hodgdon of Hoquiam to issue the currency.

The crisis continued until March before real money again became available. Grays Harbor certificates were redeemed without the loss of a single dollar and without a banking failure.

The three months' period when Grays Harbor money prevailed was particularly noticeable because hard money consisting of gold and silver was all the loggers would take prior to that time. This was because their pokes often became soaked during a squall or an unexpected dunking in a lake or river and paper money wouldn't stand that treatment.[10]

By the spring of 1908 the panic had run its course. Certificates issued in Seattle were also redeemed in full and banking returned to a normal basis. Even with restrictions on withdrawals, however, Seattle banks had suffered a substantial loss in deposits during the panic. In the latter part of 1907 the shrinkage was $12 million, almost 17 per cent of all deposits. The decline at the National Bank of Commerce totaled $1,381,000, or 12 per cent, the smallest decline among the city's four major banks. Deposits at Dexter Horton fell 15 per cent, Scandinavian American 30 per cent, and Puget Sound National almost 34 per cent.

The economy was slow to recover from the setback of 1907. A year and a half passed before deposits at Seattle banks returned to the pre-panic total. By late 1909 the total moved to a new high and then remained on a plateau with almost no change for five years. This was far different from the bubbling early years of the century. Construction of downtown business blocks and of stores and houses that had drawn thousands of carpenters, painters, bricklayers, and other craftsmen was tapering off.

Lumber, the state's basic industry, suffered from excess capacity and the competition of southern mills in supplying markets of the Midwest and East. In the panic of 1907 prices tumbled. One small mill after another disappeared from business, and the number of producing mills shrank unbelievably from 1,036 in 1906 to only 389 in 1915.[1]

The demand in San Francisco for lumber to rebuild from the earthquake and fire in 1906 pushed Washington's output to a new high. But in the next two years, production fell by almost one-third, from 4.3 billion board feet in 1906 to 2.9 billion in 1908. Not until 1913 did Washington mills cut as much lumber as they did in 1906. Even the rise in 1913 could not be sustained, and production fell in each of the next two years. The turnabout came only with the onset of World War I.

The manufacture of cedar shingles ranked in importance with lumbering during the early years of the century. A small shingle mill cost much less to build than a sawmill, and production of shingles remained largely in the hands of small operators.

Giant cedars, with long, tight-grain, knot-free trunks, were abundant in the valleys leading back from Puget Sound into the Cascade and Olympic Mountains. These trees had to be felled before the valley bottoms could be put to farming. For easier handling, cedar logs were sawed and split into bolts about 50 inches long, from which three lengths of 16-inch shingles were sawed. A generous allowance was included for trim because the soft cedar bolts, floated down rivers to shingle mills, were often badly scuffed on the rocks.

In 1909, when the all-time high in production of wooden shingles in the United States was reached, Washington cut more than eight billion shingles (1,000 shingles were packed into five bundles, equivalent to 1¼ squares in present-day measurement).[2] About this time Washington mills turned out 84 per cent of all cedar shingles made in the United States. Mills in Ballard, on the edge of Seattle, shipped as much as a trainload of shingles a week. The Seattle, Lake Shore & Eastern Railroad (later the Northern Pacific), which ran along the east side of Lake Washington north to the Canadian border, sent entire trainloads of shingles east, sometimes as often as one a day. Along this rail line one was never out of sound of a shingle mill's whistle. The little town of Arlington alone had 14 mills.[3]

The shingle industry, however, where even a new mill required relatively little capital, was plagued even more than the lumber industry by excess capacity. On and off for two decades leaders sought to curtail production and strengthen prices. In 1911 manufacturers signed agreements to close one day a week. The agreement was not universally accepted and prices continued generally unsatisfactory.

Gradually, as cedar disappeared from the valleys and loggers moved up the mountain slopes, the supply diminished. At the same

time the development of the automobile brought, indirectly, stiff
new competition that cut deeply into markets for cedar shingles.
The rising production of gasoline for automobiles yielded asphalt
as a by-product. From asphalt later came composition shingles that
replaced cedar on roofs of millions of houses.

As 1913 opened, Backus had a somber report for his stockholders:

All things considered the year 1912 has been a hard one. It appears to
have been the culmination of about three years of depression throughout the country, which has adversely affected our chief staple industry
—the lumber business. Interest rates have tended downward, while the
amount of interest paid on deposits has steadily increased.[4]

FINANCING FOR FOREST PRODUCTS

In the early years of the century, logs, lumber, and shingles
accounted for the biggest part of loans at many a city and cross-
roads bank in western Washington. Certainly that was true in the
Grays Harbor area, where the first small mills sprang up in the
1880's. In 1909, the earliest year covered by records at the Port
of Grays Harbor, 618 vessels, most of them three- and four-masted
schooners, carried 457 million board feet of lumber to markets in
California and ports on the Pacific Rim. By the mid-1920's outbound lumber shipments from Grays Harbor reached 1.4 billion
board feet, an all-time high that gave the area a reputation as the
greatest lumber seaport in the world.

Logs were plentiful and cheap. E. K. Bishop, who headed the
Aberdeen lumber company of that name, recounted in 1963 that
when he came to the Harbor around the turn of the century "the
finest timber that ever grew could be bought for $1 a thousand
board feet on the stump," a price that by the late 1960's had risen
a hundred fold. "Hemlock, considered worthless, was thrown in
free. Cruising [estimating the volume of standing timber] was
haphazard, and the overrun would make more recent buyers turn
green with envy."[5]

With timber so abundant, Mr. Bishop said, "the mills had the
money and the loggers were their slaves. The loggers were not well
heeled, and the banks and the sawmill companies carried the financial load. As time went on this situation was reversed."

Financing began with the logger, who would contract to cut a
tract of timber and would need money for payroll, cookhouse,
feed for oxen or horses, and other expenses. The logger would

Second Avenue and Spring Street, Seattle, about 1910. The corner building, originally a department store, later expanded, now houses the bank headquarters. (Webster & Stevens photo.)

borrow from his bank on a 90-day acceptance or note. The logs would be put in a river and floated to large rafting areas on the Chehalis River, where they were sorted by the owner's brand. When the logs were delivered to the mill, the logger got his money and paid the bank.

Lending on a raft of logs was common, too. Here a mill would buy a raft and give a note to the bank payable in 90 days. The discount ranged generally between 2 and 3 per cent for 90 days, equivalent to 8 to 12 per cent a year. If times were good, a mill had money enough to buy logs outright, but often as an accommodation it would let the bank handle an acceptance.

After the San Francisco earthquake and fire in 1906, numerous sawmills were set up on Grays Harbor with headquarters in San Francisco, and their financing was taken care of at headquarters. As smaller, locally owned mills started up, they turned to their local banks for financing. A common form of loan, then and now, was an advance of 75 to 80 per cent of an invoice at the time a mill made a shipment. The loan would be repaid when the lumber or shingles reached the destination and the buyer sent his check.

Will France of Montesano, who became dean of bankers in southwestern Washington, said that when logs were selling for $8 to $12 a thousand board feet, a bank would advance $3 to $4 a thousand on a 90-day note.[6] With this advance the logger could get his timber moving downstream to mills on Grays Harbor.

In the opening years of the century bankers had great leeway in making loans and depended largely on their personal judgment of the man who wanted to borrow money. E. K. Bishop, a bank director in Aberdeen who later served in that capacity for many years with the National Bank of Commerce, recalled: "Banking depended on the way the lender sized up the borrower. If the banker liked you he would not even look at your financial statement—if you had one."

When Bishop started the manufacture of shingles he took over a small mill from a bank in Montesano, signed "a sheaf of papers" and was in business. At that time there was no limit as to how much a state-chartered bank could lend to one customer, and Bishop said long afterward that many a time he had the equivalent of the bank's entire capital and surplus tied up in shingles.

One effect of this was to make banking more hazardous. Only one bank on Grays Harbor survived from the earliest day—

Lumber for the world. The schooner Alert took on a full cargo at the E. K. Wood Company mill in Hoquiam about 1922. (Jones Photo Co.)

Aberdeen State Bank. It was founded in 1901, ultimately became a branch of the National Bank of Commerce, and for two long periods—from late 1931 to 1938 and again from 1942 to 1953—was the only bank in Aberdeen.

WEALTH FROM THE SEA

An industry growing in size in the early years of the century and helping the economy balance wide swings in forest products was salmon packing. The first cannery in the Pacific Northwest opened on the Columbia River in 1867. By 1888, just before Washington became a state, 28 canneries were operating on the Washington and Oregon shores of the lower Columbia, a number that has never since been equalled. By 1895 production had reached 635,000 cases, an all-time high, about six times the average of the 1960's.[7]

On Puget Sound, salmon canning began in 1877. By 1915 production reached a record high of 2,583,000 cases. Then, as it did on the Columbia River, the salmon resource began to decline with the growth of cities and industries, the disturbance of spawning streams, and overfishing. In time, fish traps were outlawed on Puget Sound, and efforts were undertaken to rebuild the salmon runs.

In Alaska, the richest source of salmon in North America, the first cannery opened in 1878. Gradually additional plants were erected. In 1895 output reached one million cases; two years later it topped two million cases.

Much of the early fishing was concentrated on Bristol Bay, north of the Aleutian chain, the chief area for the prized red salmon. The story of the bonanza of the North drew fishermen from Puget Sound, New England, and Scandinavia, and canneries sprang up on remote bays and coves. In 1912 production reached four million cases. In 1914, with a slightly larger total pack, more than half of it in red salmon, output of this industry swelled to a value of $19,700,000 landed at Seattle. In that year salmon displaced gold in Alaska in value of output, a leadership that salmon has held ever since.[8]

For almost four decades a four-million-case pack was a base seldom missed and more often substantially exceeded. Then came a long decline and not a single year from 1950 through 1968 saw production as large as it was in 1914, though with a half-century of

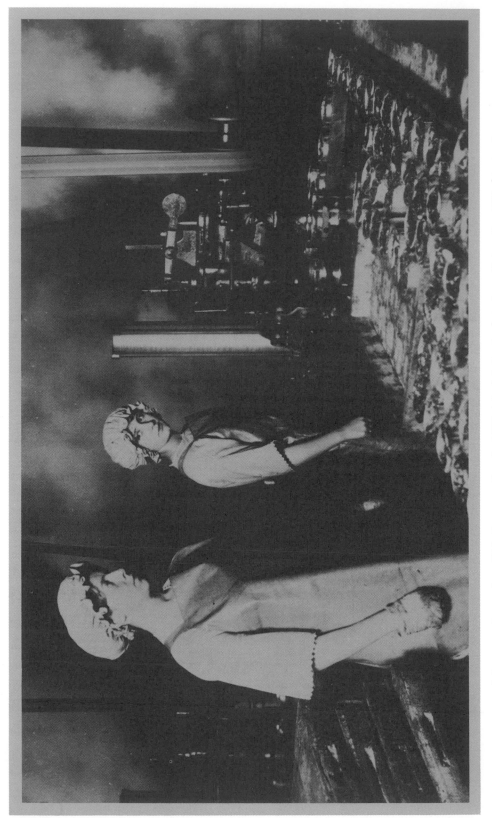

Salmon canning at Apex Fish Company, Seattle, 1913. (Asahel Curtis photo from University of Washington.)

inflation the wholesale value of the pack nowadays approximates $100 million.

Early in the century Seattle became established as the capital of the salmon industry. In the spring ships sailed north with building materials and machinery, cans, salt and other supplies, plus foodstuffs for thousands of workers. In the summer and fall, deep-laden vessels discharged their rich cargo on the docks at Seattle for warehousing, labeling, and ultimate shipment to markets of the nation and the world.

Few industries in America carry such risks as salmon packing in Alaska, and the risks were even greater in the early years when little was known about where the various runs of salmon would appear or how long they would last. The industry once was made up of many small companies, as many as 80 to 100 at one time. Most of the early canners operated at only one location, and the failure of a salmon run at that location could be disastrous.

Salmon was, and still is, a feast or famine business. A cannery may be 2,000 miles from its source of supplies on Puget Sound, but men, cans, and equipment must be ready in the hope that the salmon will return as expected from the ocean to spawn. Undoubtedly the willingness of men to gamble for this harvest of the sea contributed to the spirit of adventure in Seattle as a young city.

Backus and Spencer as bankers were called on to help finance salmon packers, and the National Bank of Commerce became a leader in this specialty. Spencer himself owned stock in San Juan Fishing & Packing Company, from early times one of the important operators on Puget Sound and in Alaska. At his death Spencer was a vice president of San Juan Fishing & Packing Company, which merged in recent years into New England Fish Company, Seattle.[9]

In the days of Spencer and Backus a canner would deliver his pack to a warehouse on Puget Sound, primarily those of the Port of Seattle. There a consignment would be inspected for swelled or puffed cans, and samples would be opened for examination of quality. A bank then would lend against warehouse receipts.

Selling in those days was largely through independent brokers. When a sale was made, the bank would issue a trust receipt and release the stocks from the warehouse. A draft was made out with an order bill of lading attached. When the shipment reached its

Chinook salmon on the Columbia River, brought in by horse-drawn nets (no longer allowed). This picture is believed to have been taken along Sand Island near Ilwaco, in the early 1930's.

destination, perhaps in the Midwest or East, the buyer would pay the draft to a correspondent of the Seattle bank.

In later years a number of larger canners established their own sales organizations. With the gradual consolidation of small packers into larger organizations, canners obtained a wider geographical spread that provided protection against the failure of a run in a single location. In time, too, as the industry grew and as individual packers built their net worth, banks loaned against the net worth of a company at the start of the season as well as against the merchandise at the completion of the season.

WEALTH FROM THE LAND

In the early years of the century businessmen like Backus looked primarily to the forest and sea to nourish the economy of young cities on Puget Sound. Agriculture, while gaining in importance, was slow to start in the Puget Sound basin, and the state's leading crop, wheat, grew almost entirely in the eastern section beyond the barrier of the Cascade Mountains and at that time far outside the service area of Seattle banks. Nevertheless, agriculture was entering a new phase of expansion. From 1900 to 1910 the number of farms doubled to 66,300, an increase unmatched in the state's history. In the same period the land in farms increased 55 per cent to 13.2 million acres, a rise unmatched in this century.

Cattle and sheep raising during the 1860's and 1870's made up the earliest agricultural enterprises of size in Washington and continue important to this day.

As the heavy bunch grass of eastern rangelands yielded to the plough, wheat took the position of dominance it has held ever since. During the 1880's, Walla Walla wheat was quoted on the Liverpool exchange. When the new railroads made distant markets accessible at home and abroad, the production of wheat spread over the fertile slopes of the Walla Walla, Snake, and Palouse River valleys and to the Big Bend country of the Columbia River. The harvest of wheat in 1909 reached 41 million bushels, almost doubled in 10 years. By the first decade of this century the wheat counties of Whitman, Columbia, Garfield, Lincoln, and Douglas south and west of Spokane had reached a peak in population never since equalled.

In western Washington, farming was concentrated on the valleys

"Unusual opportunities to men who want to succeed" carried the appeal in advertising by the Great Northern Railway in 1907 as it sought to build population in the Pacific Northwest. (Burlington Northern Archives.)

and lowlands, but there the richness of the soil that produced forests of such giant Douglas fir and red cedar gave settlers the grim task of removing mammoth stumps, and the richer the soil the bigger the stumps. In early pastures stumps were often left standing, but for large cultivated areas there was nothing to do but laboriously work the stumps out by blasting and burning and then using horses to pull out broken sections and roots. Various ingenious stump-pullers were developed, some operated by hand and others powered by horse, but there was no easy shortcut to a cleared field.

Dairying, berries, and intensive truck farming took over much of the bottom land, and poultry and fruit were produced on benchlands. The markets lay primarily in the new cities that fringed Puget Sound. Gradually also canneries came in to process fruits and vegetables for more distant markets.

A new phase in agriculture began with large-scale development of irrigation soon after the turn of the century. Some of the earliest irrigation canals were built in the Yakima Valley during the 1880's. Construction was stimulated by the arrival of the Northern Pacific, then slowed by the panic of '93 and the difficulty of financing new ventures. In 1902 the National Irrigation Act was passed, and in 1905 the newly formed Bureau of Reclamation bought out Washington Irrigation Company, which had contracted to supply more water than its canal could carry or was even available. Subsequently the Bureau undertook new projects larger and more ambitious than private companies could finance.

From 1900 to 1910 the land under irrigation increased from 135,470 acres to 334,378. By 1920 the total converted from parched dusty desert to lush green farmland reached 529,899 acres and included some of the most productive areas in the West.

Irrigation of the deep volcanic soil characteristic of central Washington brought heavy plantings of apples in the area near Wenatchee, of apples, soft fruits, and vegetables in the Yakima Valley, and of alfalfa and potatoes in the Kittitas Valley near Ellensburg.

The state's output of apples, originally grown mainly west of the Cascades, averaged close to 3 million bushels a year from 1900 to 1910, then rose sharply as young orchards on newly irrigated lands east of the Cascades began bearing. By 1914 production approached 10 million bushels. In 1919 the harvest exceeded 25

Wheat grew belly-high near Almira, Washington, in 1911. A combine required 25 horses and six men to do what one man handles today with power equipment.

million bushels for the first time, and the average return of $1.95 a bushel, highest in years, gave growers a bonanza of more than $49 million.[10] Among crops, apples came next to wheat in value in 1919, a ranking that holds to this day.

Not until the opening of the Columbia Basin after World War II did Washington again see such an expansion in its agricultural base. But the concept of damming the Columbia River at Grand Coulee and diverting the water to a million parched acres far to the south came out of the success with irrigation in the Wenatchee area. As far as is known, the first published proposal for a dam at Grand Coulee was carried in the *Wenatchee Daily World* in 1918, an idea worked out by Billy Clapp, a Wenatchee lawyer, and Rufus Woods, the publisher.

The crops of fruits and vegetables that came from the first major irrigation projects were much too large to be absorbed in the Pacific Northwest alone. For apples and soft fruit the big markets lay in major cities as far distant as the East Coast. To reach those markets growers sometimes formed their own sales organizations.

In 1902 a group of 300 growers in the Yakima Valley put up $1 each and formed the Yakima County Horticultural Union, regarded as the oldest grower-owned marketing organization in the West.[11] A year later membership dropped to 50, with each grower putting up $100 in capital. In 1906 the Hort Union, as it became known, built one of the first warehouses on Fruit Row in Yakima. Today the organization, known as the Snokist Growers, takes its name from its leading brand and, expanded in recent mergers, has built sales to $17 million a year. In the Wenatchee area Skookum and Wenoka became apple brand names known across the country and in Europe.

WAR AND BOOM TIMES

Two events in 1914 brought far-reaching changes in the economy of the young state. The first was the opening of the Panama Canal, which in time helped West Coast lumbermen deliver an increasing volume to the East Coast. The second was the outbreak of war in Europe.

America's entry into the war in 1917 brought tremendous growth in shipping and shipbuilding at Seattle, strong markets for products like wheat, and a burst of activity that carried into almost every

Emigrants unloading possessions from freight cars, about 1910–1915. (Burlington Northern Railway photo.)

business. Something of the feeling of the times comes from Backus's report to stockholders in January, 1918:

This gigantic struggle [the war] now dominates every industry . . . As no one can read the future, the only policy to follow seems to be to do today's business on today's market, keeping always in mind that we are possibly at the height of our prosperity for the time being . . . .

This city now has become the fourth port in the United States, its commerce amounting in round figures to $500,000,000, or about $130,000,000 more than that of San Francisco. Seattle is now first in importance in shipbuilding on the Pacific Coast and is probably surpassed by only one or two cities on the Atlantic side . . . . Merchants report larger sales in value than ever before—while more goods are sold for cash than on credit. Collections were never so good.

The peak came in 1919, the year after the war. Deposits at the National Bank of Commerce swelled to $22 million, up almost 80 per cent from 1915; for all the city's banks, deposits more than doubled to reach $186 million.

Backus cautioned repeatedly of the readjustment that he was sure would come. He told stockholders at the start of 1920: "The nation's business for the year 1919 surpassed all previous records, but the value of the dollar has continued to decline and great economic problems confront us. I believe that the year 1920 bids fair to be one of the most critical in the history of the republic." A year later Backus reported the largest earnings of the bank's history, but he added realistically, "I very much regret to say the losses incurred were also unequalled."

Backus recognized that business could not continue at the wartime level, yet growth of the bank had been so great that it had to seek larger quarters. Only a few years before, in 1909, the bank had outgrown its offices in the Bailey Building (now the Second and Cherry Building) and had moved to the new Leary Building (now 1000 Second Avenue Building) at Second and Madison. These quarters were expected to be ample to serve the bank for many years.

But in less than a decade the bank again had almost doubled in size. In July, 1918, the board approved purchase of the Baillargeon Building, one block north of Second and Spring, for $490,000. The building did not become available for two years and then was extensively remodeled for banking offices. Subsequently enlarged to more than double its original size, it remains the bank's headquarters.

The recession of 1921 proved short though sharp. From the peak in 1919 to 1921, Seattle's bank clearings, a measure of business activity, fell by 25 per cent; bank deposits city-wide tumbled almost 30 per cent. Then began a period of expansion in the economy of both the city and the state that continued through the 1920's.

In each of the last four years of the decade, the state's production of lumber topped seven billion board feet—almost half of all the lumber cut in the West and 20 per cent in the nation. This was the golden era for Washington lumber, an output never equalled before or since. In this decade, also, Washington took first rank in apples, and a good volume of apples as well as lumber moved over the docks of Washington seaports to markets in distant lands.

The population grew, though at a more moderate rate. To the count of 315,312 in 1920, Seattle added 50,000 residents during the decade. In total population and in actual growth Seattle accounted for almost one-fourth of all the state's residents.

The National Bank of Commerce prospered with the times and paid its stockholders well. After the consolidation in 1906, the bank raised its dividend from 12 per cent a year to 16 per cent, and later to 20 per cent. In 1928 Backus asked George Bringolf, then the bank's auditor, to figure just how stockholders had fared in the 39 years since he founded the Washington National Bank. Bringolf's simple penciled notation, which Backus proudly kept, showed that an investor who bought a share of stock for $100 in 1889 had received $5,439 in cash and stock dividends, a return averaging 140 per cent each year.[12]

A BUYER FOR THE BANK

Acquisition and merger of banks continued during the first three decades of the century. In 1910 consolidation of Puget Sound National Bank of Seattle into the First National Bank took from the National Bank of Commerce the position it had held for four years as the state's largest. In subsequent years the National Bank of Commerce maintained rank as second or third largest. The bank remained respected and profitable, and Backus showed no sign of wanting to acquire other banks just to gain size.

In 1916 Backus headed a committee of directors to look into a three-way amalgamation of the National Bank of Commerce,

Dexter Horton, and Metropolitan National. This project died in a few days, but a two-way merger of the National Bank of Commerce and Metropolitan was under active study for most of the latter half of the year. In preparation for this merger the National Bank of Commerce paid its stockholders a 45 per cent cash dividend, a distribution of $450,000. But leaders of the two banks could not agree on a basis for exchange of shares, and the consolidation fell apart.

In 1921 efforts to save the Scandinavian-American Bank from collapse included a proposal to consolidate with the National Bank of Commerce and the First National. But Scandinavian-American's loans were impaired, and a basis for the pooling of assets could not be found. Soon afterward Scandinavian-American closed its doors.

In 1928 Backus was approached by a new buyer, Andrew Price, a leader in the new generation in Seattle financing. Backus, after almost forty years in Seattle banking, recognized that the time was coming when he would have to lighten his load. His bank was at an all-time high in size and in earnings. The time was favorable to sell. When Price telephoned and asked if Backus would meet him at the Olympic Hotel, two blocks from the National Bank of Commerce, Backus readily said "Yes."

PART III

ANDREW PRICE / Banking Goes to the People

Manson Backus and Andrew Price, meeting alone at the hotel on April 2, 1928, exchanged pleasantries before Backus turned to the business at hand and said he assumed Price wanted to discuss the National Bank of Commerce. Yes, Price quickly replied, and on what basis would Backus sell his stock?[1] Out of the negotiations thus begun was to come the largest acquisition in Price's career and a turning point in Pacific Northwest banking history.

Backus and Price made a sharp contrast as individuals and as bankers. Backus, white-haired and 75, proud dean of Seattle bankers, had learned banking in the decades after the Civil War. He came from the old school in which bankers fashioned their services primarily for businessmen, who came to the bank when they wanted help. Backus had hoped that his son LeRoy might succeed him, but the son's interest lay outside the bank. Now Backus was going to deal with Price, this man so tall and thin, bubbling with energy yet deferential to one almost twice his age.

Backus had long known Andrew's father, John E. Price, a respected leader in investment banking. Of course he knew Andrew Price, although he could not agree with his notions about taking banking to the people and seeking the accounts of those who had no more than what they got in their Saturday pay envelope.

Who was Andrew Price, the man who *Fortune* magazine would report a little later was the *"enfant terrible* of Seattle banking"?[2] How had he come up in banking? And how did he propose to buy the National Bank of Commerce?

Price's earliest employment had been with the investment banking firm of John E. Price & Co., which his father had founded. The elder Price, born in Tennessee in 1857, fought in Indian wars in the Southwest, worked in railroad construction, then settled in Denver in 1888 and became secretary-treasurer of Bellan-Price Investment Company, Bankers and Brokers.

To a school chum, J. K. Bothwell, living in Seattle, the elder Price wrote from Denver in 1891: "We are doing a loan and financial brokerage business . . . . Though we are not, so far as capital is concerned, one of the largest institutions in town, yet we know we can . . . be ranked among the safest."[3] The emphasis on *safety* was to become characteristic of the financial enterprises of John E. Price.

JOHN E. PRICE & CO. FORMED

In 1902, when doctors insisted that Price's son Andrew must be taken to a different climate, the family moved from Denver to Seattle. The year before, Price had looked the young city over for a possible business connection and now he opened up the investment banking firm, John E. Price & Co. The company specialized in underwriting municipal bonds. It also dealt in bank stocks, and to gain recognition in this field, the firm published quarterly data on each Seattle bank.

The elder Price not only bought and sold bank stocks for investors, but also occasionally worked on transactions for the outright sale of a bank. In 1907 he assisted three men in obtaining control of the First National Bank of Seattle, then located on Pioneer Square. The three were Morris A. Arnold; his brother-in-law, David Hickman Moss; and Lester Turner, vice president and cashier. Arnold had been in banking in Billings, Montana. His wife and Mrs. Price were second cousins. Years later, Arnold became an eminent Seattle banker, head of Seattle-First National Bank. Price took his commission in stock of the bank.

Price also negotiated on two occasions with Manson Backus and Robert Spencer to buy the National Bank of Commerce, first in 1910 on behalf of the president of Hudson Trust Co., New York, and a year later, for a Kansas City bank whose identity now is lost. But Backus and Spencer were in no hurry to sell and set a price no one would meet.

John E. Price was never a commercial banker, but his son Andrew appeared headed in that direction from boyhood. Two weeks after the Union Savings & Trust Bank opened in November, 1903, Andrew, at the age of 13, got a job soliciting savings accounts from his school classmates. He was paid 30 cents for each account and earned about $18 in the first month.

Later, as a student at Seattle High School (subsequently named Broadway), Price made a study of school savings accounts and checked by mail with bankers and school superintendents across the country. School savings plans were beginning to spread, and in 1908 he wrote a booklet, "Teaching Thrift as a Branch of Public Instruction—The School Savings Bank System." In that same year an advisory committee of Seattle school principals recommended establishment of a school savings system.

Price studied two years at Yale, then left because his father needed him in the business. Andrew joined the firm and later became a partner. He traveled throughout the Pacific Northwest, searching out and buying the municipal bond issues that are used to finance construction of schools, bridges, irrigation systems, and other improvements. He also visited eastern financial centers to develop markets for issues the company bought.

On a trip to the Yakima Valley in 1914, Price met Homer Boyd, who then headed the Seattle bond office of the Lumbermen's Bank of Portland, later part of the United States National Bank. The two men, studying the financing of a proposed drainage system at Sunnyside, pooled their efforts. Price liked the way Boyd analyzed the situation and suggested that Boyd, five years his elder, talk to John E. Price about joining the company. Some months later, Boyd did so, and thus began a close association that continued until Andrew Price's death in 1955.

The bond work was unquestionably good training for Price,

Water for parched acres is essential for intensive agriculture in the sagebrush land east of the Cascade Mountains. This 1913 photograph shows a section of the canal above the Naches Power Station, built for irrigation and electric power.

particularly in the analysis of what to buy and how to sell issues, but he chafed under the limitations that he felt this work carried. He wrote a college friend in 1912 that Seattle, "too far removed from the vast accumulations of money," was not in a "strategic location" for bond work. Yet he liked Seattle and thought great opportunity could be found in commercial banking. He talked constantly to his associates about banks and banking and of innovations that might be made—if only he could find the capital to start a bank of his own.

With American entry into World War I, Price tried repeatedly to enlist, only to be rejected because of health. He persisted and finally was accepted and commissioned in the Army and went off to training camp. In his absence, his father and Homer Boyd carried on the business, assisted by a new bookkeeper who took over the accounting that Andrew had handled. The Armistice came just before Price's unit was to sail for Europe.

Price returned to Seattle and devoted virtually his full energies to founding a bank. From training camp he had written his father frequently about banking, and already some preparatory steps had been taken. Andrew was convinced that the means for establishing a bank lay with John E. Price & Co. and its clientele of investors in bank stocks. He anticipated that the family bond house and a new bank could operate together so that each would build business for the other with a saving in costs. His problem was not just to raise the initial capital, but to do so in a way that would enable him to retain control. What he projected was a Price venture, one that he would plan, organize, and direct.

John E. Price & Co. had never been a large company; in 1918 its total assets were hardly $100,000. But through some intricate financial maneuvering the company became the base for Andrew Price's bank. The first step in June, 1918 converted John E. Price & Co. from a partnership to a corporation. The capitalization of the corporation was set at $200,000, half in preferred stock, half in common stock.

Before transferring the partnership to the corporation the Prices first increased the book value of the partnership by almost $90,000. This was done by an accounting entry that gave to good will—not previously carried as an asset—a value of $89,359.33. The entry lifted the net worth from just over $60,000 to $150,000, and for that sum, the partners received all the common stock in the corporation plus half the preferred, a total value of $150,000. The Prices then sold the $50,000 remaining in preferred stock to an estate.

The plan of incorporation required that John E. Price & Co. maintain net assets at all times equal to 110 per cent of the value of preferred stock. To provide this protection, Andrew Price transferred to the company $20,000 in 6 per cent promissory notes secured by deeds of trust on Texas land owned jointly with his brother Hickman, who did not participate in the Seattle ventures. The company agreed not to sell or use the notes unless necessary to protect creditors or preferred stockholders. It also agreed that after paying 7 per cent dividends on both the preferred and common stock it would set at least 50 per cent of remaining earnings into a surplus fund to retire the notes and return them to Andrew Price. By this means, Price used his equity in Texas farm land to expand the base underlying the outstanding preferred stock in John E. Price & Co. The objective was to contribute equity capital to a new corporation without putting up any cash.

In the spring of 1919 additional preferred shares were sold. The largest block, $10,000, went to J. Cebert Baillargeon, later president of Seattle Trust & Savings Bank. Homer Boyd put in $5,000, a major commitment on his part that required sale of some property in Portland, and Blake D. Mills $5,000. About this time, Boyd also bought from John E. Price 10 per cent of the stock of John E. Price & Co. and sold his previous one share to Andrew Price. With these changes Andrew took over controlling interest in John E. Price & Co.

MARINE STATE BANK

Armed with new working capital from sale of preferred stock, the Prices were ready now to launch a bank. On June 30, 1919, the organizational meeting of Marine State Bank was held by John E. Price, Andrew Price, and Homer Boyd from John E. Price & Co., and two outsiders—Frank Waterhouse, millionaire shipping operator with diverse other interests, and Charles S. Wills, treasurer of Seattle Hardware Co. The initial capital to be raised was $200,000. Of this amount the two Prices subscribed for $128,000, but the subsequent sale went so well that their subscription was reduced.

Years later, Price wrote an inquiring stockholder that the "capital for this bank was provided partially from private funds of my father and myself, part from business associates and new interests we desired connected with the bank and part from John E. Price & Co. We retained control of the bank in John E. Price & Co." [4]

Use of John E. Price & Co. as a vehicle to finance a new bank proved so successful that in September 1919 the three common stockholders of the company authorized an increase from $100,000 to $500,000 in preferred stock. Within a month $66,300 was sold to give the company further working capital. The problem of raising capital had been solved once and for all. Now to get on with the business at hand, starting the new bank.

Marine State Bank differed from competing Seattle banks from the outset. Andrew Price knew that the big accounts were already tied up at established banks, so he appealed to the man in the street and sought to build volume from small accounts. One of his early advertisements said, "The whole plan of this bank is built upon the central idea of serving the man with the moderate account."

Later copy proclaimed: "A bank prospers not so much by the amount of deposits as by the number of its depositors."

At a time when commercial banks made little effort to get savings accounts, Marine went hard after this business in a series of newspaper advertisements based on slogans to encourage thrift and the opening of savings accounts. Examples included:

The man who "spends as he goes" goes no farther than spending.

Saving ten cents a day and staying with it is far better than starting with a dollar—and stopping.

Banks at that time remained open on Saturday. Price went one better and announced that his bank would be opened Saturday evenings from six to eight "for the convenience of patrons of the savings department."

Early Marine advertising urged the salaried man to use a checking or a savings account, or both, "to save, to lessen his expenses, to keep track of his income and outgo, to meet emergencies, to establish credit—to handle all of his financial affairs safely and sanely." It didn't matter how much or little a man was paid, "you will be welcome—even more than your money."

By the end of 1919, six months after opening, Marine had 460 deposit accounts for a total of $555,633. Of these, 75 were savings

Horse-drawn wagons brought fruit to warehouses located on rail sidings. This warehouse on Produce Row in Yakima was built in 1901 for the Yakima County Horticultural Union (now Snokist Growers). It was later destroyed by fire.

accounts. Among the checking accounts only 48 were classified as from business firms.

Growth and profit came in 1920. The bank added 122 savings accounts and 275 checking accounts, and year-end deposits topped $710,000. In that first full year of operation the bank made a net profit of $20,036, against a loss of $1,920 in the opening year. Stockholders received their first dividend, $3.00 a share. Late in 1920, the bank converted from a state to a national charter to become Marine National Bank. Prominent stockholders at this time included Mrs. E. H. Stuart, whose husband was president of Carnation Milk Products Co.; Joshua Green, Sr., who had not yet acquired Peoples Savings Bank; J. W. Bullock, mining; J. E. Pinkham, lumber broker; Dr. A. I. Bouffleur, western head of a subsidiary of the Milwaukee Railroad; and F. G. Black of F. D. Black, Inc., investment firm.

In 1920 Price added to the board of directors attorney Bruce C. Shorts, who subsequently was to play an important role in development of Marine Bancorporation and the National Bank of Commerce. Albert Brygger was brought in as cashier. In that year also Price established a new-business department to build deposits and loans.

GROWTH THROUGH ACQUISITION

These were uneasy times in business and in banking. The economy was settling down from the war boom to a peacetime basis. The swollen payrolls of the shipyards were gone, and the short but sharp postwar recession was taking hold. During 1920 the deposits of Seattle banks, as a group, shrank $31 million from the postwar high of late 1919. The decline continued during most of 1921, until at the end of the year deposits totaling $137 million were down a full $50 million from the 1919 peak. Marine National Bank bucked this trend and gained in deposits while other banks were losing. There was reason to be optimistic and to look about for a chance to grow by acquisition.

One of the institutions hurt in the general decline was State Bank of Seattle. In the last twelve months of its independent existence, it lost one-third of its deposits, one-third of its loans, and almost half of its reserves. Andrew Price talked to officers of State Bank about consolidation. What made State Bank particularly attractive to him was its relatively small capital in comparison with deposits. In those days book value, rather than earnings, was a guide to the market for bank shares. State Bank with 2,000 shares having a book value of $123 had less capital than Marine, yet had three times its deposits. To Price this appeared to be a good opportunity to get a substantial increase in deposits at relatively little cost.

The directors of Marine National on November 4, 1920, talked over acquisition, particularly the possibility that the stockholders might buy controlling interest in State Bank. But the directors were not ready to act yet and decided simply to leave the door open. A few months later State Bank went over to Northwest Trust and Savings Bank, which in the merger changed its name to Northwest Trust and State Bank. Although this first try at expansion through acquisition was lost, there was soon another opportunity.

Marine National continued to grow. By the end of 1921 its deposits reached $1,150,000. Price organized bank employees into two teams to compete for new deposit accounts. A vigorous effort was made to build the volume of loans, which had eased a bit at the end of 1921 to $678,000. To encourage the transfer of accounts from other banks, Marine National offered liberal credit lines, but as a condition required the customer to carry larger deposits. The bank also loaned on a substantial volume of paper from Miners and Merchants Bank of Ketchikan, Alaska, and continued to lend to lumber manufacturers.

As the recession of 1921 put further pressure on banks, Price watched for weakness among his smaller competitors. One of the hardest pressed institutions was Northwest Trust and State Bank, which by now had absorbed not only State Bank of Seattle but also Guaranty Bank & Trust Co., the latter with about $1 million in deposits. These acquisitions, however, did not bring stability, and in the last half of 1921 Northwest lost substantially more in deposits than it gained from merger with Guaranty.

As another complication, the decline in the price of government bonds impaired the capital of Northwest Trust. The merger of State Bank of Seattle and Guaranty Trust had brought $500,000 of additional capital to Northwest Trust, yet by the end of 1921 its total capital accounts were down to $395,000. Time was running out.

Rescue of the depositors of Northwest Trust presented a glowing opportunity to Marine National. The plan of consolidation, approved by directors on March 23, 1922, was simple: Marine National would take over the deposit liabilities of Northwest Trust and would receive an equivalent dollar amount of Northwest's "best paper"; Marine would pay nothing to Northwest's stockholders.

The consolidation was a master stroke. Without putting out a dollar in capital funds, Price almost tripled the deposits of his bank. When the transfer took place April 1, 1922, Marine National's deposits rose to $4,827,891. In less than three years Price had pushed his new bank to rank eighth in size among Seattle's 22 commercial banks. Later some of Northwest Trust's "best paper" turned out to be a little soggy, but Price did not complain.[5]

With the increase in deposits Marine National's stockholders put in additional money to swell the paid-in capital from $200,000 to $300,000, and thus place total capital funds close to $400,000. Stockholders had the right to buy half a share for each share held. New shares not taken up by other stockholders were bought by Andrew Price and his father; this extended their control from 58 per cent to 64 per cent. From the outset, purchases by the two Prices had been financed largely by John E. Price & Co.; funds advanced for this purpose were carried on the books of the corporation as "permanent investments."

The addition of the business of Northwest Trust crowded Marine National out of the quarters it had occupied in the investment house of John E. Price & Co. at Second and Columbia. Two blocks north at Second and Madison, the National Bank of Commerce had just vacated ground-floor offices to move to the present-day headquarters at Second and Spring. Marine National took over the old Commerce location.

BRANCH BANKING—DEAD END

Price had hardly completed consolidation with Northwest Trust when he went to work on another avenue of expansion—branch banking. The minutes of Marine National's directors, meeting on June 29, 1922, record: "It is the sense of this meeting that we purchase the Scandinavian–American Bank Ballard Branch property as a private venture, in the hope that same may be used for branch banking, at a price of $15,000."

Price drove ahead with what he projected as a group of branches

Sixth location of the bank at the corner of Second Avenue and Madison Street, Seattle, now the 1000 Second Avenue Building. Car at extreme left is a Baker Electric, the second is believed to be an import, and coming up behind is a Winton.

overshadowing the home office in size. But first there were some difficult legal questions to clear away, because the efforts of the First National Bank of St. Louis to establish branches had already brought on a controversy of nationwide proportion.

The St. Louis bank, without approval of regulatory officials, opened a downtown branch and had a second branch fully equipped and ready to open. Beyond this there were reports of as many as 15 branches to come. But Missouri law forbade branches. Could state law restrict a national bank? The Missouri attorney general thought so and got a court order to block the opening of any more branches. Thus began a test case that delayed for many years Andrew Price's ambitions to bring branch banking to Washington State.

The controversy over branches pointed up the difference in rules that apply to national banks, which operate under federal law and regulations, and state banks, which operate under laws and regulations of individual states.

National banking law stated that "the usual business of such national banking association shall be transacted at an office or banking house located in the place specified in its organization certificate." From the outset this had been interpreted as prohibiting branches. On the other hand a number of states permitted state-chartered banks to operate branches. In California, in a notable example, the restless A. P. Giannini was pushing the Bank of Italy (now the Bank of America) throughout the state. In 1922 alone he added 20 branches to bring the total to 61. Concern was expressed that the competition of large state banks with branches might impair the national bank system. The Comptroller of the Currency, the regulatory official for national banks, sought some way to break through the ban on branches.

In Washington State the law was clear. The Legislature in 1909 enacted a flat prohibition on branches: "No bank in this state, or any officer or director thereof, should thereafter open any office of deposit or discount other than its principal place of business." When the law became effective, 13 branches already in operation were allowed to continue. The prohibition in Washington was similar to that in Missouri, and Price, in seeking to open a branch in Ballard, was in the same position as the First National Bank of St. Louis.

Price moved cautiously. He sent Bruce Shorts to present the

case to the Comptroller of the Currency, John Crissinger. To get around the state prohibition against branches, Price set out in a letter to Shorts the argument that "as national banks operate under the laws and regulations of the United States," the Comptroller could approve Marine National's request for a branch; the bank would then be free to follow that authorization without respect to the state prohibition.

The Comptroller listened, but not wanting another controversy like that in Missouri, asked for a written statement from the Washington Superintendent of Banks that the state did not object. Price got verbal assurance from Olympia that the banking department would not object to the branch, but the department refused to commit itself in writing. Failure to get the required statement from authorities forced Price to abandon the effort to open a branch, a bitter disappointment.

He had one hope left: That the Supreme Court would rule in the Missouri case in favor of branches. But in January, 1924, with three justices dissenting, the court held that a state had the right to prevent national banks within its borders from establishing branches. The decision blocked Marine National from setting up branches in Washington, and it left a curious competitive situation that allowed Dexter Horton National Bank to operate with branches.

Dexter Horton at that time was contending with Seattle National Bank and the National Bank of Commerce for first rank in the city. Early in 1924, Dexter Horton acquired Union National Bank (formerly Union Savings & Trust Co.), which stood fifth in size. The merger gave Dexter Horton resources in excess of $36 million, first rank in the city, and two branches as well. In its early years as a state-chartered bank, Union had established branches in the Ballard and Georgetown districts. When Union gave up its state charter and became a national bank, it was allowed to continue these branches. Now they became part of Dexter Horton.

What distressed Price was not just that Dexter Horton operated with branches which other banks were denied, but that Dexter Horton also moved the Georgetown branch to a more strategic downtown location. In 1931 Price renewed his request to the Comptroller of the Currency for authority to open branches. He based his plea on the fact that Dexter Horton had been permitted to transfer branches "from districts not competitive to districts highly competitive with ours and other Seattle banks." [6] But the Comptroller's position remained unchanged.

MARINE NATIONAL COMPANY

Branch banking was only one avenue of expansion that Andrew Price pushed. In the spring of 1923, he broadened the Marine organization through formation of Marine National Company, an investment affiliate for the bank and a vehicle for drawing further investment capital into the Marine group. The manner in which Price set the company up was characteristic: He would attract outside investors but retain control in his hands and those of his close associates.

Authorized capital of Marine National Company was $100,000. Of this, 30 per cent was in common stock, sale of which was limited on a share-for-share basis to owners of stock in Marine National Bank; 70 per cent was preferred stock offered to investors. Through a voting trust agreement stockholders assigned their voting rights in Marine National Company to a group of trustees comprised initially of the incorporators—John E. and Andrew Price, E. Shorrock, Albert Brygger, George E. Hardenbergh, and R. H. Miller—plus Bruce Shorts. The trust assured that directors of Marine National Bank would control Marine National Company.

Stock in the new company was readily subscribed. By the first annual meeting of the shareholders, January 8, 1924, almost all the common stock had been sold and more than half the preferred stock. The trustees also had authorized sale of $150,000 in 7 per cent collateral trust bonds, and these sold quickly. The bonds were in small denominations, $500 and $100, so as to attract broader investment interest.

Armed with approximately $200,000 of capital funds, Marine National Company launched operations in the summer of 1923. What were these operations? The stated purpose was to conduct the security business of the Marine National Bank, a common function of security affiliates in that day. Yet in this respect the company was in competition with John E. Price & Co. Both did a general investment business including retail bond operations, and control of both was in the hands of the Prices. Indeed, the management of the two companies as well as Marine National Bank was in almost identical hands.

The bank moved to its seventh and present location at Second and Spring in 1921. When this picture was taken, the Seattle branch of the Federal Reserve Bank was a tenant on the second floor. (Pierson photo.)

To begin with, trustees of Marine National Company authorized purchase of up to "$180,000 face value of mortgages, real estate contracts, bonds, secured notes and other obligations . . . from the Marine National Bank." [7] Within two months the balance sheet revealed "real estate contracts, first mortgages, etc." of $112,-975. Thus, one of the first functions of the investment affiliate was to clean up the balance sheet of its parent, the Marine National Bank. In a letter to a stockholder of the bank, written just before the company was organized, Price confided: "The real purpose of this company will be to finance and take out of the bank real estate contracts which as I have told you are not a legal investment for us." [8] Most, and perhaps all, of these contracts had come in the acquisition of Northwest Trust & State Bank.[9] Acquiring these contracts was the immediate task of Marine National Company, but it went on to play a much larger role in the development of the Price institutions.

Marine National and its affiliated organizations were expanding steadily—both in the scope of operations and in capital. New capital had originally been obtained from sale of preferred stock in John E. Price & Co., then from sale of stock in Marine State Bank. Now additional funds were brought in through the Marine National Company—a small amount from sale of common stock, a larger amount from preferred stock, and for the first time, from sale of bonds.

Blocked in his efforts to set up branches, Andrew Price cast about for other ways to extend the reach of his bank. On a vacation trip to southern California in the winter of 1924–25 he visited what impressed him as "the most aggressive branch bank organizations," the Bank of Italy and First National of Los Angeles. Of particular interest to him was the First National organization: a commercial bank, a trust and savings bank, a securities company, and a realty company. Proportionate ownership in the capital of each was represented by First National Bank Beneficial Certificates, which were the only securities issued to the public and were actively traded on the Los Angeles Stock Exchange.

Price noted that the securities affiliate owned the realty company outright and he saw that his own securities affiliate, Marine National Company, could be used for acquiring banks that might give him the equivalent of branch operations. He wrote Bruce Shorts from Ojai, California, on March 2, 1925: "I have the details of the realty company pretty well in mind and it has some good suggestions for us in handling a situation like the Peoples or King County State Bank." These Seattle banks, the former a small downtown institution soon to be acquired from an estate by Joshua Green, Sr., and the latter located in the University district, Price felt were candidates for purchase or merger.

Price continued in his letter to Shorts:

It is my positive conviction that branching at least within the metro-politan boundaries of cities has come to stay and that the bank in Seat-tle which directly or indirectly gets in on the ground floor will have a great advantage. The only way I see at the present is to acquire and hold under common ownership the stocks of such nominally independent banks as we would count advantageous to the whole.

Returning to Seattle, Price plunged into a series of acquisitions that within three years went far toward establishing the structure of banking in both Seattle and the state for many decades. He worked first on King County State Bank, in which Blake D. Mills, owner of Cascade Coal Company, an early stockholder in Marine and a long-time friend of the Prices, recently had become a di-rector. On behalf of Marine National Company, Price offered $165 a share, or a total of $85,635, for 519 shares of 1,000 outstand-ing. In June, 1925, the offer was accepted, and King County State Bank became Marine State Bank. The following January Blake Mills was elected president and Andrew Price vice president. Thus the Marine group expanded into the fast-growing University district, a relatively clear field with only one other bank.

The concept of the Marine group as a series of banks under common ownership and direction was quickly presented to the city through billboards and newspaper advertising. An indication of Marine's course came in this remark by John E. Price, quoted in a local newspaper in January, 1926: "We realize that to serve our customers best we must make our facilities readily available to them. We have unbounded confidence in the growth and de-velopment of Seattle." [10]

Three years later Andrew Price looked back on the direction his organization was taking and gave this explanation:

Perhaps we who were with smaller institutions felt stronger the urge of doing something than those who enjoyed the benefits of a larger organization, and so it fell to our lot to undertake to find ways and means to increase the size, scope and influence of our own organization . . . .

We had become strongly impressed with the fact that the public's convenience was playing an increasingly important part in where they did their banking business, just as where they bought their groceries and so the idea of branch or associated banks was a natural first step in the endeavor to contact an increasing share of the public.[11]

ANOTHER BANK IS FORMED

As he looked about for places to extend the Marine group, Andrew Price was struck by the opportunity that existed in the downtown shopping district which was fast building up in the vicinity of Westlake and Pine. A few years earlier Frederick & Nelson had moved its big department store from the edge of the lower financial district eight blocks north to Fifth and Pine. In this shift Frederick & Nelson leapfrogged past the established retail district to an area that the store management insisted—quite correctly, it turned out—would become the center of downtown shopping. Gradually other stores followed, and in 1925 the 17-story Medical & Dental Building was built on the Olive Street side of the Frederick & Nelson block.

One thing was clear to Price: The new shopping district, far from the financial center of the city, needed banking facilities, and if interested he had better step fast. Already, Dexter Horton National Bank had moved its branch from the quiet Georgetown section to the bustling downtown corner of Fourth and Pike. Not allowed to open a new branch, it simply moved the Georgetown branch downtown and then created a new state bank to carry on in Georgetown.

Price's answer was the establishment of a new bank, the Marine Central, on the ground floor of the Medical & Dental Building. In January 1926 Price wrote of his plans to a group of businessmen in the area, pointing out that "the rapidly developing north end business district of Seattle presents a distinct banking opportunity." The bank, he said, would begin with capital and surplus of $250,000, and Marine National Company would subscribe for a "substantial" block of the stock. Shares were priced at $125, "the same to everybody and without profit to ourselves,"[12] Price said, adding that shares of Marine National Bank, which sold originally for $125, currently were bid at $172.50 with none offered.

Approximately 55 per cent of the initial capital for Marine Central Bank was subscribed by Marine National Company. The balance was widely spread, with no individual holding more than 50 shares and many holding 10 shares or less.

Directors were John E. and Andrew Price, Albert Brygger and Bruce Shorts, plus George E. Hardenbergh, general manager of Hofius Steel & Equipment Co.; E. H. Hatch, president of Tru-Blu Biscuit Company; R. H. Miller, president of Mutual Paper Company; and C. W. Stimson, manager of Stimson Timber Company. Later in the year Hatch and Stimson of Marine Central and Blake Mills of Marine State Bank joined the board of Marine National Bank, thereby providing almost the same directorship for each of the Marine banks.

John E. Price, who had retired the year before from active management in Marine interests, was chairman of the board. Andrew Price was president and Brygger and Lester R. McCash were vice presidents. McCash, who was manager, later was succeeded by A. W. Faragher, formerly assistant treasurer of the Milwaukee Railroad, whom Price brought into Marine Central at the outset with sale of stock a part of his job.

At 9:00 A.M. on Saturday, April 10, 1926, Marine Central opened for business, and what a day that was! Thousands of persons streamed into the bank—some just to see the interior, so different from that of any other bank, some to congratulate the officials, many to open new accounts. *Fortune* magazine, in its first issue in February, 1930, carried a nationwide analysis of group banking in which it said of Andrew Price: "He opened the Marine Central Bank on the outskirts of the town and shocked the wiseacres by bringing in the greatest opening day deposits ever recorded in Seattle." [13]

That first day's deposits added up to $450,000. Among customers was the state treasurer, W. G. Potts, who came up from Olympia for the opening.

A bank designed to appeal to the general public, Marine Central was distinctive in appearance. The *Seattle Times* described it as incorporating the "newest ideas in bank architecture." The *Seattle Post-Intelligencer* reported:

Unique among the banks of the city, perhaps of all the West, the new Marine Central, third of the Marine Bank line, opened hospitable doors yesterday . . . and disclosed not the cold grill work and barred doors of the usual bank, but quarters as informal as a lounging room. Gone were the cages, gone the long countered corridor and private offices. To the left the officers' desks stood in an easy group, a bit luxurious with heavy rugs and easy chairs. Beyond were the tellers' booths separated only by low divisions of heavy glass—no bolts nor bars.[14]

The Marine group now consisted of three banks, and Price set about to achieve some of the economies possible in branch banking. Each of the three banks operated as a separate unit, but many of the functions were centralized including auditing, purchasing, personnel, publicity, and legal. Efforts to develop new business and decisions on major loans also were centralized.

These were busy days for Andrew Price. At the end of a letter dictated to his brother Hickman in March, 1927, Price added in longhand: "Never in my business career have I had as many perplexing problems as during the past six months. Organization, personnel, financing, in fact all aspects of current operation, to say nothing of making progress, seem to have occupied my every moment awake and some when I am asleep."

Price was wholly engrossed in business. He drove himself relentlessly, seven days a week. Not for some twenty years would the heavy toll to his health become apparent.

Months passed. The Seattle banking scene appeared relatively calm—no mergers, no new holding companies. The banks in the Marine group prospered, but they were still small and Price was looking far beyond them. He had proved the holding company successful as a device to expand banking within the city. Why couldn't it be used to push Marine out through the state and to create a group of banks stronger together than any would be alone? Price worked on the idea, but to buy banks in outlying cities would take more money than the Marine group could put up. Clearly the financing for any major expansion would have to come from new investors.

What about forming a new and much larger holding company, one that would first absorb the present Marine institutions, and then be ready to acquire banks anywhere in the state? Would investors buy stock in such a company? The chances looked good. This was 1927. Money was easy. The speculative fever of Wall Street was spreading across the country. People bought stocks for the first

127

time in their lives, made money, and were hungry for more. Price had never known a climate so favorable for new ventures.

Several factors, he felt, should help launch the holding company. One was its leadership. In the eight years since the first Marine bank began business, Price had become known throughout the business community; he had proved he could make money for investors. Another was the extraordinary growth in California of the Bank of Italy and its holding company, Bancitaly Corporation, and a spectacular rise in the market for their shares.

Price was pleased with the name he selected: Marine Bancorporation. He had coined the word *bancorporation*. It carried the connotation both of banking and of a corporation such as a holding company. It was distinctive. The word caught on, so much so that some months after its first public use, Bruce Shorts sought to register bancorporation as a trade name or otherwise protect it, but to no avail.

Andrew Price now set himself to the difficult task of working out the capital structure for the holding company. No matter how much stock the public might buy, he wanted to retain control, and particularly to have the flexibility to negotiate and buy banks without each time having to go through the delay of getting approval of his stockholders. The obvious way for him to retain control was to use non-voting stock for the public. But this type of security was under some criticism. Only a year before, the Investment Bankers Association had expressed the opinion that major considerations of the public welfare required that non-voting common stocks not be issued.[1]

Price saw no alternative, however. He was satisfied also that investors would accept non-voting stock. He set up Marine Bancorporation with authorization to sell 9,000 "initial" shares; these shares were to be used in the acquisition of the existing Marine institutions and they alone would carry voting rights. The balance, called "fully participating," would have no voting rights but would be preferred to the extent of $25 in liquidation. The stocks would share equally in profits.

Formation of Marine Bancorporation was announced on September 11, 1927. The directors were John E. and Andrew Price, Homer Boyd, and Bruce Shorts, from the management of Marine interests, and the following from among the directors of Marine banks: E. H. Hatch, Wylie Hemphill of Pacific Coast Coal Co., Blake Mills, R. H. Miller, and C. W. Stimson.

At this point the Marine banks had more than 17,000 depositors, and the resources of the entire Marine group approximated $10 million, still small in Seattle banking.

A week after formation of Marine Bancorporation was announced, the directors authorized acquisition of all the stock in various Marine interests in exchange for stock of the new holding company. The exchange was complex; it involved no cash but a package containing two types of Marine stock—"initial" or voting shares and "fully participating" or non-voting shares. The exchange was on this basis: For each share of Marine National Bank, one share of Bancorporation voting stock and five of non-voting stock; for each share in Marine Central Bank and Marine State Bank, one share of voting stock, four of non-voting; for each share of Marine National Company, one share of voting stock, one of non-voting. The Bancorporation also acquired the retail bond business of John E. Price & Co. in exchange for 6,000 shares, all non-voting.

Since Marine National Company was owned entirely by stockholders of Marine National Bank, the shares of the Bancorporation which the company received in the exchange went automatically to stockholders of the bank. These stockholders received one further distribution. At the time of the exchange Marine National Company owned 58.9 per cent of the stock of Marine Central Bank and 66.6 per cent of Marine State Bank. For these holdings the company received 1,845 shares of Bancorporation voting stock. This block, in turn, was offered for sale to the bank's stockholders on the basis of six-tenths of a share for each bank share held. On these terms, 1,601 Bancorporation shares were sold.

When the exchange was completed, Marine Bancorporation had issued approximately 45,000 shares of stock having a market value of $1,250,000. Of these shares, 8,852 were "initial" or voting stock, of which John E. Price was the largest holder. He, Andrew Price, and Homer Boyd owned, either in their own name or through John E. Price & Co., 4,015 voting shares. No more voting shares were ever issued. In 1955, when Marine National Company was dissolved, 971 shares of Bancorporation voting stock which the company had bought years before and held in the treasury were retired. This reduced Bancorporation voting shares to 7,881, the number outstanding until the reorganization in 1969.

The use of a small issue of voting shares distributed primarily to stockholders in Marine National Bank enabled the Price organization to retain control of Marine Bancorporation. The capital that the Bancorporation required to expand into group banking came through a much larger issue of non-voting stock, sold to the public and used in acquisition of new banks. In May 1933 the number of non-voting shares reached 352,806, a number that remained unchanged until 1969.

As soon as Andrew Price had brought all the Marine interests into a single corporation, he turned to the task of raising $1 million in new capital through public sale of 36,000 "fully participating" shares. He already had his own sales organization in Marine National Company. Now he launched an imaginative sales campaign such as Pacific Northwest banking had never seen.

Heavy newspaper advertising opened the promotion. At the same time, Marine Bancorporation mailed to a long list of prospects "stock purchase rights" that were engraved to look like an actual stock certificate and that gave a discount of $1.50 a share from the established sales price of $29.50. Depositors, borrowers, and other customers of Marine banks were mailed "customer's rights" that took $1.00 off. To encourage small investors, Price allowed payments to be spread over six months. Employees also had a special inducement—a payroll deduction of $1.10 spread over 24 months, making the price $26.40 per share.

The decision to sell stock to depositors and other customers, Price recognized, had its hazards. The very novelty of the scheme was a drawback. And what if stock prices declined? Could the market for Marine Bancorporation shares be maintained? Before making his decision he coolly set down the pros and cons on a single sheet of paper. He was drawn to the plan because it would give broad distribution at low cost and it should help the popularity of bank stocks. But he was worried mainly about the negative effect if the plan were not outstandingly successful.[2]

The rights plan however was successful beyond any doubt. The offering of "fully participating" stock sold quickly and realized $1,024,422.50. After deduction of a 5 per cent sales commission, Marine National turned over to the Bancorporation $973,311 in new capital. By the end of the year Marine Bancorporation had 1,800 stockholders including 1 of every 10 depositors in Marine banks.

These stockholders, far more numerous than those of any bank in the Pacific Northwest and living not just in Seattle but throughout the state, gave Price another means to spread the story of Marine Bancorporation. On January 2, 1928, he put on a stockholders' breakfast at the Olympic Hotel with talks about Marine and the outlook. The printed program at each guest's place carried a message which caught the feeling of the times:

> There is a new era in business. This is the day of quantity production, of rapid turnover, of concentrated and economical operation. It is the hour of specialization and big capitalization—mergers and branches. Practically every branch of industry and commerce has felt the quickening pulse of these fundamental changes in our business structure. Banks cannot escape the necessity of keeping pace with the instrumentalities which must be financed by them. The spirit of the day in banking is favorable to fewer but stronger and more helpful banks.
>
> Another equally, if not more important, development of the present era is the democratization of business. The largest, most successful enterprises in every field of business are now owned by thousands of individual stockholders. The personal interest of these stockholders is of greater value than the capital they bring. Such organizations are growing in size, in service, in popularity and in profits in contrast with many of the older type of so-called "close corporations. . . ."

Price stood as a leader who recognized the changing times and the opportunities they presented. The public responded by buying more Marine stock. The issue was listed on the Seattle Stock and Bond Exchange, and Price announced that Marine National Company would continue to offer new stock at the bid shown on the market.

In the early weeks of 1928 trading was light, but by February it picked up sharply. The stock was bid at $35 and Marine National Company was pouring money into the parent company's treasury. The trickle of new capital became a deluge. The capital accounts of Marine Bancorporation passed $10 million. They were the largest of any financial institution in the state, second largest of all companies in the state, and soon were to reach $14 million. Now Price had the funds he needed to acquire new banks.

From the time he formed Marine Bancorporation, Andrew Price had made it clear that he was looking beyond Seattle. One of the stated purposes of the company was expressed thus: "To provide for gathering under unified ownership outstanding banks and financial institutions in leading cities and towns of Washington." [3] Advertisements announcing the formation of the Bancorporation were placed not just in the Seattle area but in 30 daily and weekly newspapers across the state.

CAPITAL NATIONAL BANK

Even though Price had made it plain that he was looking beyond the Seattle banking community, his first move caught investors by surprise. On February 15, 1928, he announced that Marine had acquired control of Capital National Bank of Olympia, an old and highly respected bank headed by C. J. Lord.

Capital National, with deposits of $3 million, was not large, but Lord had made it highly profitable. He had grown up in New York State and had been a partner with his father in the importation of French coach horses and the first Holstein-Friesian cattle brought to America. At the age of 25 Lord told his father that he wanted to become a banker. He saw little opportunity in the East and so he turned West. Lord recounted afterward that he stopped at Tacoma long enough to make up his mind that Olympia, capital of the new state, offered him an excellent opportunity.[4] In 1890 he opened the Capital National Bank. The stockholders included not only prominent residents of Olympia but also an impressive group of bankers and investors in other parts of the state.

The bank began with $100,000 in capital. In the next 37 years its stockholders received dividends totaling $1,600,000—16 times the original investment. Part of that prosperity came from the handling of state funds. During the early years of his bank, Lord had the reputation of hand-picking state treasurers.

Price and Lord reached agreement on the telephone five days before the public announcement. Marine would buy Lord's majority holdings plus any other shares that stockholders might offer. Lord drove a hard bargain—$700 a share. The price, far in excess of the bank's book value, was not publicly divulged.

Why C. J. Lord would sell the bank he had created stirred up speculation at the time. To be sure, sale would enable him to realize a large profit on his investment, but he did not need the money. He had other investments and was the largest stockholder in the National Bank of Commerce. But Lord, already 63, had no successor. He chose Price and Marine Bancorporation to provide continuity for the institution he had built. In turn, he proved of great help in some of Price's later acquisitions.

NATIONAL CITY BANK

Even before purchase of Capital National had been completed, Andrew Price was in the midst of another acquisition. On March 7, he laid before a special meeting of directors of Marine Bancorporation the purchase of controlling interest in National City Bank, a middle-sized Seattle institution with deposits approaching $5 million and capital of almost $900,000.

Price had begun work on National City months earlier, even before the first entries had been made in the books of Marine Bancorporation. On December 6, 1927, the Bancorporation contracted to buy 250 shares of National City Bank at $250 each from the A. H. Anderson Estate, Inc. Marine also received an option to buy 500 additional shares at $210 per share up to May 1, 1928.

Price reviewed these matters with his board on March 7, and reported that J. W. Maxwell, president of National City, had agreed to deliver at least two-thirds of the bank's 5,000 shares at $300 each. Along with Maxwell, who owned 600 shares, the largest stockholders were N. J. Moldstad, who was president of the First National Bank of Mount Vernon, Harriet Rhodes, John Backland, and Jennie Baker.

The directors agreed to the purchase. Three days later written confirmation of the agreement called for purchase of all National City shares at $300 each. On the back of the letter, the following was written in ink and signed by Andrew Price:

> It is my understanding that upon consolidation of the National City Bank with the Marine National Bank the official personnel of the consolidated bank shall be John E. Price, Chairman of the Board; J. W. Maxwell, President and Andrew Price, Vice President.[5]

This promise of the presidency of a much larger bank, along with the attractive price, was, no doubt, an important consideration for Maxwell, a strong individualist not accustomed to a secondary role. A few days later the *Seattle Times* carried public confirmation of the agreement under the headline: "Maxwell Will Be at Head of Merged Banks." [6]

Purchase of National City moved rapidly. Within two weeks Marine had picked up 2,817 shares for a 56.3 per cent interest. For this it issued 1,064 shares of "fully participating" stock plus $444,018 in cash.

Price was gathering in new banks fast, and before National City was merged into Marine National, a far larger acquisition intervened. Maxwell never did become president, but he remained with Marine for the rest of his career.

GRAYS HARBOR NATIONAL BANK

Acquisition of two banks in little more than a month might have called for a period of digestion. But not at Marine Bancorporation. Price and his associates were negotiating with not one bank but with several simultaneously. On March 12, Price wrote W. H. Tucker, cashier-manager of the Grays Harbor National Bank of Aberdeen, Washington:

> . . . This will constitute your authority to purchase for us up to the entire capital, but not less than 66⅔ of the capital stock of the Grays Harbor National Bank at $——— per share. In the event your stockholders desire to become interested in the Marine Bancorporation, we will be pleased to furnish them Fully Participating Stock in the Marine Bancorporation . . . in an amount not to exceed in the aggregate for any individual his present proportionate interest in the Grays Harbor National Bank.

Grays Harbor National Bank, the largest in southwestern Washington, was active in financing the lumber industry. This was a period of great activity, and ships leaving Grays Harbor carried more than 1.4 billion board feet in 1926 and again in 1927, a volume never equaled before or since.

In the letter to Tucker, Price left blank the amount to be paid for the shares. Tucker, either on his own or after a telephone conversation with Price, made the terms $300 a share, a nice profit for those stockholders who paid $150 a share when the bank doubled its capital a year earlier. The purchase was subject to the condition that directors and officers in the main would agree to continue. Curiously, Tucker added as a condition "that Mr. E. K.

Bishop and Messrs. Maxwell Carlson and Lawrence Carlson be given an opportunity to exercise their option as to whether or not they would take the offer made by Marine." The caution of these men was resolved in favor of sale to Marine. The next year Bishop became a director of Marine and in 1938 of the National Bank of Commerce as well, and years later, Maxwell Carlson became the bank's president.

FOUR UNSUCCESSFUL ACQUISITION EFFORTS

Not all of Price's efforts to bring new banks into Marine met with success. He sought to acquire control of Peoples Savings Bank but Joshua Green, who had just bought the bank at what he later called "a bargain price," was not about to sell.

Price tried to move into Tacoma, the state's third largest city, through acquisition of the National Bank of Tacoma (later named the National Bank of Washington), but was turned down.

C. J. Lord suggested that Price acquire the First National Bank in Bellingham, which was under the control of E. W. Purdy, a pioneer banker and an old friend of Lord and Manson Backus. But Purdy was in no hurry to sell and turned Price down. Reporting this on March 24, 1928, the *Bellingham American* said:

> The only way the chain banking systems can get into Bellingham and most of the other cities of the state is by the purchase of existing banks . . . . This is the reason fancy prices are being paid for existing banks in cities which the new chain wishes to enter.

The biggest bank Price sought was First National Bank of Seattle. First National began business November 10, 1882, as successor to the private banking firm of George W. Harris & Co. It was the first bank in Seattle and the second in the state to operate under a national charter. In 1928 its deposits were approximately $14 million, fourth largest in Seattle and almost equal to all the Marine banks combined.

The president of First National was Morris A. Arnold, who in 1907 had bought control of the bank through John E. Price & Co. On March 22 Andrew Price submitted Arnold a written offer of $900 a share cash or 20 shares of Marine Bancorporation's fully participating shares. The offer specified that if Arnold could not deliver two-thirds of the stock by March 31 the deal was dead.

The offer implied that negotiations had reached the point where

Arnold should lay a specific proposal before his directors. The directors, however, refused to consider selling, and thus Price's efforts to take over the First National fell through. Why? Almost forty years afterward, Lawrence Arnold, the retired chairman of Seattle–First National Bank, son of Morris Arnold, and a director of First National at the time Price made his offer, recalled that a majority of directors felt strongly that First National should remain an independent institution.[7]

Had Price acquired First National, one can surmise that Arnold might have found himself in a difficult role, though discussion at the directors' meeting did not reach this point. At that time, it had already been announced that J. W. Maxwell would become president when the Marine National and National City banks merged. If First National had gone into Marine Bancorporation, First National would have become much the largest of Marine's operating units, yet Arnold could not have aspired to more than a subordinate position. For an able and ambitious banker who had been building his own organization for twenty years, there was obviously far greater appeal in remaining head of his own bank.

Moreover, Lawrence Arnold recalled in 1966, Andrew Price had demonstrated to the Seattle financial community how a bank with a holding company could acquire other banks. Less than a year after Price and Arnold terminated negotiations, First National Bank, operating through its affiliate First National Corporation, acquired Metropolitan National Bank. Soon it became apparent that Arnold and Price would go their separate ways, rivals as each built a statewide banking system.

Rebuffed by the First National Bank, Price set his sights higher—on the National Bank of Commerce, one of the city's largest banks, with deposits exceeding $21 million.

Just who brought Price together with Manson Backus, president of the National Bank of Commerce, is not clear. Joshua Green, Sr., a close friend of Backus, said almost forty years later that he told Price to see Backus.[1] There were other, perhaps closer, ties. Backus and C. J. Lord had been associates for years. Lord was also the largest stockholder in Backus's bank, owning almost 11 per cent of the shares. The two, heading toward retirement, had many common problems. Unquestionably Lord discussed with Backus the sale of Lord's Olympia bank to Marine, and Lord must have mentioned how eager Price was for acquisitions. When Price telephoned Backus on April 2, 1928, Backus was ready.

Backus and Price quickly got down to discussion of the National Bank of Commerce. Price asked on what basis Backus would sell his stock and noted afterward: "He evidently had been giving the

137

matter some consideration and promptly responded that he would be willing to accept $700.00 a share." [2]

Price must have been startled. This was almost three times the book value of approximately $250. Five weeks earlier a newspaper in Hoquiam, Washington, referring to C. J. Lord, said that he valued his Commerce shares at "better than $300 a share." The highest price in the market was $435 or $440, Price acknowledged later in reporting that Backus "nevertheless insisted, and stated that this price was satisfactory to him and he would so recommend to his stockholders."

A clue to the thinking at Marine on Backus's terms is contained in a note dated April 26, 1928, from Price to Henry Broderick, head of the Seattle real estate firm of that name:

We believe we are frankly discounting the future when we offer $700 a share for this stock. If we can in reality obtain the good will or the larger portion of it that goes with the bank, we are satisfied that it will be a good deal for the Marine Bancorporation, even though the price is high, as it rounds out our plans . . . in Seattle.[3]

Negotiations moved rapidly, and next day the agreement was reduced to writing for presentation to stockholders. At this point it looked as though the acquisition would proceed in uneventful routine. But Price was to find that it was one thing to buy a country bank and quite another thing to go after a major metropolitan bank where he would meet opposition from some directors and officers and stiff competition from other bankers.

The first sign of trouble came with startling suddenness ten minutes before the Executive Committee of the National Bank of Commerce was to meet at noon on April 5 to discuss Marine's offer. Backus called to tell Price that he had received a counter proposal which he felt obliged to place before the Committee. The new proposal, which came from Morris Arnold, called for three-way amalgamation of First National, Metropolitan National, and National Bank of Commerce. To Price's dismay, Proposition No. 1, as it became known, was approved by the Committee with Backus dissenting. The Committee was comprised largely of officers of the National Bank of Commerce, and Backus assured Price that the Committee members other than Backus owned less than 5 per cent of the bank's stock. Still, it was plain to see that the proposal to sell to Marine had split the bank. Price could not at that time have surmised the full consequences of the opposition to him that was building up among officers and directors.

In the face of the Committee's opposition, should Marine withdraw its offer? Price talked this over with William Calvert, a director of the bank and a large stockholder. Calvert, urging Price not to withdraw, said he would take the lead to see that the Marine offer was reviewed by the bank's directors for submission to stockholders. Price telegraphed for the advice of Bruce Shorts and C. J. Lord, both of whom were out of town. Shorts approved Calvert's course of action but felt strongly that Marine should insist on getting not less than two-thirds of the stock, that being the minimum required for the anticipated merger of National City Bank and Marine National Bank into Commerce. Calvert and Lord, however, felt that Marine's offer should be contingent on getting 51 per cent, rather than two-thirds, and it was on that basis that Marine tendered its formal proposal on April 12. Marine gave stockholders three alternatives: Proposition 1 called for $700 a share in cash; Plan 2 called for $388 in cash and six shares of "fully participating" Marine Bancorporation stock; Plan 3 provided for exchange of 13.46 shares of Marine stock for each share of Commerce.

On the Thursday that Marine submitted its proposal, the Executive Committee of the National Bank of Commerce, with a larger attendance than on April 5, modified its earlier stand and recommended that the proposals of both Price and Arnold be presented to the stockholders.

The rival groups now plunged into a fight for votes of shareholders across the nation. A stockholder near Cleveland wired Price that on returning from five weeks' absence he "found several telegrams from Seattle brokers making increasingly generous offers for my stock."

The struggle to obtain the votes of shareholders turned up ominous signs of opposition to Price within the bank. A Walla Walla stockholder, John R. Robb, received an offer of $500 a share from Easter & Co., Seattle securities house. The next day, April 13, Easter came back with a price of $520. Marine's offer of $700 a share was not yet public. Puzzled by the unexpected market activity, Robb phoned Robert Walker, executive vice president of the National Bank of Commerce. Walker, the next man in the bank to Manson Backus, must have been aware of the details of Marine's offer, but he told Robb he knew of no reason for the price increase. As a result Robb sold his own stock and that of his sister at $520 a share—and realized $7,200 less than if he had got $700 a share.

On April 16, H. D. Campbell of Seaboard National Bank in New York telephoned Price that Caspar Clarke, cashier and a director of Commerce, had solicited the vote of Seaboard Bank on 40 shares of Commerce stock held in trust. Clarke asked for a vote against Marine.

From within the investment community Price ran into opposition, too. A summary published by the Seattle investment house of Baillargeon, Winslow & Co. reached a conclusion adverse to Marine. The firm explained that Morris Arnold's rival plan "contemplates a company to be known as the First National Corporation, the shares of which would be exchanged for the existing shares of the First National Bank, the Metropolitan National Bank and the National Bank of Commerce." The exchange would be on the basis of 7.86 shares of the holding company for each share in National Bank of Commerce, equivalent, the firm concluded, to "something in excess of $766 per share, either in cash or stock."

This conclusion Price disputed. For one thing there was no assurance that merger into First National Corporation would be carried out or that the necessary two-thirds vote could be obtained from stockholders for merger of the banks involved. More to the point, he wrote a stockholder that with a $60 market for Marine Bancorporation shares "it is our belief that our proposition is equivalent to $807.60 per share" for Commerce stock.[4]

Massive new opposition to Marine's offer came to the surface on April 19. A powerful group of Seattle businessmen, some identified with the National Bank of Commerce and some with Metropolitan National Bank, wrote to all Commerce stockholders urging acceptance of the offer of First National Corporation.[5]

The letter carried the signatures of eight directors of Commerce: Timothy Jerome, Dietrich Schmitz, Caspar Clarke, Joshua Green, Sr., LeRoy Backus, Evan S. McCord, Moritz Thomsen, and Langdon C. Henry. The chairman of those signing, Langdon Henry, was the son of H. C. Henry, an early president and later chairman of the National Bank of Commerce. LeRoy Backus was the son of Manson Backus, and the son's signature was looked upon as endorsement by his father.

The names on the letter included also those of four large stock-holders in Metropolitan National Bank: C. D. Stimson Co., H. C. Henry Investment Co., O. D. Fisher Investment Co., and Dr. A. I. Bouffleur. Why those identified with Metropolitan National Bank signed was not made clear; possibly Arnold already had begun negotiations which were to bring Metropolitan into First National's holding company. Others who signed were Frank Carpenter, long-time president of Cle Elum State Bank; E. W. Brownell, a vice president at Commerce, who was soon to move to First National; A. W. Leonard, president of Puget Sound Power & Light and a director at First National; Milnor Roberts, Dean of Mines at the University of Washington and an investor; and James Eddy, prominent lumberman.

The arguments in the letter centered on loss of control that the stockholders and directors of the bank would suffer if Commerce were to go into Marine Bancorporation. In contrast to Marine's offer of non-voting stock, the letter set out that "the plan of organization of The First National Corporation provides for only one class of stock, all of which carries equal voting rights." This must have been an important consideration to the substantial men signing the letter, men accustomed to exercising their vote as shareholders.

The letter stressed that the First National organization would be "actively officered and guided by the officers and directors who have in the past led these three institutions to their present favored standing in this community." By contrast the Marine Bancorporation board was small, and directors of the National Bank of Commerce obviously feared they would lose their voice in management. The fact that three officers, Brownell, Clarke, and Schmitz, signed the letter indicated concern over a change in top staff under Marine, though Price continually denied such a possibility.

The key issue, it was becoming apparent, was Andrew Price himself. Should the National Bank of Commerce be transferred from conventional bank management and control to a holding company which was dominated by Price, one in the management of which present Commerce stockholders would have no voice? In commercial banking, Price was regarded as an outsider. The banks he had formed were still small, and he had never headed a large institution. His activities had centered on mergers, acquisitions, and stock promotion. His holding company, Marine Bancorporation, was new in concept; its direction was still not established, and it had not yet been tested in adversity.

In the midst of the battle for control of the National Bank of Commerce, Price cast about for other acquisitions. He and Bruce Shorts worked over the possibility of picking up Metropolitan National Bank, perhaps as an effort to soften the opposition of Metropolitan's large stockholders. Shorts suggested that Marine retain from the Commerce negotiations enough Marine shares to deal with Metropolitan.

On April 12 Price asked C. J. Lord's advice on still another acquisition—Seattle National Bank, which then ranked second to Dexter Horton in size and was substantially larger than the National Bank of Commerce. Seattle National was organized in 1890, consolidated with Boston National in 1903, and in 1910 acquired Puget Sound National, which Jacob Furth founded in Seattle in 1882 (this is not to be confused with the present Puget Sound National Bank in Tacoma, which was founded in 1890).

Price telegraphed Lord that he had been approached on a confidential basis by Seattle National for a strictly cash deal with control to be delivered immediately.[6] Who approached Price was not indicated, but at that time in excess of 40 per cent of the bank's stock was lodged with its president, Daniel Kelleher, directly or as a trustee, the Furth Investment Co., and the F. H. Brownell family. Undoubtedly the size of Marine's cash offer for the National Bank of Commerce impressed large stockholders in Seattle National.

Lord agreed that acquisition of Seattle National was desirable but urged postponement of any action until negotiations with the National Bank of Commerce were concluded, successfully or unsuccessfully. Lord, who shared Price's long look ahead, went further to suggest that Price consider obtaining control of all three banks in the proposed First National Corporation plan. Specifically, Lord said he preferred acquisition of Metropolitan over that of Seattle National.

Price laid aside these other acquisitions to concentrate on the battle for the National Bank of Commerce. One stalwart on his side, thanks to the intervention of C. J. Lord, was Mark E. Reed, head of Simpson Logging Co., Shelton. Lord said that Price's proposition was "by far the best for the shareholders,"[7] and Reed observed to George de Steiguer, whose family held a substantial block of Commerce stock: "How any other conclusion than that to sell to the Marine can be arrived at from a cold-blooded business analysis, is beyond me." Reed figured that "it would take Commerce stock nine years to approach a market value of $650." [8] This support must have had telling effect on such Commerce stockholders as were still undecided.

A week after the rival offers had been submitted to Commerce stockholders, the Marine directors made a strategic move. They told Commerce stockholders that Marine would pay $700 cash regardless of whether Marine got 51 per cent of the stock. This offer ran the risk that Marine might end up with a big investment in the National Bank of Commerce but without control. Price felt, however, that the offer of $700 cash would bring in enough shares, coupled with commitments already in hand, to give Marine at least 51 per cent.

Price telegraphed this offer to stockholders on April 27 as he strove to bring negotiations to an early close, far ahead of the May 31 deadline. Marine officials were increasingly concerned, fearing that the long struggle would undermine morale at the bank and play into the hands of competitors, and that the premium they were paying for good-will would yield nothing.

The next day Burle Bramhall, vice president of Marine Bancorporation, carried the issue to C. W. Stimson, a leader in the group of stockholders opposed to Marine. Bramhall said Price was confident he would win control and "the more pressing problem and the situation to which Marine officers had now turned their attention, was maintenance of the business and goodwill of the National Bank of Commerce." They indicated that "impairment of efficiency [was] . . . being capitalized on by competitors." [9]

On May 2, L. C. Henry, again representing the writers of the dissident letter, capitulated. He advised Commerce stockholders that a merger between Commerce and other units of the proposed First National Corporation was clearly an impossibility, and it was the "intention of the stockholders who signed the former letter to deposit their stock with that of the majority in favor of the sale to the Marine Bancorporation." [10]

The battle was over. On May 4, Commerce stockholders were advised that more than 51 per cent of the shares had been voted for the Marine offer. Price had acquired a strong headquarters bank in Seattle. Now he could go on building the Marine group of banks.

MARINE STOCK

The acquisition of banks in Olympia, Aberdeen, and Seattle had caught the interest of investors and speculators. Marine stock rose from $29.50 at the first public offering in the fall of 1927 to $35 early in March 1928. Then the market began to respond to Price's expansion program. With acquisition of Capital National the stock jumped more than $2, and one publication reported: "The financial district of Seattle seethed with rumors and forecasts and this was reflected in a buying movement that was soon to become frenzied." [11]

On March 12, two days before the announcement of acquisition of the Grays Harbor National Bank, the stock sold for $41.25; at the end of the week it touched $43.75. The next week, with confirmation of acquisition of another bank, National City, the stock jumped to $47.50. This was an era of rumor and speculation, and the public was scrambling for shares. L. E. Hill, financial editor of the Seattle *Post-Intelligencer,* reported on March 23 "a stampede for Marine Bancorporation stock." He added:

The volume of purchases of Marine Bancorporation this week has been unprecedented in Seattle. It is estimated that more than $2,500,000 worth has been bought or contracted for in three days. . . . According to shrewd estimates over $4,500,000 of this stock has been bought since March 12, and the amount undoubtedly could have been much greater if the management had been willing to fill thousand-share orders.

Late Wednesday, when worn out accounting clerks and auditors had footed up share commitments, it was found that about 300,000 of the authorized 500,000 had been bought, reserved or subscribed for.

People crowded into the lobby to buy stock. Years afterward Merle Johnson Harp, who was secretary to Andrew Price from this period until the end of his career and who served also as assistant secretary of Marine Bancorporation, recalled:

That lobby! It was so crowded you had to work your way through to get to the counter or your desk. People clutching a handful of bills would attempt to thrust the money into the hands of anyone they recognized worked there and say: "Give me ten shares!" Or "Give me five shares!" Or "Give me what I can get!" It was like a store at the height of the Christmas rush, and it was weeks before the accounts were straight and the books audited.

Mr. Price kept issuing statements trying to keep people from speculating, but that only made matters worse.[12]

In an attempt to quiet the frenzy, Marine stopped the sale of new shares from its treasury, but that only drove buyers to bid for shares already on the market. The price rose to $51.

Realizing their mistake in this effort to stop a runaway market, Marine officers resumed sale of new stock but at no more than $49.75 a share and with no more than twenty shares per applicant. This served only to goad buyers. L. E. Hill on Saturday, March 24, described the result: "Early yesterday there were long queues in the bank premises, buyers lining up and awaiting their turn to buy 20 shares and '20 for the wife.'"

The limited offering failed to satisfy the demand, and the price on the exchange moved up on Monday, March 26, to $56 and the next day to $60. Then buying temporarily wore out, and at the end of the week shares dropped back to $50.

These swings in the market worried Price. He counted on spreading the ownership of Marine widely and converting owners into customers for his banks. He wondered how much support he would get from shareholders exposed to such an erratic market. He wrote stockholders on March 31: "We would deplore any speculation in Bancorporation stock, and it will be the constant effort of your officers and directors to discourage by every means within their power any such tendencies."

The public's interest continued unabated, however. A curious example was a tailor's advertisement in the *Post-Intelligencer* of April 9:

Marine Bancorporation stock worth $75.00 to me. Here's a proposition you can't beat. I mean exactly what I say. One of my regular $75 suits for a share of Marine Bancorporation stock. Come in and see for yourself. You'll say, "Rubenark, it's a go." If you haven't a share, buy one today and bring it to me for your suit. This offer will hold good for this week only, so act today. A. Fred Rubenark, Inc. Merchant Tailor.

Speculators who pressed for Marine stock saw a parallel between this organization as it embarked on statewide banking and the Bank of Italy, whose branches A. P. Giannini by now had established in many parts of California. The Bank of Italy (later the Bank of America) split its shares in April 1927 four for one to widen distribution. After the split in 1927 the price rose from $172 to $263 by the end of the year, then soared past $315. Giannini himself publicly discouraged purchases of the bank's stock at these prices, and on a visit in New York, took the unusual step of asking eastern correspondents of Giannini banks to withhold credit "from persons who are attempting to promote speculation in our securities." [13]

Efforts to restrain speculation only increased the urge to buy. The *San Francisco Examiner* on April 23, 1928, in describing the buying of Bank of Italy stock reported: "Not even the wild days of the Comstock and the old mining exchange had witnessed such 'plunge,' such a fierce rush 'to get aboard' the latest favorite."

In early May, Price's acquisition of the National Bank of Commerce renewed interest in Marine shares, and the market held between $50 and $60. Trading in Marine opened on the San Francisco Curb Exchange on May 7, and the *New York Times* reported of that first day: "A flood of buying orders sent it [the stock] from around $60 to $75 in the course of the day's trading, where it hesitated for awhile and then dropped to $61 after a turnover of 21,000 shares, which swamped the machinery of the exchange." [14] Shares traded in that one exchange in one day had a value of more than $1 million.

Marine was at a pinnacle of public interest. By May 1928 it had more than 6,000 stockholders, a number greater than that of any Washington corporation except Puget Sound Power & Light Co. But difficult days lay ahead for Price. Events over which he had no control soon sent Marine stock plummeting to half the peak reached in May, bringing Price the greatest disappointment of his career.

DISSENSION AND WALKOUT

Andrew Price was well aware that the battle for control of the National Bank of Commerce had left a serious split among its directors and officers, but he was not prepared for the action that followed. On June 4, scarcely five weeks after Marine had won control of Commerce, Seattle papers carried the chilling news that a group of directors and officers would walk out of the National Bank of Commerce and form a new institution, Pacific National Bank. Price had won the vote of a majority of stockholders but he had been unable to sell himself to some of the key officers and directors. Almost forty years afterward one of Price's former associates said the split grew out of a feeling in the dissident group that Andrew Price did not have the background or experience to conduct a bank the size of Commerce.[15]

The chairman of the organization committee for the new bank, and subsequently chairman of the board, was a Commerce director, William Calvert, who at a critical juncture had kept alive negotiations for the sale to Marine. Calvert turned in his Commerce shares for Marine stock, then sold these shares in San Francisco with the help of a phone call from Price. As a result Calvert came out better than if he had taken the offer of $700 cash.

Among other Commerce directors who left for Pacific National were T. A. Davies, president of the automobile agency of that name; J. H. Fox, president of Commercial Boiler Works; H. F. Ostrander, president of Pioneer Sand and Gravel Company; and Moritz Thomsen, president of Centennial Mills and Pacific Coast Biscuit Company.

Robert S. Walker, who, as executive vice president and a director, stood second in command at Commerce, became first vice president and a director of Pacific National. Dietrich Schmitz, vice president in charge of the investment department at Commerce and a relatively new director, moved down the street to Pacific National as vice president and a director. Another Commerce department head, Alfred V. Godsave, vice president and trust officer, went to Pacific National in a similar position.

Nor were these all to leave. LeRoy M. Backus and Langdon Henry sold all their Commerce stock and thereby disqualified themselves as directors. Several others who were directors at Commerce before Marine's acquisition left the board—E. B. Deming, Judge George Donworth, and Timothy Jerome of Merrill & Ring Logging Company.

Pacific National Bank in turn had a strong board—seven from the National Bank of Commerce, and fourteen others, including a number of prominent businessmen.

The loss of Schmitz was particularly disappointing to Price. The two had known each other for years. Both were in the municipal bond business before they entered banking. Schmitz started his banking career with Union National. When that institution merged with Dexter Horton in 1923, he found himself in the No. 3

position in the bond department, and moved to Commerce, where he headed the bond department and made it highly profitable.

Years later Schmitz said he left Commerce because Price already had a complete investment department in the combined operations of John E. Price & Company and Marine National Company, and there was no place for Schmitz as a department head.[16] In addition, as an employee of Marine National he would be selling Bancorporation stock to the public, and Schmitz told Price it was against his principles to sell non-voting stock in such a company. Schmitz was a close personal friend of William E. Boeing, then chairman of the Boeing Airplane Company and a key man in the formation of Pacific National Bank, which he served as bank director from the outset. As head of Pacific National's investment affiliate, Schmitz handled in 1928 the first public offering of Boeing stock. He recalled long afterward that the profit on that underwriting alone was enough to pay the bank's dividends for a couple of years.

Andrew Price's reaction to the exodus was set out in a letter to J. R. Robb, the Walla Walla stockholder. Robb complained that he had sold his National Bank of Commerce shares at $520 each on the basis of what proved to be faulty information from an officer who subsequently left Commerce. Price replied on June 8:

> You can readily appreciate that our views are very sympathetic with your own, when, having paid $700 per share for the stock of this bank, we are now confronted with the organization of a new bank, largely at the instance of former directors of the National Bank of Commerce, who after accepting this price for their stock, are parties to an organization who are strongly soliciting the business of the bank which they sold to us.

Other banks were also after the customers of Commerce. Jay Larson, who came into Dexter Horton National Bank as an officer in the spring of 1928 and subsequently became executive vice president of Seattle–First National Bank, said not long before his death in 1965: "Competition directed at Price and the National Bank of Commerce during this period was intense, often bitter. Everyone was sniping at the Marine organization, attempting to lure away depositors and other customers."[17]

T. A. Davies told a Commerce officer several years later: "I would not have given your bank two years after we went out, but I was mistaken." [18]

Manson Backus put his finger on the trouble a year after sale to Marine: "Price and Shorts made just one mistake. They should have stipulated that the directors would not engage in the banking business in Seattle for a two-year period." Backus added that if Pacific National had not been organized, Commerce would have been the largest bank in Seattle. [19] In subsequent agreements for purchase of banks Price included a restrictive clause on officers and directors.

Manson Backus and C. J. Lord stood by Price and continued on an enlarged board of directors, more than half of whose members after the defection were new, some drawn from Marine Bancorporation and its other banks and some from the business community. John E. Price might have gone on the board at this time, but he had been in ill health for several months and died on July 31, 1928, at the age of 71.

Backus remained president of the bank to which he had devoted so much of his life. Then 76, he was still keen and alert, going to the bank daily and pursuing his cherished hobbies, the collection of etchings and Northwest Americana. An associate who knew him only in these later years recalled him as "a sweet little man, but hard as nails." [20] In 1929 Price took the title of first vice president, which had been vacant since the death of the founder, Robert R. Spencer. In the business of the bank Price consulted with Backus, but, titles aside, Price was the executive head. Late in 1931 Backus was seriously ill with pneumonia, and early the next year at the age of 78 he relinquished the presidency to Price and took the honorary position of chairman of the board, where he continued until his death in 1935.

The rebuffs that Andrew Price received after the acquisition of the National Bank of Commerce drove him to new efforts to build this institution as the cornerstone of his banking organization. In mid-June 1928 he merged Marine National—the bank that he, his father, and Homer Boyd had founded in 1919 for their start in banking—into Commerce. This added a little over $5 million to the deposits at the National Bank of Commerce and pushed the mid-year total a little over $25.6 million. By the end of the year the deposits fell to $24.2 million, a drop surprisingly small in view of the growth of Pacific National's deposits to almost $6.7 million at the year-end.

In January, 1929, Price merged National City Bank into the National Bank of Commerce. This added almost $5 million more in deposits to swell the total shown in the bank call on March 27, 1929, past $28.7 million. Excluding the infusion of deposits from the two mergers, the National Bank of Commerce in the year of defection lost less than 10 per cent of its deposits, which suggests the effectiveness of efforts to build new business.

THE MERGER THAT NEVER HAPPENED

Within a month after Marine acquired Commerce, Morris Arnold and his associates set up their bank holding company—First National Corporation. Through this company Arnold established the First National Group of banks that included First National, Metropolitan National, Rainier Valley Bank, Greenwood National Bank, the Canal Bank, First Security Bank, and First Securities Company.

The creation of First National Corporation alongside Marine Bancorporation altered the balance of power in Seattle banking. For a number of years Dexter Horton National had rested comfortably at the top in deposits and capital. Now Dexter Horton was challenged, and W. H. Parsons, its president, felt that he could no longer remain outside group banking. He was ready to talk to Price.

It is uncertain now who initiated negotiations, but Price and Bruce Shorts met with Parsons and on August 15, 1928, Price gave Marine directors a formal report on negotiations. Parsons proposed merger under Dexter Horton's name, thus retaining the branch banking authorities that had come from an earlier merger with Union National. Dexter Horton would increase the number of its shares from 22,000 to 38,000 and exchange the 16,000 new shares for Marine's Seattle banks. Marine Bancorporation on its own would continue its development of out-of-Seattle branches. Parsons recognized that Price would object that while Marine would be the largest single stockholder, control would reside with Dexter Horton. So he proposed that the 16,000 shares to be issued to Marine and approximately an equal number of Dexter Horton shares be voted by a committee of eight, half representing Marine and half Dexter Horton.

Parsons labeled his proposal a suggestion and asked Marine to come back with a counter proposal. The next day, Price talked to J. D. Hoge, one of the largest stockholders in Dexter Horton. Hoge seemed more receptive to Price's idea for exchanging Marine shares for those of Dexter Horton but spoke of the difficulty of reaching an equitable valuation. Both issues were traded on the Seattle Stock Exchange, and on the basis of current quotations, 13 shares of Marine would be worth 1 share of Dexter Horton. However, negotiators did not feel that this took into account some of the complex factors in the relative value of a large well-established bank in contrast with a young holding company. Price thought a 10 for 1 exchange would be fairer, even though this would give Dexter Horton a premium of about 10 per cent over its book value.

Various compromises were studied, but by early November it was evident that a means of establishing a ratio of exchange was not the only roadblock. More difficult in some ways was the question of voting rights in Marine stock. Price reported to his directors on November 4: "The voting power being limited has centralized control and proven a great advantage in carrying on negotiations for bank acquisition on a purchase basis, but has been raised as an objection by the Dexter Horton group to merger plans."

It was time to reappraise continued use of two classes of stock with voting control restricted to a small group of initial investors. Such control, he recognized, guaranteed "non-interruption of original programs." He thought managerial results also would be better because of management's holding of voting shares.

At the same time Price recognized some advantages in eliminating non-voting stock. For example, there would be no question, now or later, as to selfish objectives of those owning voting stock. Control also would be placed "reasonably beyond reach" of any individual or group. Voting shares, he also noted, were more popular with the public and thus recapitalization would broaden the market.[21]

Price concluded his appraisal by deciding to make no change and thus to retain non-voting stock. He recognized, however, that in a merger with Dexter Horton the voting shares could not be kept solely in the Marine group. He proposed an increase in the authorized number of shares of voting stock from 9,000 to 50,000. Of this number, present Dexter Horton stockholders would receive 22,000, the present holdings of Marine voting stock would be increased to 22,000, and 6,000 would be held for sale to directors and officers. Of the total issue, 26,000 would be pooled for joint control for ten years. This proposal, however, brought no agreement.

For four months negotiations continued in secrecy. Then when the news began to leak out, the organizations announced that consolidation was imminent.

A week later Price tested out Parsons to be sure that a merger would bring the full support of Dexter Horton's directors; Price wanted no repetition of the unhappy walkout at the National Bank of Commerce. He got this assurance and with his associates met on November 28 with Parsons, Mark Reed, J. A. Swalwell, and J. D. Hoge to work out final terms.

Marine offered 12 shares for each share of Dexter Horton. Parsons and his group held out for 13. Price suggested 12½. Dexter Horton balked and the talks ended. A week passed. Price called Parsons to say that Marine would meet Dexter Horton's requirement of 13 shares. Price and Parsons agreed next on the tangible per share value of $24 for Marine and $210 for Dexter Horton, and on December 12 the boards of both institutions unanimously approved the consolidation plan.

The name would be Dexter Horton National Bank of Commerce. Its resources would exceed $95 million, much the largest in the Pacific Northwest. The officers, drawn equally from Dexter Horton and Marine, were agreed upon, and the list was imposing. The patriarch Manson Backus would be chairman; J. D. Hoge and J. W. Maxwell, vice chairmen; W. H. Parsons, president; J. A. Swalwell, chairman of the executive committee; Andrew Price, executive vice president; and W. W. Scruby, vice president and cashier. The directors would include all the directors of the banks in the merger.

Marine Bancorporation, in turn, would become Dexter Horton Marine Corporation with Mark Reed, chairman; Andrew Price, president; and six vice presidents chosen equally from Marine and Dexter Horton. The corporation would have up to 24 trustees, chosen equally from Marine and Dexter Horton, and that balance was to remain for four years.

Price had yielded on two crucial issues without obtaining concessions in return: Dexter Horton stockholders would get 13 shares for each share issued to Marine stockholders, and all shares in the new bank would be voting. Yet this merger, publicly announced and complete even to the selection of officers, never came to pass.

Why? No precise answer is available. The newspapers reported the collapse was due to undisclosed "legal obstacles"—a handy way for officials to avoid discussion of other issues.

Homer Boyd, who was close to Price throughout the negotiations, reported that Price received a telephone call from the Dexter Horton group one morning saying, "Let's not go ahead." [22] Difficulty with details was the reason given. The details on which it was so hard to find acceptance included satisfactory positions for officials, some of whom had already been covered by the public announcement. One who was close to Price at this period observed long afterward: "Too many top men would have been submerged." [23]

The acceptance of the valuations set on the stock of Dexter Horton and Marine proved a barrier, too. Jay Larson, who headed the Dexter Horton committee on the evaluation of Marine's assets, attributed the collapse of the merger to inability to agree on asset values. He felt that exchange on the basis of 13 to 1 was not appropriate. He called Dexter Horton a "clean operation" but he felt values in Marine were inflated, and in particular, that Marine had paid too much for Capital National, National Bank of Commerce, and National City Bank. [24]

Larson, incidentally, did want to see Dexter Horton merge with Marine and suggested that Marine buy the Exchange Bank in Spokane, a $10-million institution which could have been obtained for 10 per cent over book value. Such an acquisition, he said, would have enabled Marine "to even down the prices paid for Commerce and Capital National." Parsons at Dexter Horton turned down this suggestion. Larson thought it would appeal to Price, but nothing came of it.

Perhaps a more serious factor in the collapse of negotiations was the opposition of some of Dexter Horton's large stockholders. Parsons found his stockholders split, and the depth of the split may not have been apparent until after the plan for merger had been made public. The split was another sign that Price simply was not acceptable to some important financial interests in the city. The opposition included that of the Anderson Estate, one of the largest stockholders in several Seattle banks. In 1927, the Anderson Estate, which was represented on the board of the National Bank of Commerce by Mrs. A. H. Anderson, bought the shares of J. W. Clise, Sr. in Seattle National Bank. Soon after this purchase and long before Price and Parsons sat down to negotiate, representatives of the Brownell interests at Seattle National talked to Mrs. Anderson about a consolidation of Dexter Horton and Seattle National.[25] It is likely that Price, and perhaps Parsons as well, knew nothing of this.

After the merger with Marine had fallen apart, negotiations opened between Dexter Horton and First National. Whether Morris Arnold at First National already had initiated talks earlier with some of Dexter Horton's stockholders in order to keep Dexter Horton from going to Marine is not known. For Arnold this was a crucial juncture. Soon he made Dexter Horton the center of his expanding banking system, and it was Arnold, not Price, who headed the largest bank in Seattle.

RESUSCITATION FOR MARINE STOCK

Many in the Marine organization were glad to see the Dexter Horton merger die.[26] There was some feeling that Marine, young and aggressive, would have been inhibited in its expansion if teamed with Dexter Horton. An officer of Marine Central, C. L. Stewart, wrote to Price early in 1929: ". . . The morale of our stockholders and friends in this part of the city seems much improved, and the unanimous opinion seems to prevail that we may now really accomplish something in the way of expansion."

The collapse of the merger left the Marine organization robust, but the same certainly could not be said about Marine stock. In the summer of 1928, with the split in National Bank of Commerce and establishment of Pacific National, the market for Marine fell to $36, little more than half the peak reached a few weeks before. Early in 1929 renewed selling drove the market down toward $29.50, the price at which shares had first been sold. And while Marine shares were falling, the stocks of other Seattle banks were rising.

The wide swings in Marine stock disturbed Price. He regarded the market as a measure of the investing public's appraisal of a company. He felt that this appraisal was of particular importance for a new and expanding organization. Price had an analysis prepared in February 1929 of Marine's 6,984 stockholders. He was pleased to find that 6,000 of them still held their original stock certificates. More than 70 per cent of the shareholders lived in Seattle and 80 per cent in Washington State. But because so many stockholders had bought for investment and tucked their shares away, the market was thin and susceptible to wide swings.

In an effort to stabilize its shares Marine entered the market in 1929. When prices weakened, Marine bought its own stock. Then it turned around and sold these shares to investors on an installment plan, $10 down and $2.50 a month. The investor was not allowed to accelerate payments.

Late in March 1929 Price left for New York City, "looking for a broader distribution of our stock." He had hardly arrived when Homer Boyd, president of Marine National Company, wrote:

On March 26th . . . the local market crashed and conditions have been more or less hectic ever since. Marine suffered rather badly inasmuch as we were in no position to give any support. . . . We need some assistance on Marine and if it could come from the outside (I mean outside the State of Washington) it would be more helpful, of course. We are now working on a local situation which may make it possible to interest a group in the stock here.[27]

Boyd said that Bruce Shorts opposed the idea of interesting a local group in Marine shares and preferred to sell more stock that would be held rather than traded on the market. But Boyd added: "Even if he is right . . . we just cannot do that under these conditions."

Price spent weeks talking with financial men in New York. Toward the end of April, he was reasonably confident that either Seaboard Securities Company or Kuhn, Loeb & Company would agree to buy 22,000 shares at $40 a share. But Kuhn, Loeb indicated it was not interested in such a small transaction unless there were "associated reasons," which Price interpreted to mean the "possibility of some larger development." Price, not wanting to force the issue with Kuhn, Loeb, made the same proposal to Seaboard and offered in return to concentrate Marine's banking and security business with Seaboard. But Seaboard already had substantial business from Seattle and if it took on Marine it might lose as much as it gained.

By May 2, Price reported the situation had worsened. Neither Kuhn, Loeb nor Seaboard would make a commitment and Seaboard insisted on detailed earnings reports of all Marine banks, Marine National Company, and Marine Bancorporation. Price confided to Boyd: "The figures look spotted as we well know and don't come up to proving a high earnings per share. The results for April are encouraging it's true, but nevertheless, it was very evident that the figures did not help our cause."

Price talked also to representatives of the Old Colony Trust Company. From them came a suggestion that Price sell a large block of stock in each of Marine's banks. This would conserve capital and permit spreading it over a larger number of subsidiary banks; it would also strengthen the bank operations and the market for Marine. Price considered issuing to Marine stockholders rights to buy shares of the National Bank of Commerce but did not go ahead.

Marine leaders considered other plans. One was to manipulate the price of Marine shares upward, but Price feared that in such an operation he would be at the mercy of stockbrokers who might get the market up, sell out, and leave Marine's market in worse shape than before. He understood that this was characteristic of the operations of at least one securities firm mentioned in relation to the plan.

Price's contacts at Kuhn, Loeb and Seaboard strongly urged getting investment distribution through a house like Blyth & Co., and Price asked Boyd to check with Blyth at Seattle on redistribution of perhaps 25,000 shares.

Kuhn, Loeb and Seaboard officials also urged listing of Marine stock on the San Francisco Exchange, though Old Colony opposed this because it would subject the stock to wide swings under price rigging by professionals.

Price talked also to A. P. Giannini, who was in New York to complete arrangements for Bancitaly to acquire an investment banking firm. News of their meetings got about and revived rumors that Price and Giannini would join forces. Giannini was determined to get into Washington, and for more than a year financial publications had carried rumors—labeled as unconfirmed, but nonetheless persistent—that Marine would be merged with the Giannini group, either into Bancitaly Corporation or United Security Bank and Trust.

Returning to Seattle in May 1929, Price denied that he and Giannini had discussed the linking of their organizations. Unquestionably he felt that he had to make such a denial lest the acknowledgment of Giannini's interest touch off a new wave of speculation, but the two had indeed discussed consolidation of Bancitaly and Marine. On the desirability of such a merger, Price wrote to Boyd in Seattle: "From our personal standpoints if we could get a premium for our initial [voting] stock this would likely have attractive possibilities." [28]

Price also was offered an attractive salary with Bancitaly and a position that might ultimately have led to the presidency of that organization. But Price and Giannini never reached agreement. Nor, after weeks of discussions with eastern financial men, did Price come back from New York with anything tangible to buoy the market for Marine shares.

To this extent the trip was a failure, but the long discussions of what might be done with Marine and the perspective gained from a distance fortified a basic decision: Price would remain at the head of Marine Bancorporation and would make it his life work. He was not again tempted to leave Seattle.

Price's determination to concentrate on Marine and its cornerstone, the National Bank of Commerce, was strengthened by conversations he had in New York with two men prominent in Seattle National Bank. One was Frank H. Brownell, who was chairman of Seattle National Bank and a director of Chase National Bank in New York. The other was one of the two sons of Daniel Kelleher. Daniel Kelleher, until his unexpected death the previous February, had been chairman of Seattle National and the largest stockholder. Price's memo does not indicate which of Kelleher's sons he talked with; presumably it was Hugh, who lived in New York, rather than Campbell, whose banking career was spent in Seattle.

Brownell recognized in talking to Price that group banking, which Price had brought to Seattle, was forcing a new alignment of major banks in the city. Seattle National for years had maintained second rank, behind Dexter Horton. Brownell felt strongly that a bank should be big. He remarked to Joshua Green, Sr. that the largest bank "got first crack at all the big, new business." [29]

To make Seattle National the first in the city would require merger. Brownell wanted to explore the chances of putting together Seattle National, First National, and the National Bank of Commerce.

Price thought the likelihood of such a merger was slight. He noted to an associate that Brownell and Kelleher were "clearly afraid of our control" and "didn't like our initial [voting] share set up." Moreover, Price suspected that Brownell might be using these discussions as a smokescreen for a deal with Dexter Horton, a bank which Price said "they have hardly mentioned."

Brownell returned to Seattle in July 1929. On August 9, newspapers carried the announcement of the biggest merger in the city's history, one that would bring together Dexter Horton, First National, and Seattle National. The new institution would be known as First Seattle Dexter Horton National Bank (later shortened to Seattle-First National Bank). The president would be Morris A. Arnold of the First National.

The merger was completed in November, and at the end of the year, First Seattle Dexter Horton reported deposits of $78 million, almost half from Dexter Horton alone. This left the National Bank of Commerce, though second in the city, far behind with deposits of not quite $29 million. The inclusion of affiliated banks in Seattle increased the deposits of the Arnold group to $92 million, almost three times the total for Commerce and the other banks in the Marine group.

Thus Arnold, with the backing of financial leaders, put through a merger with Dexter Horton, succeeding where Price had tried so hard but failed. With the amalgamations of 1928 and 1929— one under Arnold, the other under Price—the structure of banking in Seattle was largely established, and these groups in years to come built the two big statewide banking systems of Washington.

GROUP BANKING—AN INTERIM STEP

On his return from New York, Price was more certain than ever that nothing could long prevent branch banking from coming to Washington State: the advantages to the public and to banking were too great. He took the leadership in speaking on behalf of branch banking. He also resumed negotiations for banks that would expand Marine and place its units—perhaps branches, later—where they would serve important areas of the state's economy. Meantime, he pushed ahead with group banking.

On August 10, 1929, stockholders of two banks in southwestern Washington, the Montesano State Bank and the Bank of Elma, agreed to sell to Marine. The price for the two together was $481 a share, paid for with 9,165 Marine shares that were carried on the books at $339,105, roughly $37 a share. The Montesano bank, organized in 1897, was the second oldest in the Grays Harbor area.

Three weeks later, on September 4, Price concluded acquisition of 56.2 per cent of the stock of the First National Bank of Mount Vernon, on which negotiations had begun almost 18 months before. The bank, founded in 1889, was the oldest and largest in the rich agricultural Skagit Valley. It had resources of $1.6 million.

Price and Boyd had gone to Mount Vernon in April 1928 to talk with N. J. Moldstad, the largest stockholder, owning almost 30 per cent. After the visit, Price noted: "Moldstad seemed very favorable," [30] but a year passed without any action. In the spring of 1929, L. E. Younger, auditor of Marine Bancorporation, advised Price that exchange of stock on the basis of 9 shares of Marine for 1 of Mount Vernon "would be a good deal," and the maximum should be 10 to 1. Marine's stock then stood at $32, and Younger calculated the value of Mount Vernon stock between $288 and $320 a share. Younger was constantly preparing studies such as this for Price's guidance.

But Mount Vernon stockholders wouldn't budge at the values Younger suggested. Price found that he had to pay $350 a share in cash, a total of $196,700, to get majority ownership. Even so, Moldstad declined to sell.

The Mount Vernon acquisition during the expansive era of the late twenties was another example of Price's willingness to pay a premium for a bank that could contribute to Marine's growth. After the depression, Price was a more restrained buyer, and on occasion bid so close that a competitor picked up a bank Price was anxious to add to Marine. [31]

A few days after the purchase at Mount Vernon in 1929, Marine acquired 68 per cent of the stock of LaConner State Bank, ownership of which was largely the same as that of the Mount Vernon bank. Marine paid $275 a share, a total of $46,750.

The Marine group of affiliated banks now numbered nine—three in Seattle and six in outlying cities of western Washington. Marine was gaining in diversity as well as size. But group banking was cumbersome, and Price regarded it only as a step toward branch banking.

In group banking the ties are loose. Each bank remains a separate operation and in time of crisis must stand on its own. The obvious advantage is to the owners who, by holding shares in the parent organization, spread their investment over a number of banks and who, incidentally, fend off other banks which might also be building a chain.

In branch banking the individual banks are merged into a single institution that is stronger than any of the separate units. The advantages to customers are obvious; depositors have the protection of the capital and surplus of a large bank, and borrowers have access to greater funds and wider services. Costs of operation are somewhat lower in branch banking. A large institution also can provide trained management that is often hard to obtain in a small bank under owner-management.

Barriers against branch banking were beginning to come down by 1927. In that year Congress passed the McFadden Act, which cautiously allowed national banks to establish branches on a city-wide basis—provided that state law permitted branches. Then in October 1929 the Comptroller of the Currency, J. W. Pole, told the American Bankers Association: "I have come to the conclusion that an extension of branch banking privileges should be granted to national banks."

Developments such as these drove Price to new efforts to lift the state ban on branches. He carried the issue to a meeting of independent bankers in 1929. The text of his talk he retained in his files but the name of the group was not indicated. Price said that group banking was only a transition to branch banking. "Group banks today," he said, "are doing only what chain stores did yesterday—buying out tired independents."

Most of the banks of the state then in business had been founded thirty to forty years before, during the last two decades of the previous century. Many of these banks were still in charge of the founders. Speaking with unnatural sharpness as though to shake these older men into facing the changing times, Price told the group:

The halo still encircles the patriarchal head of many an old banker, but the corners of the notes in the pouch are worn round, and the cobwebs are over the face of the credit files in many an institution with this leadership. . . .

Mr. Independent Banker, I tell you that by the grace of God and the fact that your state and national laws have surrounded you with a certain franchise right, that you had best capitalize upon this exclusive privilege as quickly as possible, put your house in order, seek out your association—be it group or branch organization—get in the big tent while you may. It is impossible to build a successful organization by hiring men at the top.

This was late in 1929. In October the stock market crashed. The decade of the twenties—a decade of merger, acquisition, and speculation—was coming to a close. Depression was beginning to take hold in America, and before the depression had run its course, the banks of many of the men to whom Price spoke so sharply were closed and branch banking had become inevitable.

The depression spread hardship and suffering across the land. Millions of persons lost their jobs and went month after bleak month without work or paycheck, sometimes even several years. Collapsing prices of commodities like lumber, shingles, wheat, and apples dragged down the economy of Washington State, a producer essentially of basic commodities.

The depression relentlessly tested the worth of every venture, whether a speculation in stocks or an investment in a sawmill. Companies that had not had time or foresight to build up reserves found themselves in trouble—or out of business. Some once regarded as sound and profitable found that as prices fell and sales shrank they had no option but to close.

Reserves were exhausted not only on the balance sheet, but also, which was far more serious, in the minds and spirits of countless men and women. A hope in the early 1930's that the worst had passed gave way to a realization that 1931 was a recession year and that 1932 might be blacker still. There seemed no way out.

The start of the depression is commonly pegged to the collapse of the New York stock market in October 1929, but in numerous industries the decline began much earlier. Lumber is an example. *Timber and Men,* the Weyerhaeuser history, records:

In the middle 1920's lumbermen watched industries other than theirs making prodigious profits. Their own were either nominal or non-existent. Prices for standing timber were declining. Mill capacity had expanded far beyond limits warranted by market demand, and lumbermen were waging continuous war against wood substitutes.[1]

If excess capacity in lumber was burdensome in the 1920's, it became devastating in the 1930's. The nation's production of softwood lumber reached a peak in 1925, then began to decline. In Washington, the peak output came in 1927 at 7.5 billion board feet, a volume never equaled since. By 1932 production had fallen to less than 2.3 million board feet.[2] Where there had been jobs in logging and lumbering for three men in 1925, there was a job for only one in 1932.

Lumber prices worked downward for ten years. In the Douglas fir region, mills averaged $27.82 per thousand board feet on lumber sold in 1923. By 1932 mills averaged only $11.50.[3]

House building, the big outlet for lumber, likewise passed its peak in the middle 1920's. For the nation, the number of new housing units fell from 937,000 in 1925 to only 93,000 in 1933. Not until the postwar housing boom in 1949 would the 1925 peak be surpassed.

In Seattle construction shrank even farther. In the big year of 1925 the city issued building permits for 3,618 single-family houses. Save for the wartime surge in 1918, that stands as the city's all-time high. For the decade after 1925 residential construction declined relentlessly year after year.[4] At the bottom in 1934, work was undertaken on only 150 new houses. Jobs vanished. In 1934 there was employment for only 1 out of every 24 carpenters employed nine years earlier.

Construction of office buildings, stores, warehouses, and factories ceased. In Seattle, the high in value covered by building permits came in 1926 when work was started on $36 million in buildings; for 20 years that figure stood as the record. By 1934, new construction, including even remodeling and renovation, had shrunk to less than $2 million.

Farming areas were hard hit. Farm prices plummeted until they brought less than the cost of production. In the big year of 1925, wheat growers of Washington sold their crop for an average of $1.36 a bushel; at the bottom of the depression they averaged only 36 cents a bushel. Potatoes that yielded farmers a statewide average of $2.50 a bushel in 1925 brought only 65 cents in 1932.[5]

For apples the plunge was even greater. At the peak in 1927, Washington growers averaged $1.32 a bushel delivered to the packinghouse door; in 1932 and again in 1933, the return came to only 32 cents a bushel. On street corners of distant cities men without jobs sold apples for a nickel apiece to try to earn a few cents.

Business profits almost disappeared. In 1932 corporate net income for the nation fell to one-fifth the 1929 level. In Washington, harder hit, it dropped to scarcely one-tenth of the peak. Washington corporations filing income tax returns for 1929 reported total net income of $76.2 million; in 1932 they reported only $7.7 million.[6] There is no record of how large the losses were for companies that operated in the red or later went out of business and filed no tax return.

As the depression dragged on, factories went onto a short week to spread work and payrolls as widely as possible. Many companies, from manufacturing to retailing, had more help than there was any chance of using, and each week more men found themselves entirely out of work. For those who still had a job, pay cuts were almost universal.

Just how many were unemployed in the depths of the depression no one knows. The machinery for gathering such statistics came later. To get some measure of the problem, the Washington Emergency Relief Administration made a survey in the eleven largest cities in Washington in December 1934, well after the bottom had been passed. This showed just over 25 per cent of all wage-earners out of work. The average unemployed person had 2.34 dependents to feed; he had had no work at all for 10 months and had not worked at his usual occupation for 19 months.[7]

For bank management the depression became the greatest test in this century. As the economy tightened, people withdrew their savings and deposits shrank. The manager of a small bank which subsequently closed spoke grimly thirty years later of the loss in deposits as "a seepage, a persistent withdrawal of funds, week after week, month after month, and there was nothing you could do about it. Some of the withdrawal was from fear, but most of it was money that was needed." [8]

At national banks in Washington, deposits fell from $296 million at the end of 1929 to $180 million at the end of 1933. For the smaller and more numerous state banks, many of them located in hard-hit farming and lumbering communities, the plunge was even greater, from $157 million in 1929 to just under $70 million in 1933.

Deposits held best in the large city banks. At the National Bank of Commerce the drop from the end of 1929 to the end of 1932 (just prior to merger of affiliated banks) was only 9 per cent. This compares with a drop of 16 per cent for Seattle banks as a group and 39 per cent for all banks in the state.

As deposits shrank, banks struggled to gain liquidity, seeking somehow to get cash to meet tomorrow's withdrawals. A loan might be made for 90 days, but if the borrower was a sawmill operator who had to shut down for lack of orders or an apple grower who couldn't even recover his costs from the sale of his crop, the bank could only wait. [9]

Many banks also held bonds of foreign governments. Commonly, the bonds had been pushed out by New York banks to institutions throughout the country. But the market for bonds plunged, particularly foreign bonds. To sell meant taking a loss, and even if the bonds had been of top value, who was going to buy them? People wanted money.

Banks could take some types of collateral to the Federal Reserve Bank and borrow money, but banks that were the hardest pressed no longer had acceptable collateral. Some time later, the new Reconstruction Finance Corporation made funds available for banks with frozen assets, but by then thousands of banks had closed.

As the depression deepened, the runs on banks spread like a disease through the nation. In mid-February 1933 the governor of Michigan, seeking to protect banks in Detroit that had been weakened by heavy withdrawals, declared an eight-day banking holiday. The eight days stretched into two weeks with the banks still closed under the governor's order. Runs then spread to other states and banking holidays followed. On March 2, Oregon and

California declared holidays, making 17 states with not a bank open for business.

The next day, a Friday, apprehension spread to Washington and runs developed. The *Seattle Times* cautiously reported:

Withdrawals were heavy from local institutions and lower Second Avenue for a time was clogged with vehicles parked two and three abreast as depositors thronged to the banks. Every check presented was honored in full.

Governor Clarence D. Martin then stepped in and ordered banks closed for three days. The next day Franklin D. Roosevelt took office as President and the federal government ordered all banks in the nation closed, a holiday that was to last ten days. When banks reopened, nervous officials prepared for a resumption of withdrawals but found, instead, that customers swarmed back to make deposits. In Seattle the newspapers reported that one customer brought in $50,000 in gold. On the New York Stock Exchange the Dow Jones industrial average soared $8.26 to $62.10.

Years afterward Chester B. Starks, who left commercial banking to serve under the Washington State Supervisor of Banking as a liquidator of closed banks, observed: "Each bank had exactly the same assets at the end of the holiday that it had at the beginning, but the holiday had taken the fight and the fear out of people." [10]

The panic was over, but long reconstruction lay ahead, reconstruction that would see innovations such as the establishment of the Civilian Conservation Corps to give jobless young men useful work, especially in the forests; emergency food relief for families that had exhausted their funds; and the launching of widespread public works projects.

The mortality among banks was on a scale never before known. In the nation from mid-1929 to mid-1933 the number of commercial banks shrank from 24,970 to 14,207.[11] Thus, two out of every five banks in the United States closed.

In Washington, 16 national banks and 54 state banks closed.[12] A few that closed ultimately paid depositors in full, but more often depositors got only part of their money and stockholders nothing. Many small banks had been under-capitalized. Thirteen state banks placed in liquidation in 1931 and 1932 had capital of less than $25,000; 5 had capital of only $10,000.[13]

The toll was heaviest among small institutions and in one-industry communities. In mill towns and farming centers of western Washington, 14 banks went under. In the apple country from Wenatchee north to the Canadian border, 8 banks closed; in the Yakima Valley, 6; and in the wheat country of eastern Washington, 12.

No section of the nation escaped the closings. So great a shock to the economy brought measures to strengthen the banking system. One was insurance of deposits, a protection set up under federal law and paid for by banks. Another was the lifting of federal restrictions on branch banking.

BRANCH BANKING AUTHORIZED

The first step toward the legalizing of branch banking in Washington came in February 1933. The legislature, worried by the ominous spread of bank holidays across the nation, sought to strengthen state banks by allowing larger institutions—those with at least $500,000 of paid-in capital—to operate branches. The law applied directly only to state-chartered banks, but it automatically allowed national banks to take advantage of the McFadden Act and establish branches in their own city.

Apparently in preparation for this legislation, Price converted his two state banks in Seattle to national charters so as to simplify ultimate merger with the National Bank of Commerce. In this interim step, Marine Central Bank became Central National Bank of Commerce and Marine State Bank became Washington National Bank of Commerce. An April 1, 1933, these two banks became the first branches of the National Bank of Commerce.

In June Congress passed the Banking Act of 1933 as part of a broad program of reconstruction and reform. The Act allowed national banks to establish branches wherever state banks had this authority.

Price, who had worked so hard to bring branch banking to Washington State, was ready. Up to this point Marine Bancorporation had been his vehicle for bringing together a group of banks under common ownership and direction. But as soon as branch banking became legal, he converted the separate units owned by Marine into branches of the National Bank of Commerce. Later he added new branches to form a unified statewide bank.

Just before Congress passed the banking act, Price took another step in preparation for consolidation; he wrote down the premiums Marine had paid for banks it acquired in 1928 and 1929. This called for a re-appraisal in terms of the harsh realities of the depression and was announced to stockholders in a letter dated May 1, 1933.

Price began the letter by recounting with pride that all of Marine's banks had reopened immediately after the banking holiday and added that of 253 banks in Washington, only 143 were similarly allowed to reopen. He continued:

In spite of the unprecedented demands occasioned by a country-wide run, the National Bank of Commerce was one of the few large banks in the country which did not have to borrow any money, or rediscount any of its paper, or sell any of its securities. Instead, it promptly met all demands upon it, assisted many of its correspondents, and upon declaration of the holiday, had a larger cash reserve than usually necessary under normal conditions. The same can be said of all bank members of the Marine group.

Price then reported that those capital funds in Marine Bancorporation in excess of $25 par value per share would be transferred from capital to surplus. This would provide almost $5 million "for reserves, charge-offs and other corporate purposes" and would place Marine "among the leaders in the banking business in the country in adjusting its affairs to conditions and values as they are, not as we hope subsequent developments may justify."

From the funds thus set up, $2,342,685 went to write down the costs at which Marine carried its subsidiary banks on the books. In addition, $2,500,000 went into a special reserve against the price at which Marine carried the National Bank of Commerce itself. This reserve, incidentally, was never used and in 1945 was released as no longer needed. The establishment of these reserves gave Price a solid foundation for going ahead with acquisitions.

Three weeks after the new banking act became law, Price opened a branch in Centralia, which for seven months had had no bank. Next he opened a branch at Bremerton to take over a substantial part of the deposits and assets of the closed First National Bank. These branches filled a void left by the failure of local banks. Later in the year he converted Marine's banks in Olympia, Aberdeen, Montesano, and Elma to branches of the National Bank of Commerce.

Yakima grew as a shipping center for a rich agricultural valley, made fruitful by irrigation. The view is west in downtown Yakima in the 1920's.

In 1935, with a gradual improvement in business and agriculture, Price was ready for further expansion. He looked across the Cascade Mountains to the state's agricultural heartland where no Seattle bank had yet penetrated. His sights were set on Yakima First National, a respected institution that had begun as a private bank in 1883 and ranked as the largest bank between Seattle and Spokane. Yakima, the leading city of a rich, irrigated valley, would give Commerce not just opportunity for growth but also diversification in the economy it served. A branch in Yakima would be the first by any Seattle bank east of the Cascades, though late in December 1935 Seattle–First National Bank leapfrogged to Spokane with acquisition of Spokane and Eastern Trust Co.

Robert M. Hardy, president of the Yakima bank and president also for many years of Sunshine Mining Co., announced sale of the bank to Commerce in September 1935. The consolidation, he said, would give Yakima "facilities which we as a smaller institution could not have (and) since local management is coupled with larger resources, it will enable us to do a better job in taking care of the financial needs of the community." [14]

Stockholders of Yakima First National Bank received book value for their shares plus $200,000 for goodwill. At that time the bank had deposits of a little over $9 million. In 1969 the Yakima branch had deposits of $40 million and was the largest outside Seattle in the statewide system of the National Bank of Commerce.

Three years later the bank moved into Wenatchee through acquisition of the Columbia Valley Bank. Wenatchee, the apple capital, was then hard hit by a recurrence of devastatingly low prices for apples, but Price was confident of better days. By 1969 deposits of the Wenatchee Branch exceeded $21 million.

The transition from group to branch banking was nearly complete. In time, Marine acquired the remaining shares of banks in which it held a majority interest and merged these institutions into the National Bank of Commerce. Thus, Marine had served its original purpose of bringing together a group of banks before branch banking was permitted.

In the operation of the National Bank of Commerce, Price relied at this time on three officers above others. Two were commercial bankers of long experience—Ira W. Bedle and L. E. Younger. The third was the attorney Bruce Shorts, whose counsel extended far beyond that relating strictly to legal matters. A fourth to whom Price turned frequently was Homer Boyd, close associate from early days in John E. Price & Co. but, like Price, one with training in investments rather than in commercial banking.

Bedle in 1935 was in his middle fifties. In his early years he had been with Washington Trust Company in Spokane and later joined Price at Marine National Bank. In 1935 Bedle was a vice president and director of Commerce. He was primarily a credit or loan man and thus concentrated in the area where conventional banks made their money, but having come through banking in the days before there was great specialization, he also knew operations well. He became senior vice president in 1946 and retired in 1948.

Younger, who in 1935 was in his late forties, was a self-taught man with no formal schooling beyond the eighth grade. He was meticulous about detail and became thoroughly grounded in banking. For a number of years he was with Scandinavian American Bank, then became a state bank examiner and ultimately joined Price at Marine National Bank. Price made Younger auditor of Marine Bancorporation, a strategic position in the evaluation of banks that Price considered acquiring. Later Younger became controller of the National Bank of Commerce, and on retirement in 1951 was a vice president. He acquired a coast-wide reputation as an auditor; in the bank's management he was outspoken.

Shorts' association with Price went back to the days of John E. Price & Co., when the law firm of Shorts & Denney was adviser on municipal bonds. Both Shorts and Homer Boyd were directors of Marine Bancorporation from its founding. When Marine acquired Commerce, they both became directors of the bank and served until death—Shorts in 1945 and Boyd in 1965.

Together Bedle, Younger, and Shorts constituted a balance wheel for Price, the builder and innovator. That relationship, however, at times meant great frustration for Price as he sought to take the National Bank of Commerce into fields unfamiliar to conventional bankers.

Another senior officer important at this time was Herbert Witherspoon, who was in his late fifties. Witherspoon had spent 25 years with the Spokane and Eastern Trust Co., before coming to National City Bank in Seattle in 1919. On consolidation of National City Bank into the National Bank of Commerce in 1929 Witherspoon became a director and served as such until his death in 1962. He became a vice president in 1929.

One officer whose name, along with that of Manson Backus, Price always placed above his own in the formal listing of officers was J. W. Maxwell, who by 1935 was in his early seventies, Price's senior by a quarter century.

Maxwell first came into the National Bank of Commerce in 1906 as cashier under Robert Spencer, but left soon after the merger in which Manson Backus became president. Later Maxwell was cashier at Seattle National, then president of National City Bank. When Price bought National City, expecting to merge it into Marine National, Maxwell was assured the presidency. But before that consolidation was made, Price also acquired the National Bank of Commerce. When National City was merged into Commerce in 1929, Backus remained president of Commerce. The best that Maxwell could do was to accept the title of chairman of the executive committee. This position, created for the situation, was a curious one for Maxwell, a man of great positiveness who scorned committees when decisions were to be made.

In 1932 Backus became chairman of the board and Price, as the active head of the bank, became president. With the death of Backus in 1935, Maxwell moved up to chairman of the board. He served as a director of both Commerce and Marine Bancorporation from 1928 to his death in 1951.

Recovery from the depression came slowly. Consumer buying power could be rebuilt only as men and women found work, yet unemployment held stubbornly high through the rest of the decade. In 1937 a sharp unexpected recession broke the upward swing and jolted confidence. Prices of major farm products again turned distressingly soft. As late as 1939, in spite of growth in population, the number employed in manufacturing in Washington remained 27 per cent short of the 1929 total.

But entirely new factors began to broaden and strengthen the economy of Washington. At Bonneville, where the Columbia River cuts through the Cascade Mountains and upstream at Grand Coulee in central Washington, great power projects were under construction. Soon the Pacific Northwest's abundant cheap power began to attract new heavy industry, and water from melting snow and glaciers on the Rocky Mountains in the United States and Canada converted rich but desert land into farms of great productivity. At Seattle, a small manufacturer of aircraft began to

175

expand, and from employment of 1,780 in early 1938, the Boeing
Airplane Company—its name shortened later to just the Boeing
Company—built its work force in two years past the 6,000 mark.
In timber areas new mills were built to convert the finest Douglas
fir logs into plywood and the weed tree, hemlock, into pulp for
paper.

Then came war and mobilization of the nation's manpower.
Shipyards sprang up on the Columbia River at Vancouver and
on Puget Sound; from employment of less than 1,000 at the end
of 1939, shipyards of the state built their work force to a mighty
wartime peak of 117,554.[1]

Boeing stepped up output of its Flying Fortress, the bomber that
helped pound Germany into submission. Rosie the Riveter came to
work by the thousands, and by early 1945, Boeing's employment
at Seattle passed 47,000.

Aluminum smelters at Vancouver, Longview, Wenatchee, and
Spokane began pouring out the metal so essential for airplanes.
Washington and Oregon, which until 1939 had never made a
pound of aluminum, produced 28 per cent of the nation's output
in 1943.[2]

The total effort was prodigious. In spite of shortages of manpower, manufacturers in Washington employed at the peak of
war production just over 315,000 men and women, a level that has
never since been equaled even in August 1968, the biggest month
in the boom of the late 1960's, when the total was 300,100.

When the war ended, thousands of men and women returned
from service to their homes in Washington. Countless others who
had been stationed at some time in the Pacific Northwest came
back to look for work. Would there be jobs for all? Shipyards
lay quiet. Boeing's employment fell to less than 8,000. But from
the limitations of the civilian economy in the war and from the
belt-tightening during the depression years, shortages had arisen
in housing, in consumer goods, in industrial equipment. Out of
the need to fill these shortages came the industrial expansion
that, broken by short uneasy periods of recession, has dominated
the years since 1946.

The decade of the forties brought the greatest gain in population in Washington's history, a net increase of 642,772. The fifties
brought an increase of 472,251, which swelled the state's total to

2,853,214, a doubling of population in not much more than 30 years.

The postwar years brought also a change in the character of manufacturing in Washington—away from the production of commodities such as lumber and coal and toward an increasing diversity of end products. This was the sort of expansion the state had been reaching for since its earliest days.

Forest products continue important but no longer dominate. In March 1940, for example, 55 per cent of all jobs in manufacturing were in forest products, 47 per cent in lumber alone. With growth in other industries and a decline in lumber, forest products in 1969 provided only 23 per cent of all jobs in manufacturing.

Within the forest industry there have been wide changes. As the harvest of old-growth timber tapered off, output of lumber fell. But at the same time the pulp and paper industry, able to use lower-grade raw material, expanded sharply. From 1947 through 1968, output of pulp increased more than two and a half times, but this growth was not so fast as in some areas of the South, and Washington yielded to Georgia its rank as the nation's leading producer of pulp.[3] With growth in western markets, more of Washington's pulp was converted to end products, and as a result output of paper and paperboard increased more than three and a half times from 1947 to 1968.

The raw material for this expansion came not from a larger harvest of logs—indeed, pulp-mill use of whole logs has declined in recent years—but from chips made from the leftovers of lumber and plywood plants and from salvage logging.

Other manufacturing has grown, too. In 1957 employment in the aerospace industry for the first time moved ahead of that in the lumber and plywood industry. Boeing, like others in aerospace, has known wide swings in the total work force, yet even at the lowest point during the cutbacks of 1963 and 1964, its employment easily topped the peak of World War II.

Aluminum smelters have expanded, and more of their output is manufactured here into plates, extrusions, wire, and rod for use in the West. Kenworth trucks built in Seattle rumble through the oil fields of the Middle East and the forests of the Philippines. Ski wear made for the slopes of the Cascade Mountains finds buyers in New York and New England. Luggage made in Seattle carries

This peaceful rural scene is strictly camouflage against air attack. It was built on the roof of the Seattle Boeing plant that turned out B-17 Flying Fortresses during World War II.

the belongings of travelers the world over. Frozen fruits and vegetables from Washington are served by housewives in every state.

The postwar years also have seen new farm lands come into production in the rich Columbia Basin. Today Washington ranks as the leading state in apples, hops, late-summer potatoes, mint, and dry field peas. It is second in green peas for processing, pears and apricots, and generally fourth or fifth in wheat.[4] It is an important producer of sugar beets.

Along with expansion in basic industry and agriculture the past twenty years have brought development of houses, apartments, schools, shopping centers, freeways, pipelines, and power dams —the greatest period of construction the state has ever known.

Recovery from the depression brought not simply growth in banking but also a change in the character of banking. When Manson Backus headed the National Bank of Commerce, a bank consisted of one office, usually dominated by one man who wielded real authority in the business community; the bank dealt primarily with business firms rather than wage-earners. This was wholesale banking. But in the years since the depression the trend in America has been toward retail banking, toward taking banking to the people via branches and providing a wide range of services for consumers as well as for business firms.

Retail banking had its earliest development in the West. One of the pioneers was A. P. Giannini, founder at San Francisco of the Bank of Italy, now the Bank of America. Giannini, finding it hard to get the business of large firms for his new bank, went to the Italian colony in San Francisco, soliciting small savings accounts and making loans to individuals. Conventional bankers scorned this business as risky and costly to handle, but Giannini proved that it could be substantial in volume and profitable.

Andrew Price, constantly searching for ideas, watched Giannini with admiration. Like Giannini, Price at the beginning found that the big accounts were already well established at other banks. To build growth Price had to go after business that other bankers didn't see or didn't think was worth handling. He was forced to innovate, to promote.

Fortunately for Price, this was an approach he liked. He was a builder, a developer, a promoter in the sense that everything new has to have a promoter. Because he had come into commercial banking through the investment side, he was free of many of the inhibitions and restraints of men who had spent their lives as commercial bankers and were seared by the depression into conservatism.

Price was constantly putting on stunts to build business. Early in the depression when the going was rough he ran a contest for the staff in which he gave points for new accounts, new loans, and other types of added business. Price made the awards substantial; one officer recalled recently that he won enough to join a golf club, which later in the depression went broke.[1]

In 1929 Price brought in Wylie Hemphill to head the business development department. Hemphill, formerly president of Pacific Coast Coal Company, had just finished a term as president of the Seattle Chamber of Commerce and was widely known and respected. He worked to get new customers, whether a new manufacturer such as Northwestern Glass Company or a secretary with a $15 savings account. Hemphill, Price, and Bruce Shorts constituted a close-working unit in developing the bank. Price was the idea man, Shorts the steadying hand, and Hemphill the business builder.

Price was always reaching for ideas. He would return from a banking convention or a trip around the country with a hatful of notes and suggestions to toss out for discussion at staff meetings. Sometimes an idea would be accepted; sometimes it would be trampled on, but Price was undaunted. The willingness to search for the new, to innovate, and to promote made Price a pioneer as the industry moved into retail banking.[2]

A BROADENING INTO CONSUMER LOANS

As business built up from the depression, Price sought to broaden the bank's activity and to lend directly to consumers for purchases of such major items as automobiles and appliances. Conventional bankers—and there were plenty in the National Bank of Commerce just as there are now in every successful commercial bank —scoffed: If a consumer can't pay cash for a car he shouldn't have one. Price was convinced to the contrary and looked for a way to start.

Soon after the Federal Housing Administration's Title I Program for home-improvement loans was organized, Price set up a parallel Title I program within the bank—a one-man operation. In 1937 he extended the effort to include personal loans other than those for home improvement and turned this job over to Wendell Sizemore, who had been with the bank since 1920. Under Sizemore the bank loaned directly to individuals, but the volume remained small and almost no loans were made on automobiles, which today constitute such a large segment of instalment credit.

When the United States entered the war in December 1941, it was obvious that expansion in consumer financing must wait. In the conversion to a war economy, the manufacture of automobiles and many other civilian products ceased, and as long as the war lasted there was little need for consumer financing. As one result, the directors of Marine Bancorporation voted to liquidate a subsidiary, National Credit Company, which had been in the financing business since 1928 and had extended its operations into Oregon and Idaho.

Looking far ahead to the end of fighting and a new outpouring of civilian goods, Price was certain that consumers would need help in financing and he wanted the bank to have a department staffed and trained for this work. He laid his ideas before Homer Boyd, who backed him all the way. In 1942, the bank set up an instalment loan department.

Here as in several other instances where the bank was charting a new field, Price brought in a man from outside commercial banking. The man for instalment loans was Edgar A. Ruth, who had been in consumer finance with Chrysler, then with General Motors Acceptance Corporation, and finally with National Credit Company. Ruth came in under Sizemore and subsequently became head of the department, where he remained until he became chairman of the senior loan committee in 1967. He was succeeded in instalment credit by Chester C. MacNeill.

The decision to expand into instalment loans on a full scale

The 5000th Boeing Flying Fortress being rolled out of the Seattle plant during World War II. (Boeing Co. photo.)

was "one of the most difficult that Andrew Price made," Ruth recalled a quarter century later.[3] Right off there was a question whether lending to consumers in amounts much smaller than commercial bankers were accustomed to handling could ever become profitable. Beyond this, consumer instalment loans were not an accepted part of commercial banking, and Price was concerned as to how customers and the financial community would react.

But Price saw also some distinct advantages—a chance to expand, to reach wage-earners and heads of families who were not customers, and to expose them to other services of the bank, such as savings accounts and mortgage loans. Price decided to take banking to the people. The vigorous move into instalment lending was a turning point in the bank's development, the first important step in the transition from commercial or wholesale banking to retail banking.

Today instalment credit has become an accepted part of retail banking everywhere and a major department at the National Bank of Commerce. Consumer borrowers numbered more than 90,000 at the end of 1969, and their loans totaled $129 million, almost 20 per cent of the bank's entire domestic loans (excluding the London branch). Although the amount in instalment loans is substantial, the average loan runs for only a little more than eight months, and hence turnover is rapid.

RESIDENTIAL MORTGAGES

Soon after setting up the instalment loan department, Price pushed farther into retail banking and established a mortgage loan department.

Mortgage loans were far from new in commercial banking, but so far the volume was minor and the type of loan was designed more for a borrower on commercial properties than for one on residences. Before the depression, a bank would lend up to 50 per cent of the value of a residential property, but only for a short term, generally three years. During the depression when money was so tight, a borrower who could neither pay off his loan nor refinance was in trouble. So was many a bank. The real estate market was dead. A sound $8,000 house with a mortgage of $4,000 would not bring enough to pay off the mortgage. Across the country, countless people out of work and out of money gave up, left their houses empty, and moved in with relatives.

So great was the distress of both home owners and lenders that the federal government in 1933 created a rescue organization, the Home Owners' Loan Corporation. For those who could not pay interest or principal on the mortgage and faced the loss of their home, HOLC picked up the mortgage and refinanced it with payments spread over 15 years. For banks in distress, HOLC exchanged its own 4 per cent bonds for defaulted mortgages. The bonds at least could be sold. Later the Reconstruction Finance Corporation worked with HOLC to give banks in difficulty cash for mortgages.

Nationwide, HOLC made one million loans totaling $3 billion. Its loans in Washington alone went to 21,438 home owners for a total of $39 million.[4] Of houses that were eligible (non-farm, owner-occupied, with mortgage under $5,000), 21 per cent in the nation carried an HOLC loan. In Washington the proportion was higher—26 per cent, or one house in every four. In Idaho, where distress was greater, the proportion ran to 44 per cent. HOLC took on a heavy burden and at the outset heavy losses were widely predicted. In time the agency foreclosed on 19 per cent of all the loans it made during the depression. Houses taken over in default on the mortgage were generally renovated and then sold. After World War II when HOLC went out of business the agency showed a slight profit. As a long-standing policy, still in effect, the National Bank of Commerce retained the mortgage loans it made and did not go to HOLC for help.

Some bankers shook their heads at the risk in such long loans with such a small down payment. But monthly instalments proved to be less burdensome for the borrower and less risky for the lender, and this type of mortgage made possible the great spread in home ownership after World War II.

For Andrew Price, whose confidence in the consumer had just led to establishment of an instalment loan department, the self-reducing or fully amortized mortgage with monthly payments could only increase the attractiveness of real estate loans. Even more compelling, Price's plans for postwar growth called for attracting money into savings accounts. Since savings funds are invested primarily in residential mortgages, his first task was to get more real estate loans.

In late 1945, the war over, Price was ready to drive ahead on mortgage loans and to set up a major department. Characteristically, Price tried his ideas out on Homer Boyd and got Boyd's full backing; then he went outside the bank for an experienced man.

At the suggestion of Carl Phillips, a vice president, Price invited to lunch Ross Williams, who had handled mortgage financing at the University National Bank but had left the bank for other work during the war. Earlier Williams had served as president of the Seattle Mortgage Bankers Association. Price and Boyd told Williams of their plans and asked if he were interested. Indeed he was, and after taking two months to clean up other business matters, Williams came to the bank in mid-December 1945 to head the real estate loan department. On his retirement fifteen years later he was succeeded by Herndon McKay, who carried the department through its period of greatest growth. He retired in 1968 after twenty-two years in the mortgage business at Commerce and was succeeded by Stephen D. Churchill.

Until Williams' appointment, mortgages at the National Bank of Commerce were only a minor item in the commercial loan department. Williams organized a new department to handle all mortgages, residential and commercial, and set up a program to build volume at the home office and the branches.

Growth in residential mortgages came rapidly. Williams recalled after his retirement that when he began, the bank had no more than three or four million dollars in mortgage loans. Price told Williams that if he could build the total to $10 million, that would be fine. When Williams made that goal, Price said, "Maybe you can build it to $20 million." When the bank reached $20 million, Williams said, "Mr. Price never again spoke of a goal, and the total has been growing ever since." [5] Today the bank has more than $180 million in mortgage loans, and the total investment in instalment and mortgage loans is as large as the total in commercial loans, which in earlier years were the essence of banking.

Paralleling the growth in mortgage loans was a steady increase in savings accounts. Early in World War II savings or time deposits pushed past $20 million for the first time, but they still came to less than 20 per cent of the bank's total deposits. By the end of the war, savings deposits approached $100 million. In 1969 savings and time deposits exceeded $535 million and represented more than half of all deposits.

INVESTMENT BANKING

One of the early activities which Price inaugurated at the National Bank of Commerce—investment banking—has come to full development only in the past decade, but its founding goes back more than thirty years to Barrett Green, who built and headed the investment banking department. Green came to Seattle during the 1920's to represent the New York bond house of Bonbright & Company. In 1931, as the depression deepened and the bond business melted away, Bonbright closed its Seattle office, but Green chose to remain in the city on his own.

Price and Green had known one another in the investment business, and in 1932 Price asked Green to come into the bank. It was an unusual arrangement. Green had no title and no specific duties, but he was to see what was going on and to make suggestions. At that time the bank had no investment department and no investment officer. Its purchases and sales of securities were made through the affiliate, Marine National Company, which also bought and sold securities for customers.

When reform legislation in 1933 required banks to divorce themselves of investment affiliates, Marine National Company went out of this business and ultimately was dissolved. The bank's purchase and sale of bonds for its own account were then handled by a committee of directors working with senior officers. This arrangement was cumbersome, however, and in time Price took over the responsibility. He used Green for making background analyses, then gave orders to buy and to sell, and reported to the directors for approval of completed transactions.

During World War II, trading in government bonds became heavy and the bank bought and sold bonds both for its own account and for its customers. "We began trading in large amounts of securities, often a million dollars in a single transaction," Green said recently. "Because of our activity we were able to get a better price than a corporate treasurer might." [6] Out of this grew the bank's investment department of today, which buys and sells government and municipal bonds for its own investment account, for correspondent banks, and for corporate and public treasurers. The volume of municipal bonds—obligations issued by state and municipal government and by school, water, sewer, port, and other improvement districts—has increased rapidly during the past decade.

As the investment department grew, Green delegated to William R. Chouinard, now a vice president, the responsibility for expanding into the underwriting of municipal bond issues. Here the National Bank of Commerce, acting either alone or as a member of a syndicate, bids for an entire issue. It may retain some or all of the issue for its own investment account, or it may sell part to other banks and to large investors such as Washington-based insurance companies.

On retirement as manager of the investment department, Green was succeeded in 1961 by Edward R. McMillan, who began with the trust department in 1949 and after service in the Korean War, came into the investment department in 1953. The investment department's officers and staff totaled 17 by 1969.

THE TRUST DEPARTMENT

Wealth accumulates slowly in a pioneer land. The first settlers are the venturesome young. Indeed, in the first two decades after statehood it was unusual to see a white head at a public gathering in Seattle. Those who came West were starting a new life, and the wealth they would build up had to come from their own efforts. It is not surprising, therefore, that the handling of estates and trusts was an aspect of banking that took years, even decades, to develop significant volume. Not until 1903—fourteen years after statehood—did the Legislature even adopt a code for the regulation of trusts. Today the trust department is an essential part of every major metropolitan bank and at Commerce it has grown rapidly.

Trust work at the National Bank of Commerce traces back to the Northwest Trust and Safe Deposit Co., which was founded in 1900 and was one of the earliest banks in Seattle that handled trusts. In time the assets of this institution were acquired by Marine National Bank and then were merged into the National Bank of Commerce.

One of the great assets that came from Northwest was its trust officer, Robert W. Sprague. For a quarter century he headed the trust department of the National Bank of Commerce and on retirement in 1954 he was recognized as the dean of trust officers in Washington State.

Sprague grew up in Iowa not far from Iowa City, where Robert Spencer, founder of the National Bank of Commerce, began his own career. After graduation from Monmouth (Illinois) College in 1902, Sprague began work with the Farmers and Merchants State Bank in Columbus Junction, Iowa. In 1905, at the earnest solicitation of a college friend, he went to Waitsburg, Washington, and he served for a year as principal of Waitsburg Academy. He came to Seattle in 1907 and found employment with the Northwest Trust and Safe Deposit Company. In 1918 he was placed in charge of the trust department.

Ten years later when Andrew Price acquired the National Bank of Commerce, its trust officer was one of those who left to found Pacific National Bank. Sprague, then head of trust work at Marine National Bank, was placed in charge of the department at the National Bank of Commerce. He carried the department through major expansion in scope of services and in the number of trust accounts. On his retirement he was succeeded by John T. Glase, who began with Commerce in 1930, later served in the trust department in Yakima, and became a senior vice president in 1966.

Growth in the trust department, slow during the first four decades of the century, took hold about the time of the Second World War and continues at an accelerating rate. Just since 1948 the volume in the department has more than tripled. The staff grew from 9 in 1930 to 145 in 1969. Some of the added trust business came from banks acquired in Aberdeen, Olympia, Bellingham, Yakima, Waitsburg and Wenatchee.

The major part of trust work lies in the handling of estates, for which a bank may be designated in a will as both executor and trustee. Another part, growing rapidly, is the management of property which owners turn over to the bank to administer during their lifetime, perhaps, to distribute ultimately to children, grandchildren, or charities.

The department operates five investment funds for trusts and four investment funds for pension and profit-sharing plans. This gives diversification and flexibility for both large and small accounts. The earliest of these funds was established in 1947, at which time the National Bank of Commerce was the first in Washington to create a common trust fund under a new state law. The type of fund that is selected depends on an individual's needs and objectives. For a widow, for example, who wants income, investments would be placed largely in a fund made up of bonds, while for an individual seeking long-term capital growth, investments would be placed in a fund made up of common stocks only. One of the newer of the bank's common trust funds permits self-employed persons such as lawyers, physicians, and dentists to place money in a trust for income after retirement.[7]

A branch of the department operates in Yakima, where the National Bank of Commerce's trust work traces back to two early companies—Yakima Trust, founded in 1906, and Guaranty Trust, founded in 1919. Yakima Trust merged in 1925 into Yakima National Bank, which after consolidation with First National, became a branch of the National Bank of Commerce in 1935. In 1944 Commerce acquired the accounts of Guaranty Trust, reputed to be the only company in the state which concentrated solely on trust business and did not accept commercial or savings deposits. Guaranty's accounts added a substantial volume of trust work in the Yakima Valley, and Commerce set up a branch trust committee for local administration.

Trust work in eastern Washington expanded in 1955 with acquisition of First National Bank of Waitsburg, located in an area of large wheat and cattle ranches. Unlike most small banks, it had a trust department. Subsequent acquisition of banks in Clarkston, Pomeroy, Dayton, and Endicott and the founding of a new branch at Asotin gave further impetus to Commerce's trust business in that section. As a result the bank established a southeastern Washington trust advisory committee to assist the trust committee headquartered at Yakima.

Bank trusts have been put to a growing diversity of uses in recent years. A trust, for example, may provide the means for keeping together an efficient farm unit after the owner's retirement or death. The development of large farm machinery and the increased use of chemical fertilizers have cut production costs in the wheat country of eastern Washington during the past thirty years but have forced consolidation of small farms into larger units for economical management. As a result, farms of 1,000 acres, 2,000 acres, and even larger are not unusual. An owner may have several children whom he wishes to have share equally in the property, and yet a division of the farm might give each child a unit too small to operate profitably. As a result, it has become increasingly common for the owner to place the farm in trust with a bank. The bank then selects an operator or tenant—who may be one of the children—to manage the farm, and the bank distributes the net earnings among all the children.

The opening of 1946 found the nation well along on the return to a civilian economy. Millions of men and women were coming back from the armed forces. Thousands of jobs in shipyards and aircraft plants disappeared, but thousands of others were starting to open up—in construction, in sawmills, in agriculture, in retail stores, and in countless other activities which had been starved for help. Growth that war had halted took hold again across the nation.

PRICE'S ILLNESS—A NEW PRESIDENT

Price was ready. He could look with satisfaction at the institution he had built. It was eighteen years since he had acquired the National Bank of Commerce, only to see a group of officers and directors walk out and form a new bank. But in that time the deposits of the National Bank of Commerce had risen from less than $22 million to $337 million (excluding the government war-loan account). The bank ranked second in size in the state and forty-second in the nation. It had 25 branches including a group in eastern Washington that came close to fulfilling Price's early dream of a string of banks along the Columbia River. New branches were in the offing. Clearly the greatest growth, for the Pacific Northwest and the bank, lay ahead, and for this Price was preparing.

Then tragedy struck. On a Friday in February 1946, Mr. and Mrs. Price took the steamer to Victoria for a few days of rest. Price was tired and tense. The extra responsibilities thrown on banking during the war years, together with a severe shortage in staff, had left him under continuous strain. He also was state chairman of the government's final savings-bond drive. Because the war had ended, the bond quota proved exceedingly difficult to make, but Price was determined to succeed, as indeed he did. Furthermore, on the day before leaving for Victoria, Price had had a particularly unpleasant meeting regarding one of the bank's officers whose father had come in through an earlier acquisition and who thought he had not been treated properly.[8]

The morning after arriving in Victoria, Price found that he could not get up. He asked Mrs. Price to call a doctor, then, as he lost his voice and sensed his condition worsening, he scribbled on a pad of paper he always kept beside his bed: "I am going into a coma." That was the last he ever wrote with his right hand. For several weeks he lay helpless at the hotel. Later he said that he was not unconscious but heard the conversation and knew what was going on; he simply could not move a muscle, not even an eyelid, to express himself.[9] Slowly he came out of the coma, but control of his right side and of his speech remained seriously damaged. Weeks and months of rest and therapy followed in the salt air of his summer home on Bainbridge Island and in the winter sunshine of Tucson, Arizona.

Price was determined to resume active business life. His condition improved and in 1947 he returned from Tucson to the bank, but even a determined will could not repair the damage. His right arm hung useless, his speech was impaired. His mind remained keen but locked in; in speaking or writing he could communicate only with frustrating uncertainty. His walk became a slow, tortured shuffle, but walk he did and every step displayed his unshaken will to carry on.

Price had pushed himself unmercifully throughout his career. An associate remarked: "He drove himself at a fantastic pace and he loved it."[10] You might find him at 7:00 A.M., the first man in the bank, teletyping a message to a New York financial house. Or you might find him working far into the evening.

As is common among men who have built an institution, Price liked to have a hand in everything going on and was slow to delegate authority. Yet as the bank grew larger the pressures on him built up, not the least of which was the handling of proud and ambitious officers who had come in through mergers.

Price was a hard taskmaster but appreciative and quick to reward. His warmth impressed those about him. One of today's senior officers remarked fondly: "He was a tremendous guy!"[11] Another officer recounted the day in 1935 when Price, having just acquired Yakima First National Bank, visited the bank: "He stepped behind the counter, spoke with each individual, and shook hands. I was just a humble messenger boy at $65 a month, but he made me feel as important as a vice president."[12]

The training during early years in the bond business served Price in good stead. Barrett Green recalled:

He was a man of strong emotion, which he kept completely submerged. But he had a habit of subordinating himself completely to a situation. He would never let his personal feelings intervene in a business decision. Instead of justifying an error he would turn himself completely around as soon as he saw the error. That is an essential quality in a good market operator, but few people have it.

After his stroke, Price paid poignant recognition to the fact that there is a limit to how hard a man should drive himself. When he walked through the bank after hours and saw an employee still at work, he would point to the clock, point to his useless arm, and silently shake his head.[13]

Price's illness posed an immediate problem in management of the bank. No one knew to what extent he would recover or how long his recovery might take. As an interim measure Carl L. Phillips was named first vice president and placed in charge, and four of the older officers were named senior vice presidents: Ira W. Bedle, Homer L. Boyd, A. W. Faragher, and Herbert Witherspoon. Three of these—Bedle, Boyd, and Witherspoon—were also directors; Faragher soon joined them on the board.

As time ran on, the recognition grew that Price would never resume active direction of the bank. There must be a new president, someone younger than the senior officers who were filling in and yet someone having broad banking experience.

Price saw this, too. He was reluctant to step aside, but he knew that strong leadership must be continued. The time had come to call in the man he had been grooming as his successor. But first Price went to Homer Boyd to go over the decision. Boyd gave immediate assent. The selection: Maxwell Carlson. In January 1948 Carlson became president of the National Bank of Commerce, at 42 one of the youngest bank presidents in America.

Carlson had grown up in Aberdeen, Washington, the son of Gust A. Carlson, a prominent logger and a director of Grays Harbor National Bank. Young Carlson was graduated cum laude from Dartmouth in 1928 and continued a year to take a master's degree at the Amos Tuck School of Administration and Finance. His specialty was investment analysis.

Carlson began as a clerk in the Grays Harbor National Bank in the summer of 1929. Late the following year, Marine Bancorporation brought him to Seattle as an assistant auditor on branch examinations. He continued this work for eight years, a crucial period that covered the hard times of the depression with its special problems and the start of branch banking. In 1938 Carlson was transferred to the National Bank of Commerce as manager of the credit department. In 1946, Price named him vice president in charge of operations, the understudy of Ira Bedle. The following year Carlson became a director as well.

Like Price, Carlson made the bank his life and devoted his full energies to it. In early years when Price, back from a trip, would toss ideas before the Saturday morning meeting of officers, he might ask for a volunteer for checking and follow-up. Carlson was often the man to take on an assignment even though it might be outside his department. He brought to the presidency a thorough knowledge of the operation of the bank and a wide acquaintance among personnel at the head office and branches.

Price, meantime, retained the title of chairman of the board and devoted himself to limited phases of operation, particularly advertising and promotion. He laboriously learned to write with his left hand and formed words by slowly drawing each letter.

One of Price's interests at that time was the development of a symbol for the bank and a shorter name. He wanted something as simple and telling as the trade-name Coke. One of the early bank designs was a circle with the sketch of a ship, a locomotive, and a truck to suggest commerce, and around the circle the words, "The National Bank of Commerce of Seattle." In 1947 Price simplified this by substituting just the initials "NBofC" and placed them on a black circle or cartwheel with the phrase "Founded 1889."

Price was still not satisfied with the symbol. "It needs more life," he told the bank's advertising manager and the representative of the advertising agency as the three men bent over a desk one day in 1949.[14] To show what he meant he picked up a pencil in his left hand and painstakingly sketched a silver dollar turned at an angle to form an oval—a rolling cartwheel. Thus Price developed the symbol the bank has since used, a rolling dollar that today bears just the imprint: NBofC.

Price continued as chairman of the bank until March 1955. Then under a retirement plan adopted in 1943 that made retirement mandatory at age 65, he stepped down. His health had gradually deteriorated, and impairment from the stroke became more burdensome. Four months after retirement, and almost ten years after the stroke, he died.

Early in Price's illness his son Andrew, Jr. gave up a career in engineering to come into the bank. In 1943 his studies at Yale

University had been interrupted by military service. After his discharge in 1946, Andrew, Jr. returned to Yale to prepare for his chosen profession and was graduated the following year in aeronautical engineering. However, with his father's illness, Andrew, Jr. began work at the National Bank of Commerce in October 1947, starting as a trainee at the University branch. Subsequently, he served in various aspects of the bank including real estate and instalment loans, commercial loans, auditing, the controller's department, and national accounts. He was graduated from the Stonier School of Banking at Rutgers University.

In 1963 Price was named executive vice president in charge of business development and two years later became chairman of the bank. He has been president of Marine Bancorporation since 1962 and represents the bank in many civic activities.

PART IV

MAXWELL CARLSON / New Horizons for the State, for the Bank

Maxwell Carlson's presidency coincided with two decades of expansion and diversification in the Pacific Northwest economy. In this setting the bank added new customers, grew with the business of its customers, and began to offer new services in fields such as international trade, assistance to small business, and the handling of trusts. It extended its branches to create a statewide institution with 100 offices, and it established seven offices overseas.

The development of branches followed the pattern that Price pioneered. Price opened offices in industrial cities of western Washington including Aberdeen, Bellingham, Bremerton, Longview, Olympia, and Vancouver, and in the agricultural centers of Ellensburg, Wenatchee, and Yakima. By 1946 Price had taken NBofC into a dozen more cities, both in western Washington and in the agricultural interior.

When Price became incapacitated, the momentum for branching was temporarily lost. It was regained once Carlson became president and set about to broaden the bank and its services. In

199

two decades more than 70 branches were opened. Most branches added during the 1950's came through acquisition of country banks, where commonly a man who had spent a lifetime building a successful bank was ready to retire but had no one to take over management and much of his savings were tied up in the bank's stock.

During the 1960's most of the branches added were new offices established by NBofC to serve areas where no banks had existed before. Many of these offices followed the movement of population into new suburbs.

Deposits in the past twenty years tripled, from $344 million in 1949 to more than $1 billion by 1969. A big share of growth in recent years has come in savings and time deposits. In addition the London branch, opened in 1968, brings Euro-dollars to the bank's deposits. In 1969 deposits in London alone exceeded $100 million.

EARNING THE CAPITAL FOR GROWTH

Any substantial rise in deposits requires a corresponding increase in capital—those funds invested by shareholders in buying the bank's capital stock in the first place or accumulated out of earnings and appearing in the balance sheet under the headings of surplus and undivided profits. Such funds are put to work in loans and other investments, just as are deposits by the bank's customers. But depositors have a prior call on a bank's resources and thus a bank's capital, surplus, and undivided profits stand as a reserve for protection of depositors.

The rapid growth in the nation's economy during the past two decades swelled deposits throughout banking. How to match this rise in deposits with a corresponding rise in capital funds has been one of the foremost problems in bank management. Some new capital came from retained earnings. But most major banks also sold additional stock or capital notes or issued new stock in exchange for assets acquired in mergers. Of the twelve largest banks on the West Coast, including the four largest in Washington and Oregon, the National Bank of Commerce was alone in neither selling nor issuing additional stock nor borrowing with capital notes. Instead it depended solely on earnings to build capital.

Marine Bancorporation, the parent organization, followed this policy until 1969, when for the first time in more than forty years it split its shares as a part of a broader recapitalization.

In the quarter-century after World War II the bank's do-it-yourself course for creating capital allowed only about one-third of the profits to be distributed for cash dividends while two-thirds went back for growth. This compelled close concentration on effective management and sound banking. In each department, goals were carefully established and expenses closely budgeted. At the same time the quality of assets was maintained. Any loan classified by the bank's auditors, by a committee of the directors, or by the national bank examiners as "doubtful" or "loss" was immediately charged off in full. Even on this conservative basis, write-offs for losses were small, and in some years recoveries exceeded write-offs.

The results are striking. While deposits increased three-fold, the total in capital, surplus, and undivided profits rose more than four-fold—from $15 million in 1949 to $67 million in 1969.

At the same time the bank built substantial reserves against loan losses. The policy of the Carlson administration was to add to reserves when times were good, and during the 1950's and into the late 1960's it did do so regardless of whether funds thus set aside might be charged off against the federal income tax. To a Marine stockholder who asked at an annual meeting several years ago why reserves were so high, Carlson commented:

I was an auditor and branch examiner from 1930 to 1938; the losses always occurred where we least expected them. . . . In recent years our losses have been insignificant, but that is no indication of what may lie ahead. Some New York banks found that after Castro came to power in Cuba their entire reserve for losses in loans was wiped out.[1]

The bank's reliance on its own resources for capital and for liquidity goes along with another conservative policy: Never to borrow from the Federal Reserve Bank or other federal agencies. Not even during the depression did the bank borrow at the Federal Reserve window nor did it ask help through Reconstruction Finance Corporation or Home Owners' Loan Corporation. The bank, however, in recent years has borrowed so-called federal funds or temporary excess reserves from other banks, and it lends its own excess funds in this market. Through its London branch it has access to Euro-dollars.

The policy of not going to the Federal Reserve Bank for help has been in effect as long as any of the officers now serving the bank can remember—at least forty years. Perhaps it goes back to the founding of the Federal Reserve System. One of the leaders in the establishment of the Federal Reserve Bank of San Francisco in 1914 and the opening of its Seattle branch in 1917 was Manson Backus, then president of Commerce. Some years later Backus opposed extension of authority for commercial banks to borrow from Federal Reserve banks even on high-grade bonds, and he even favored withdrawal of authority granted during World War I for banks to rediscount gilt-edged Liberty Bonds.

INTERNATIONAL TRADE AND BANKING

Andrew Price used the term "department store of finance" to suggest the diversity of services offered at the National Bank of Commerce. Maxwell Carlson gave the concept added meaning as he broadened the functions of the bank still further. Not long after he became president he created the international department.

For decades the National Bank of Commerce operated a small foreign department handling mainly foreign remittances by immigrants and letters of credit to finance ocean trade. The war in 1939 cut off remittances and foreign trade with Europe. Two years later Pearl Harbor closed the Pacific. For the duration of the war the foreign department was all but out of business.[2]

The end of the war in Europe in mid-1945, however, brought a surge of remittances from residents of Washington who had been cut off from their families for six years. Soon the Philippines and China were also reopened for trade—though China not for long—and the bank's foreign transactions stepped up sharply.

Up to this point, although volume was substantial, the bank handled only relatively routine items in foreign trade. Carlson saw a much broader opportunity, one which he felt a bank in a world seaport like Seattle had a responsibility to develop. He wanted to build a full international department, one that would undertake the development of foreign business, one staffed with experts able to provide guidance to Pacific Northwest firms looking for markets overseas. In 1948 he formed the department. Early the next year he selected Clarence L. Hulford from the bank's commercial loan department to become manager, a position he has held since. Today the National Bank of Commerce has the largest international department of any bank in the Pacific Northwest.

Much the biggest part of the international department's work is in the Far East; second in importance is Latin America and third Europe. In the typical financing of imports, NBofC makes a loan, generally for 30, 60, or 90 days, to cover goods from the time of loading in a foreign port to delivery at the customer's United States warehouse.[3]

The financing of exports is more complex because a substantial volume of goods shipped from the ports of Puget Sound and the Columbia River consist of equipment and machinery for use in underdeveloped nations on the Pacific Rim. These nations are short of capital, and the money to pay for the equipment must be generated while the equipment is at work. This requires financing with term loans, commonly for three years. A typical export might consist of a heavy log-loader made in Washington State for a customer in the Philippines. The customer would go to his bank to arrange a loan under which NBofC would pay the manufacturer as soon as the equipment was aboard ship. NBofC would recover its funds in instalments over a three-year period. Generally, the loan would carry the guaranty of the customer's bank.

As an outgrowth of the international department, NBofC established in September 1964 a subsidiary, the International Bank of Commerce, with a full banking office at Hong Kong. The subsidiary was formed under the Edge Act, in which Congress authorized banks to set up foreign financial corporations under federal supervision. Speaking to a luncheon meeting in Seattle when the Hong Kong bank was announced, Carlson suggested the long-term objectives thus: "As the population of the world increases and the standard of living rises, there will be more trade in the world, not less. We want to encourage, promote, develop and finance a greater flow of trade between our area and the rest of the world, especially the Far East."

NBofC's initial investment in the International Bank of Commerce was $2 million. The risk in starting a new bank in a foreign city is substantial, but in the long run the return may be great—in helping build business through the ports that NBofC serves and in the return to the bank itself. The strong capital and reserve position of the bank was a principal reason Carlson felt able to take on this risk.

The National Bank of Commerce was the second bank in the West and the fourth in the nation to open an Edge Act banking office in the Far East. By the end of 1969 this wholly-owned

The western office of NBofC's Edge Act subsidiary, International Bank of Commerce, in Hong Kong.

subsidiary had five offices in Hong Kong. Increasing activity in sterling area currencies through Hong Kong prompted the opening of an office in London, which was established in April 1968 as a branch of NBofC, the second bank on the West Coast to establish a full-service bank in London. This was followed by the opening of a representative office in Tokyo in September 1969. A second Edge Act affiliate, the National Bank of Commerce, Seattle (International) opened in New York late in 1969, and plans were announced for a representative office in Singapore.

COMMERCIAL BANKING IN CHANGING TIMES

Through the years the addition of new departments and services has broadened the concept of the bank as a department store of finance and has made an important contribution to growth at the National Bank of Commerce. The largest single department, however, continues to be that handling commercial loans. The rise in demand for commercial loans parallels expansion in the economy of the region—an increase in the number of companies in business in Washington, in the size of companies, in their reliance on banks for financing, and in the range of bank assistance available to them.

The evolution of banking during the past four decades has brought not just growth but changes in the type of commercial loans as well. When Manson Backus was president, the National Bank of Commerce, like many banks, carried a substantial volume of loans in commercial paper. This paper essentially is an IOU issued by a large corporation of unquestioned credit with a promise to repay on a specified day one to six months later. In Backus's time, most companies that sold commercial paper were headquartered in the East; of the few in Washington State, an outstanding example was Fisher Flouring Mills Company, Seattle.

Purchase of commercial paper was an easy way for a bank to get loans at relatively little risk. Gradually, however, as banks paid greater attention to customers in their own community and particularly to middle-size and small firms, they made less use of commercial paper. It has been more than 25 years since the National Bank of Commerce has put loan funds into commercial paper.

Bank loans made on stocks or bonds as collateral to guarantee repayment were also relatively more common forty years ago. In those days there were no federal restrictions as to how much a man might borrow on securities, and it was common for a speculator to buy stocks and take them to his bank to use as collateral so that he could buy more stocks. When the market crashed in October 1929 and continued downward with little interruption for almost four years, loans that were made with stocks as collateral were reviewed daily at the National Bank of Commerce. As the decline in prices deepened, a borrower would be asked to put up additional collateral, such as real estate, or to sell the stock on which the loan was based.

During the depression many commercial loans based on inventories of raw materials or finished goods or on accounts receivable became delinquent. Collateral that a bank took over on loans in default was held sometimes for several years before it could be sold for enough to wipe out the original loss.[4] Here, as was the case during so much of the depression, the problem was liquidity. Prices fell, assets were frozen, and no one knew whether or when old values would ever return.

In the depths of the depression when a business customer asked for a loan, it was common for a representative of the bank's credit department to visit the place of business, check the books, look over the inventory, and try to determine whether the money could be put to good use and whether it could be paid back from the cash flow in the business.

As the depression receded and confidence gradually returned, business activity expanded and the volume of loans grew. But the restraints from the depression held back recovery until the extraordinary expansion during World War II.

Even before the United States entered the war, production built up under the government's Lend-Lease program of assistance to the Allies. To finance the war the government sold bonds to wage-earners and other individuals, to financial institutions and other corporations, and to millions who never before had owned a bond. The concept of payroll deductions to buy government bonds, now so common, was introduced. The government, in turn, used banks to finance war production of items as diverse as ships for the Navy and arctic sleeping bags for the Army. At one time, the National Bank of Commerce was financing six shipyards in Seattle alone, and it joined with Portland banks in financing the immense shipbuilding activity on the Columbia River at Vancouver, Washington.

Most of this financing was handled through the Assignment of Claims Act of 1940, under which the government made direct payment to a bank for amounts it had advanced to a shipyard, a machine shop with a war contract, or other producers of essential goods. Some financing also came under the V-loan program, under which the government guaranteed 90 per cent of what a war manufacturer borrowed. V-loans enabled banks to make much larger advances to companies contributing directly to the war effort—up to 10 times a bank's normal loan limit.

When the war ended, the volume of loans fell drastically but deposits remained high. Most individuals making the transition back to a peacetime economy had savings in war bonds to draw on. With money abundant, interest rates fell. For prime commercial borrowers—the largest corporations with the highest credit standing—the rate dropped as low as 1¾ per cent a year. Then, as the peacetime economy built up, money rates rose, but not until 1959 did the prime commercial rate reach 5 per cent. The return on savings rose also, and in 1966 the National Bank of Commerce boosted to 5 per cent the interest paid on one-year savings certificates, the highest in decades. In 1968 the bank offered investment certificates that guaranteed 5 per cent for three years. In 1969 it introduced the Blue Ribbon Savings Account, which paid 5 per cent and recorded interest, deposits, and withdrawals in a single bank statement issued quarterly.

The size of business loans has increased substantially in the past two decades—another reason why banks must build their capital funds. The largest loan that a national bank may make to any one borrower is 10 per cent of a base which the Comptroller of the Currency in the 1960's broadened to include not just capital and surplus but also undivided profits and certain capital and other reserves. The National Bank of Commerce has held its limit to 10 per cent of capital and surplus. Even on this more conservative basis, the bank's loan limit more than doubled in a decade, from $2.5 million in 1958 to $5.7 million in 1969. This limit permits the bank to handle in full the requirements of small and middle-size borrowers. The few corporations in the state which require larger loans obtain part of their needs from local banks and part from banks in major money centers of the nation.

In meeting the diverse needs of its borrowers the National Bank of Commerce has developed a number of specialties. One, going back almost 40 years, is the financing of large and small

contractors. At the outset Herbert Witherspoon gained for the bank a reputation for knowing the intricacies of financing construction. He was succeeded in this specialty by Elmer Satterberg. When Satterberg retired in 1962 the bank's reputation in the industry was well established. This specialty has continued as a responsibility of a group of men headed until recently by E. Carter Shannon.

The financing of construction differs from most types of lending. The risk of non-payment of a loan is great unless all the elements are recognized and properly evaluated at the inception of the loan. An officer in this work recently noted:

> The capital base of the construction industry is thin and always has been. This is coupled with extreme competition among contractors, whose risk is great. The industry also is complex and growing more so, and the collateral that provides security on loans to contractors and on new construction projects is not salable as it is on loans based on wheat, lumber, canned salmon, stocks, bonds and the like.

A large project such as an office building, hotel, or shopping center requires a wide variety of specialized subcontractors who in turn have numerous suppliers. Each of these is a separate business, separately financed. The complex of these separate contractors and suppliers becomes interdependent for satisfactory progress and timely payment for work done. Each contractor and supplier may legally file a lien for non-payment against the owner of the project, and such a lien is prior to the claim securing a bank loan.

Protection for the lender comes from knowing as much as possible about the industry and the borrower and being able to spot a problem at its inception. Officers working on this specialty at the National Bank of Commerce make it a business to attend meetings within the construction industry and to work on matters that may not be related directly to finance.

In turn the bank's understanding has proved of help to the industry. More than one subcontractor, seeking a larger line of credit to handle a new job, has gone to his banker only to be told in effect: "I'm nervous. I do not understand your business." The dismayed subcontractor, who has to have bank financing if he is to go ahead, then reports his trouble to the prime contractor and may be told: "Go see the National Bank of Commerce."

Another specialty is financing in Alaska, a business built up through many years by W. Erich Lucas, who got his start in banking at Seward, Alaska. The Alaska division at the main office handles two types of credits. One covers seasonal financing for companies packing salmon, king crab, scallops, halibut, and other seafoods of the North. It is believed that the National Bank of Commerce finances a larger share of the Alaska salmon pack than any other bank. The second covers participation with Alaska banks in loans larger than those banks can handle themselves.

The ties to Alaska have been close for many years. In the fall of 1961, Maxwell Carlson, traveling in Alaska, was surprised to find that because of lack of funds the new state would not be represented at the 1962 Seattle World's Fair. Recalling Alaska's participation in the famed Alaska-Yukon-Pacific Exposition at Seattle in 1909, Carlson thought it would be unfortunate if Alaska did not participate also in the 1962 Fair. As a result, the bank donated approximately $200,000 to provide the building for an Alaska exhibit.

In the Good Friday earthquake that struck Alaska in 1964, the first concern everywhere was for the safety of residents. Fortunately, casualties were light, surprisingly so in the face of the great physical damage. For reconstruction, the Small Business Administration made more than $80 million in disaster loans to individuals and business firms in Alaska. This assistance included $16 million for homeowners and more than $65 million for business. NBofC assigned two experienced credit men to the SBA to work with several others sent north from Washington State in processing disaster loans. Losses suffered by individual banks were small; at the National Bank of Commerce there was only one loss on a residential loan.

Agriculture is another area of NBofC loan specialization. Several years ago, noting the trend toward bigger farms and larger financial requirements, the bank asked Walter J. Funk in its Yakima office to come to Seattle so that there would be a man at the head office thoroughly familiar with the agricultural economy of eastern Washington.

Funk began his career in 1923 at the Bank of Wapato in the Yakima Valley. In those days, the loan limit at the Wapato bank was only $3,750, yet that covered most needs in the area. Today with larger farms and with greater outlays for such requirements as seed, feed, spray, fertilizer, and equipment, the financial needs

have risen sharply. A typical loan for a wheat rancher may run to $100,000 or $150,000, and some of the large diversified operations in the Columbia basin require $300,000 to $750,000 in a season.[5] In 1965 Robert H. Matthews, a former manager of the Quincy branch in the Columbia Basin, became head of the agricultural division at Seattle. In 1969, NBofC ranked twelfth among the nation's banks in the total of loans to farmers.

Most bank loans run for only short periods: in agriculture, commonly from planting to harvest, and in industry for from one to six months to finance inventory, work in process, and goods sold but not yet paid for. In recent years, however, banks have found an increasing demand for term loans— those which may run for three to five years, sometimes longer. Some large corporations borrow on term loans, but probably the greatest need for this type of money comes from small, young business ventures, hard put to raise money for working capital and for purchase of plants, machinery, and equipment.

Early in 1961 the National Bank of Commerce established a new department—term loans and small business development—and to head this up brought in Robert F. Buck, formerly regional administrator at Seattle for the Small Business Administration and later deputy administrator in Washington, D.C. This department, now headed by John D. Mangels, vice president, makes a specialty of financing for small business. The needs are usually great, in money and in guidance. Before a loan can be made, many questions must be answered, such as: Has the market for its products been tested? How able is the management? Will it accept guidance? Has it the capacity to grow? And will the cash flow liquidate the loan? Investigation for a term loan to small business takes substantially more time and more specialized skill than is required for lending larger sums to well-established companies, but in this lies the challenge. A small, young venture can be the seed of new industry. In helping such companies a bank helps the area and itself as well. There is no better example of this than Northwestern Glass Company, Seattle.

Back in the early days of the depression, Northwestern Glass was a small struggling venture, the first in the Pacific Northwest to make glass bottles and jars. Seriously underfinanced, its prospects seemed so poor that the bank then handling the company's account asked that it take its business elsewhere. The company

went from one bank to another seeking help. At the National Bank of Commerce one morning, Northwestern's founder talked to Wylie Hemphill, the man in charge of new business. Hemphill was so impressed that he took a group of the bank's officers the same afternoon to look over Northwestern's makeshift plant and to discuss the company's plans and markets. The bank followed up with a loan and financial counsel; thus began a business relationship that continues to the present.

Northwestern Glass went on to become the first manufacturer in the nation to use an electric furnace in making glass containers. Today it turns out bottles and jars for packers of food, beverages, chemicals, and other products of the Pacific Northwest. Its employees number more than 400. Its founder and retired president, Edward S. Campbell, a director of the National Bank of Commerce, says of the hard, early days: "Ours is an outstanding example of what a bank can do to get a manufacturer over the hump. I do not think we could have survived without the bank's help." [6] In 1968, Northwestern Glass became a subsidiary of Indian Head, Inc.

Term loans have grown rapidly throughout banking in the last five years. Their use gives greater flexibility in meeting the needs of customers and particularly in tailoring a loan to the customer's ability to repay out of earnings over a period of years. There are many other applications. A clothing merchant in a middle-sized city borrowed $5,000 on an NBofC term loan to buy out a partner. An automobile dealer, offered a Chevrolet franchise if he put up a building, financed construction with a term loan.

For a bank and a customer, the term loan can be a realistic and sound method of financing. A businessman, for example, may need $100,000 and under conventional practice take out a loan due in full in 90 days. Yet both the borrower and the banker know that the loan cannot be paid off in that short time and that it will have to be renewed, perhaps repeatedly. With a term loan, however, payments can be scheduled over four or five years, and payments monthly, quarterly, or semi-annually are based on anticipated cash flow—that is, on net earnings plus the allowance for depreciation and amortization of building and equipment. By the end of the term the loan will be paid off. The loan agreement may also provide that the borrower guarantee to maintain working capital above a specified minimum and supply a quarterly financial

statement. Thus any difficulties that may arise can be handled before they become overwhelming.

As equipment required in a business grows in size, complexity, and cost, banks are called on to enter new areas of financing. Some airlines, for example, turn to banks to help finance the purchase of jet transports, the cost of which ranges from $3 million for a Boeing twin-jet to $8 million for the long-range Boeing 707 and more than $20 million for the huge Boeing 747. Starting in 1964 the National Bank of Commerce joined with several other banks in buying commercial jet transports and leasing them to airlines. Lease payments are spread over several years. When the loan is paid off, the banks will sell the planes, either to the company that leased them or to other airlines.

A more unusual type of lending which the National Bank of Commerce has pioneered in the Pacific Northwest enables mining companies to obtain tax benefits under what is known as the carve-out law. Here a mining company sets up an interim corporation, which with a loan from the bank buys the next year's mining output. The result is to give the mining company two years' sales and profits in one year and none in the next year. Since the federal tax allowance for depletion of mines is based on a percentage of profit, this method saves more than enough to offset the cost of the bank loan. Money thus saved may go back into further development of the mining property. Use of the technique has been upheld by the United States Supreme Court.

SENIOR LOAN COMMITTEE

Final decisions on major new loans at the National Bank of Commerce lie with the senior loan committee, a small group whose work goes to the heart of commercial banking.[7] The committee has met daily for more than forty years. It now numbers eight men plus five alternates, and deals only with loans of more than $50,000. It confirms, or occasionally declines to confirm, loans already made by branch managers and other officers, and approves or declines applications submitted to it for unusual or difficult loans. It also reviews lines of credit and longer-term loans every 90 days.

Reliance on a committee of top officers for this critical work recognizes that in appraising changing circumstances several minds are better than one and makes certain that several officers are

familiar with each of the bank's larger loans. Beyond this, the committee provides a central review of the judgment of each loan officer in the statewide system and enables these officers to operate with unusual authority in the granting of new loans. In effect, a branch manager has authority such as he might exercise if he were president of a local bank.

The committee originated many years ago, no one knows just when. As president of the bank, Manson Backus served for many years as chairman of the loan committee, and John L. Platt was secretary. After Marine National Bank was consolidated into the National Bank of Commerce, Andrew Price became chairman of the loan committee, and Platt remained secretary until C. O. Ousdahl was elected cashier. When Price was incapacitated, Carl L. Phillips, the first vice president, succeeded as chairman of the loan committee. From 1950 to 1966 the chairman was Ralph J. Stowell, the bank's senior loan officer. Stowell began his career at NBofC in 1927, became vice president and manager of the Central branch in 1947, senior vice president in 1958 and executive vice president in 1965, when he was also elected a director. He retired as an officer in 1968 but continued on the board. In 1967, Edgar A. Ruth became chairman of the senior loan committee. When he retired two years later he was succeeded by E. Carter Shannon.

As the bank has added departments and branches, the composition of the committee has changed, but the chairman remains the senior loan officer. The secretary now is drawn from the credit department. In recent years membership has consisted of a supervisory officer from each of these departments: commercial loans, instalment credit, real estate loans, agricultural loans, and term loans and business development, plus the officer handling bank audit reports, examinations, and charge-offs. Because members are encouraged to work outside with customers and branch officials, the committee may meet with only four or five members present. To be sure that at least four would always be available, three alternates were added in 1966.

Members of the loan committee meet each morning at 10 o'clock. Their work may run well past noon, and in a single day they may review the credit extended to an average of 75 companies and individuals. Each case comes to the committee with a portfolio that summarizes the checking and analysis of a loan officer and a member of the credit department. The loan committee's policy is

to make a decision on the day it reviews an application. It may diverge from this policy and delay a decision in a period of extremely tight money. It may also refer its recommendation on larger loans—those over $250,000—to the Thursday meeting of the executive committee of bank directors.

The functioning of the committee enables the National Bank of Commerce to give its branch managers and other loan officers unusual latitude. Most banks place a limit on the loan which a branch may make and require head office approval for larger loans. By contrast NBofC sets no restriction on the size of loan; there is only a "reporting limit" beyond which the head office must be advised. This means that a branch manager can give a customer a quick Yes or No. In practice, a branch manager with a request for a loan of unusual size or nature will pick up the telephone to check with the head office supervisor.

The reporting limit usually ranges between $2,500 and $25,000, depending on the experience of the manager and the size of the branch. Loans over the reporting limit are reviewed by a supervisor in the head office, who is also a member of the senior loan committee, and those over $50,000 go to the full committee.

Most loans that reach the committee come for confirmation. If the committee refuses confirmation, the branch manager is notified, but the loan, having been made, remains in force until it comes up for renewal. If this occurs a second time the officer will get an immediate telephone call. If subsequently the responsibility proves beyond the man's judgment, he will be transferred to other work. Conversely, loan officers who are doing especially effective work anywhere in the statewide system quickly become recognized. Thus, the committee provides the means both for supervision of larger loans and for appraising the work of key men in this, the principal revenue side of banking.

THE COMPUTER AGE

Banks, like every large business in the country, have turned to electronic data-processing to take over an ever-growing volume of paperwork—the countless but essential details that must be stored for each customer's account and must be quickly available when needed. In a single day, customers of the National Bank of Commerce hand to tellers more than 300,000 checks for deposit. Later in the day each check must be compared with the deposit slip and

the total amount credited to the customer's account. Then the check must be sent along for collection, either to another account in the same office of the bank, to a branch, or to another bank.

This is a chore that tireless computers, faster and more accurate than humans, have largely taken over. In doing so computers have freed clerks and bookkeepers for other work that makes greater use of their skills. But because computers are only slave mechanisms that do no more than they are told, they have also created entirely new jobs. In number of employees the data-processing department has become the largest in the entire bank.

The tasks assigned to computers steadily grow in size and complexity, and no one can see how far this growth may carry even in as short a span as ten years. Computers, the heart of a data-processing center, are becoming ever more versatile. Perhaps more important, the industry is making great advances in development of equipment that converts information into computer language.

By 1969, NBofC's data-processing center at Seattle and a satellite computer at Yakima, operating 24 hours a day, six days a week, were handling the bookkeeping for more than 200,000 checking accounts, 150,000 savings accounts, and 300,000 BankAmericard accounts. Beyond this, the center provides a broad range of management reports that make possible more effective planning and control. The data-processing department is headed by David H. Scott, vice president.

MARINE SERVICE COMPANY

Early in the evolution of the bank's computer center, it became apparent that this tool could be of great help to many of the bank's customers in their own business—customers who might need a computer for only a few minutes a day and obviously could not afford an installation of their own.

As a result, Marine Service Company was established in 1964 as a division of the bank's affiliate, King County Building Company. The division acquired a pioneer in this work, Professional Office Systems, Inc. In 1969 this activity was transferred to the bank itself as the Customer Computer Services Division.

One early application by Marine Service Company tied together for the first time in the country a touch-tone digital telephone transmitter and a computer to move data directly from a business firm onto a bank computer. The customer, a plumbing and heating

firm, put its payroll accounting for 100 persons on an NBofC computer. Each week data on employment, such as the number of hours an individual worked, sped over telephone lines to the bank's data-processing center. The computer calculated the amount of pay, entered various deductions such as social security and income tax, then wrote a check. From the outset the installation saved the customer about eight hours a week in putting up the payroll, and in addition provided information such as allocation of costs.

Similar installations enable physicians and dentists to turn the burden of billing and record-keeping over to a computer. In a typical case a doctor's receptionist each day transmits to the computer the name of the patient and the type of treatment or service given. The computer center keeps the records, makes out the bills, and sends them to the patient in the doctor's name. The patient mails payment by an enclosed envelope to the post office box of the computer center, and payments go automatically into the doctor's account. Each morning the doctor has on his desk a complete analysis of his previous day's work. Periodically the doctor receives a summary showing past-due accounts that may need attention.

On request the computer will furnish a detailed report that lists all care the doctor has given to a patient. Currently the NBofC computer puts out the bills for more than 50,000 patients a month in Washington, believed to be the largest number from any computer center in the state.

Payrolls are handled for a wide range of other types of business that include, for example, retail store chains, car dealers, contractors, a college, and diverse manufacturing.

BANKAMERICARD

The bank credit card, probably the most important innovation in banking in many years, was made possible in the first place by the computer and its ability to store and then recall and process an almost endless amount of detail. The credit card in turn permits the further expansion of banking into consumer merchandising.

Before a bank issues a credit card, it checks a consumer's record in paying bills and sets up an account on the computer. When the consumer uses the card to charge a purchase, the retail merchant includes that charge in the day's receipts which he deposits. The computer transfers the charge automatically to the consumer's account.

The more widely a credit card is accepted in retail trade, the more useful it is to the consumer and the larger the volume of transactions. For this reason, instead of establishing a new credit card of its own, the National Bank of Commerce joined with other banks in the nation and in the world to become a franchised user of BankAmericard, which was pioneered by the Bank of America in California. Late in 1966, NBofC introduced BankAmericard in Washington State and in 1969 set up a subsidiary, Bancard, Inc., to handle BankAmericard in Alaska. Perhaps the most universal of all bank credit cards, BankAmericard is accepted in thousands of shops and by airlines, banks, and hotels throughout the United States and Canada and in large areas of Europe and Asia.

SENIOR MANAGEMENT

Within the National Bank of Commerce the senior management group was expanded during the 1960's to include two executive vice presidents and seven senior vice presidents in addition to the president and chief executive officer, Maxwell Carlson, and the chairman of the board, Andrew Price, Jr.

Carlson told bank directors and associates five years in advance that he would retire December 1, 1970, when he became 65. In his final years he concentrated on building strength and depth in leadership throughout the bank.

Carlson is one of the last leaders in Washington State banking whose career began before the days of branches and who, in coming up through the organization, worked in almost every phase of the bank. Such men have a knowledge of the details of the bank's daily work and a wide-ranging acquaintance with the staff that is unmatched.

During the span of Carlson's career, deposits at the National Bank of Commerce grew from $28 million to more than $1 billion; two-thirds of that growth came while Carlson was president. Over the same period the bank's staff expanded from approximately 35 in a single office in 1929 to more than 2,700 statewide. The greater part of this expansion likewise came under Carlson's presidency and through leaders of his selection.

With growth both in size and complexity in banks as in other large organizations, the day of one-man direction is passing. Well aware of this, Carlson expanded the bank's administrative staff and spread responsibility among a larger group.

In 1963 two positions of executive vice president were created. Those named to these positions were Ralph J. Stowell, previously senior vice president and for many years the bank's senior loan officer, and Andrew Price, Jr., who later became chairman of the board. In 1965, T. Robert Faragher returned to Seattle from California to become executive vice president with Stowell. Faragher had worked part-time for the National Bank of Commerce while a student at the University of Washington. He began his career with Guaranty Trust Company in New York, but later moved west to become a vice president of Peoples National Bank in Seattle. Later he was manager for the Bank of California in Tacoma, and in 1962 transferred to that bank's San Francisco headquarters as senior vice president.

In 1968 when Stowell retired as an officer but continued as a director, the bank had seven senior vice presidents, all heads of departments. They were Robert F. Buck, business development; Alfred A. Erickson, operation; John T. Glase, trust; Clarence L. Hulford, international banking; Ronald A. Macdonald, personnel; Edward R. McMillan, bank investment; and Edgar A. Ruth, loans. Macdonald and Ruth retired in 1969.

The role of Marine Bancorporation has changed markedly through the years. The intense activity of the late 1920's centered on acquisition of banks which were later consolidated into the National Bank of Commerce. With this consolidation largely completed by the mid-1930s, Marine operated unobtrusively for more than three decades as a bank holding company. Its assets consisted almost solely of stock in the National Bank of Commerce, where it owns all but the qualifying shares of the bank's directors.[1]

During the forties and fifties Marine broadened its investments to include common stocks in several industrial corporations, primarily in the Pacific Northwest. These investments, built out of dividends from the National Bank of Commerce, were conceived as a secondary reserve for the bank under management's firm belief that the bank should depend for liquidity on its own resources rather than on government agencies or the Federal Reserve.

The National Bank of Commerce, however, has never needed to

draw on these reserves, and, with a broad rise in market value and earnings, the outside investments themselves became a growing and significant source of income for Marine. Common stocks for which Marine paid $1,631,000 had risen in market value by 1969 to $8,045,000.

One of these investments outside banking was in Soundview Pulp Company, Everett, the nation's largest independent manufacturer of market pulp, which was acquired by Scott Paper Company in 1951 through exchange of stock. Even after selling approximately one-third of this investment, Marine's holding of Scott shares that cost $112,300 had market value in early 1969 of $1,650,000. Similarly, an investment of $198,000 in Safeco Corporation rose in market value to approximately $1,560,000, and shares in Pacific Car and Foundry Company costing $32,600 rose to $1,350,000.

Other investments include stock in Weyerhaeuser, Crown Zellerbach, Potlatch Forests, Evans Products, and two Spokane banking organizations—Old National Bank of Washington and its holding company, which has recently been renamed Washington Bancshares, Inc., and Washington Trust Bank. To balance these investments Marine bought shares in a number of other companies outside the Pacific Northwest, notably in international oils.

From 1965 through 1967, Marine also bought some of its own stock in the open market when the price was substantially below book value. This investment totaled $1,204,000 and by early 1969 had nearly doubled in market value.

Marine also set up two subsidiaries that complement the work of the bank yet have greater flexibility operating separately from the bank. The first of these, King County Building Company, buys real estate well in advance of future expansion of the National Bank of Commerce, both for the head office and various branches in the state. Until these properties are used by the bank, King County Building receives rents that add to Marine's income.

The second subsidiary, set up under King County Building Company, was Marine Service Company, the specialized organization for computer services which subsequently became a division of the bank.

During this gradual widening in activities of Marine Bancorporation, far more extensive changes were beginning to alter the structure of banking all across the country. Leaders in banks that

included the largest in the nation were discovering that they could become more useful and more competitive in the changing world of finance if they converted to a one-bank holding company like Marine.

In a typical conversion stockholders of a bank exchange their shares for those of a holding company, which in turn owns the bank and creates or acquires other corporations that provide related services such as data-processing, equipment-leasing, or mortgage finance. A bank thus becomes the center of a financial organization that provides a widening range of services for individuals and business firms.

As this development took hold it became apparent that Marine Bancorporation, far from becoming an anachronism, was in the forefront of new trends in banking. But before Marine could operate to the fullest as a one-bank holding company it had to reorganize its capital structure.

From the very beginning, control of Marine and of the National Bank of Commerce lay with the owners of its 7,881 "initial" or voting shares, the stock retained by the founder Andrew Price, Sr., his close associates, and their families. The remaining 352,806 "fully participating" shares (344,966 owned by approximately 4,100 stockholders and the rest held in Marine's treasury) participated equally in dividends but had no vote.

Because of this two-class structure, Marine's "fully participating" shares usually traded in the over-the-counter market below the initial shares and sometimes substantially below book value. In contrast, shares of most bank stocks commanded a premium over book value.

Reorganization in Marine's capital structure had been contemplated at various times in recent years, but with the spread of one-bank holding companies the need became more pressing. To make the shares more attractive to investors, Marine realized it would have to extend the voting power to all stockholders. A reorganization for this purpose would also provide an occasion to split the shares so as to bring the price down within reach of investors buying in 100-share lots.

In more than forty years Marine had neither split its stock nor declared a stock dividend. It paid out about one-third of the bank's earnings in the form of cash dividends and plowed the rest back to provide capital for growth. From 1933 through 1968, a period of

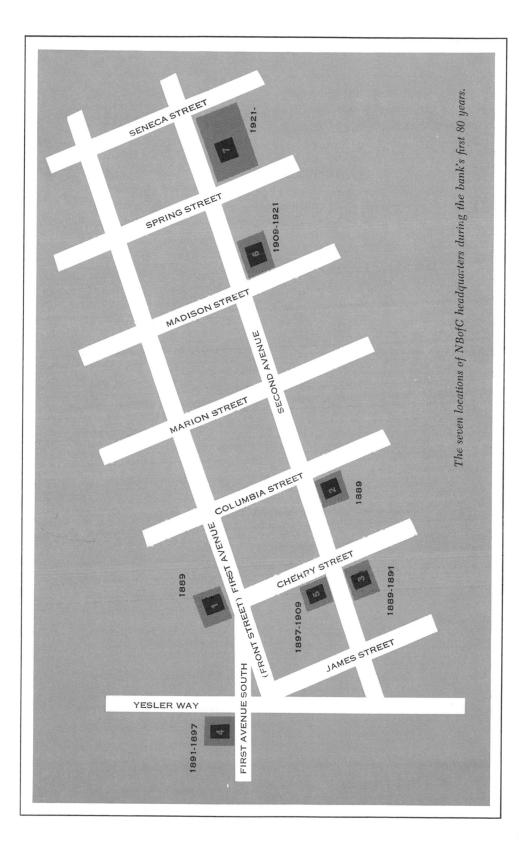

The seven locations of NBofC headquarters during the bank's first 80 years.

extraordinary expansion in all banking, the National Bank of Commerce and Marine constituted the only organization among present billion-dollar banks in the West which financed growth entirely out of earnings and without sale of stock or capital notes or issuance of stock in acquisition of other banks.

Bit by bit Marine's cash dividends increased through the years, and shares rose in price but not so rapidly as for many major banks. During most of 1967 and 1968 the market for Marine's non-voting stock ranged between $145 and $170 a share. In 1968 earnings totaled $22.78 a share and the cash dividend $6. The book value (stockholders' equity) at the year end reached $229 a share, up slightly more than $15 in the year.

In January 1969, Marine's directors brought shareholders of both classes of stock to a historic meeting. Their proposal: to create a new class of voting shares and to issue 10 new voting shares for each share of "fully participating" stock and 30 for each share of "initial" stock. The basis of exchange was recommended by two outside investment firms.

The proposal was approved overwhelmingly. The result was an increase to 3,686,000 in shares outstanding. Stockholders also authorized directors to increase the total to 10 million and to issue preferred stock. The additional shares would become available for acquisitions.

The market responded at once and subsequently new shares were bid above $30, equivalent to $300 for the old "fully participating" stock.

Just prior to the reorganization Marine announced its first major acquisition in many years—the cash purchase of Coast Mortgage and Investment Company, the largest mortgage banking firm in the Pacific Northwest and twenty-first in size in the nation. Coast and its subsidiary, Ward Smith, Inc., serviced more than $460 million in mortgages through 11 offices in western Washington. Leadership of the company remained in the hands of its president, Carl A. Sandquist, and its chairman, Ward Smith. [After Smith died in October 1969 and Sandquist in 1970, Richard A. Cady, who came to Coast in 1951, became president.]

A little later Marine's board was enlarged from 10 to 12 members. The bank's directors in 1969 numbered 24, all but·4 from outside the bank management. Ten of NBofC's directors were also directors of Marine. In 1966 the bank set the retirement

age for directors at 72 and adopted for a five-year interim period a director-emeritus status for several senior directors.

Officers of Marine, numbering seven, generally hold senior positions in the National Bank of Commerce. Marine has had only three presidents in more than forty years—Andrew Price, Sr., who served from the founding in 1927 to his retirement in 1955; Keith G. Fisken, a lumberman and a director of the National Bank of Commerce since 1928 and of Marine since 1951, who served as president of Marine from 1955 to 1962; and Andrew Price, Jr., president since 1962.

In the quiet perspective of history the eighty years that began with statehood brought extraordinary development in Washington—from thin settlements along the nation's western outposts to bustling cities and industries known around the world; from communities that offered little more than the hard, rough life of the frontier to those with institutions in education and culture that rank well among others in the nation. The gradual achievements during these years must have carried the state far beyond the dreams of its early settlers.

Growth continues, not simply in population—and in crowding—but in the diversity and sturdiness of the economy, in the fabric of human institutions, and in the contribution of people, products, and resources that Washington sends out to older parts of the nation and of the world.

How far will development carry, and what expansion in the economy may one expect by the centennial of statehood and the

bank in 1989? Some helpful clues come from today's basic industries.

FROM THE FORESTS

For decades forest products have constituted the dominant industry in the Washington economy. Mills producing lumber, plywood, shingles, pulp, and paper are dotted across the state, from tidewater to the Idaho border. Dollars harvested from trees swell the payrolls in retail shops, in banking and insurance, and in supporting manufacturing far removed from the sweet fragrance of fresh sawdust.

In total employment the forest products industry has ranked No. 1 in Washington for much of the time since the earliest settlements. The peak in recent years came in 1951 with an annual average employment of 75,800. Then with increased mechanization in the woods and the mills, employment in logging and lumbering shrank, a reduction only partly offset by construction of new mills in pulp and paper. In 1969, a depressed year in residential building and hence in markets for lumber and plywood, employment in forest products averaged 65,200.

During most of the 1960's aerospace outranked forest products in employment, just as shipbuilding did during World War II. But by 1970, cutbacks in aerospace left forest products still the state's leading employer.

The harvest of timber in Washington reached an all-time high during the 1920's. That harvest came entirely from virgin stands within relatively easy access to tidewater, river, or logging railroad —the transportation route to sawmills. New-cut lumber then moved overland by rail car or by the Panama Canal, sometimes in entire shiploads. By the time the nation's housing boom of the late 1920's collapsed, the state's most accessible stands had been largely cut off. When markets picked up again after the depression, loggers pushed back into the less hospitable hills and onto steeper mountain slopes. Some left for southern Oregon and northern California, where new stands were opening up.

Decades passed. Rich valley bottoms, which early settlers had laboriously cleared, went into farms and industry. Cities and highways spread out to claim other land. Yet away from the cities and towns much of the soil in western Washington finds its highest utilization for one product: trees, and, untroubled by war or de-

pression, trees just keep on growing. Now a new crop, already forty to eighty years old, is coming to maturity, the trunks tall and straight, the mantle of green tops stretching often for unbroken miles.

The first yield from this new growth comes as thinnings of crowded, spindly trees, which make excellent poles, pulpwood, and even lumber. In time the entire stand is logged, and another crop starts.

Year by year the harvest of second-growth logs has increased to supplement the dwindling cut of virgin stands. As a result the total harvest of timber in Washington reached seven billion board feet in 1969, the greatest since 1929.[1] During the 1970's the harvest is certain to exceed the high set 50 years earlier.

The biggest part of Washington's timber comes from the moist slopes west of the Cascades and on the Olympic Peninsula. In this section where second growth is maturing so fast, output of logs reached almost six billion board feet in 1969, a new high as a result of a sharp increase in production from private timber lands. Output from the drier, more open timberlands east of the Cascades topped one billion board feet in 1969, down slightly from the record high of 1966. From earliest times Ponderosa and white pine have been the choice species in eastern Washington, but in recent years manufacturers have expanded their resources by milling and marketing associated species such as larch, spruce, and red fir.

In timber Washington has entered the Age of Second Growth. It is the first state in the West to make the transition to the new age and to convert its far-flung forest industry to perpetual yield. In the transition, early-day mills built to handle old-growth logs of tremendous size have given way to new mills and new machinery—fast and light for processing the smaller but more uniform second growth.

In the Age of Second Growth lumbermen focus their efforts on the ability to increase productivity as measured in the cubic feet of new growth per acre per year. Nature finds new assistance in increasing the green harvest. Geneticists, for example, select and breed trees for superior qualities and faster growth. Timber owners apply chemical fertilizers to help a new crop take hold and thus shorten the growth cycle. Forest practices in reseeding, in brush control, and in thinning improve constantly. Science has just begun its work in the forests. Out of such efforts will come a larger,

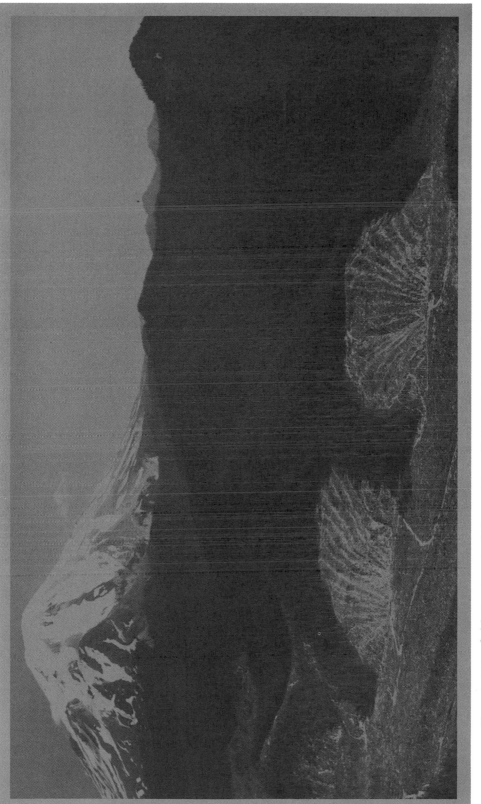

Harvest of Douglas fir forests on foothills near Mount Rainier, Washington. Seedlings of Douglas fir will not take hold in the deep shade of old trees. Hence timber is clear-cut and patches of old trees are left for seeding. (Weyerhaeuser photo.)

more dependable supply of raw material, a supply rising in value with growth in demand in the United States and overseas.

Industry, meantime, is squeezing more products, more dollars, and more jobs from every tree harvested. Leftovers from lumber and plywood mills have long since become the raw materials for pulp and for particleboard. More and more pulp, once shipped largely to converting mills elsewhere in the nation and the world, now is made in Washington into tissue, towels, writing and printing papers, cartons, and other finished products for the expanding markets of the West.

There are still waste products to utilize, and new pressures to eliminate pollution of air and water spur research efforts to utilize these products. Perhaps the greatest challenge centers on lignin, the binder in wood cells, now largely discarded at pulp mills. Some day science may find a way to extract chemicals from the extremely complex molecule of lignin and thus make trees the basis for an industry comparable to petrochemicals.

In the decades just ahead the forest industry will remain a major employer in Washington. Development of new processes and machinery will reduce the amount of labor expended on each cubic foot of wood harvested, but this trend will be somewhat offset by a rise in the amount of raw material and by the creation of new products of the log.

Forests, however, are more than just a raw material for a basic industry. They are a part of the outdoor heritage of America. Increasingly, private forestlands have been opened to hunting, fishing, camping, and other forms of recreation. With relentless growth in American population and rising interest in the outdoors, the decades ahead will bring new concepts in planning and management of forest areas, whether they are under public or private ownership.

AEROSPACE

Aerospace has contributed heavily to growth in the Puget Sound basin during the past fifteen years. Eminence in aerospace rests with a single company, Boeing, one of the corporate giants of the country and the world's foremost builder of commercial jet aircraft.

Founded more than a half-century ago, Boeing expanded into commercial aircraft when that industry was in its infancy, became a leader in production of military aircraft during World War II,

The first model 747, biggest commercial jet aircraft in the world, being rolled out of the Everett, Washington, plant of Boeing in 1968. (Boeing Co. photo.)

and manufacturer of the Minuteman missile in the years after the war. But its greatest growth came in production of commercial jet transports, which it pioneered and which in 1969 accounted for almost two-thirds of the company's sales.

Boeing developed not one but a series of commercial jet transports. First came the four-engine model 707 during the 1950's. Then followed the three-engine 727 and the twin-engine 737. In turn, each of these series was available in passenger or cargo configuration, and long-body "stretch" versions were added. In 1969 the first of the mammoth model 747s was delivered to airlines. As one model passes its peak, another tends to take up the slack. Reorders depend on growth in airline travel.

Boeing has plants in Wichita, the South, and the East, but concentrates the design and production of commercial jet aircraft in the Puget Sound area—in the 45-mile stretch from the 747 plant at Everett, through Seattle with its complex of administrative headquarters, flight-test center, and supersonic transport production, to Renton where commercial aircraft other than the 747 are manufactured, to the aerospace center at Kent, and to the immense central fabrication facility at Auburn.

In 1957 when production of commercial jet aircraft was on the rise, employment in aerospace averaged 62,500 in Washington, barely exceeding the total in forest products. From mid-1967 through 1968 the buildup at the 747 plant, which at the peak had almost 25,000 employees, helped boost employment in aerospace just over 100,000. Then with completion of several government contracts in aerospace and with a slowing down in new orders from airlines, employment shrank month by month.

In 1968 almost one in every seven wage and salary workers in the metropolitan area of Seattle-Tacoma-Everett was employed at Boeing, a concentration that made the area unusually sensitive to the wide swings characteristic of the aerospace industry.

In the long look ahead, Boeing's strength lies in its organization —in the ability to tackle extremely complex jobs, to research, design, test, and manufacture, and above all to finance and sell. One great asset in development of new business is the company's force of engineers and scientists.

Significant industrial diversity has come as a spin-off from Boeing. Boeing builds integrated systems, not components. In a number of instances engineers and scientists at Boeing have de-

veloped components or equipment useful to Boeing and others in aerospace and then left to set up their own manufacturing companies. Among corporations whose leaders or products had ties with Boeing are United Control, Rocket Research, Tally, and Heath Tecna.

OCEANOGRAPHY AND NUCLEAR ENERGY

Two young and expanding areas of scientific exploration and industrial development offer unusual potential in Washington State. These are oceanography and nuclear energy.

The sheltered waters of Puget Sound, its estuaries and shallow bays, and its ready access to the Pacific Ocean constitute a natural laboratory for man's expanding studies of the complex world of marine life and the oceans themselves. These explorations draw scientists from universities, federal and state agencies, research organizations, and private industry. In turn the state recognized the potential in this expanding field with creation in 1967 of the Oceanographic Institute of Washington.

Explorations in nuclear energy and the peaceful uses of the atom are centered at Hanford, adjoining the Tri-Cities of Richland, Kennewick, and Pasco. At Hanford, along what was once a remote stretch of the Columbia River, the Atomic Energy Commission produced plutonium in World War II. Now the facilities have been turned to man's constructive purposes. Industry seeks new uses for the products of atomic energy, for example in medicine and in food preservation. The AEC research laboratories, which employ more than 2,000 persons, have been taken over by Battelle-Northwest and expanded.

CONSUMER GOODS

Probably the greatest growth in manufacturing in the decades just ahead will come not in industrial commodities to supply national and world markets but in consumer goods made primarily for the Pacific Northwest.

Production of consumer goods follows growth in population and is aided, of course, by the cost of inbound freight, which serves as a tariff wall to protect new industry. The 3,400,000 residents of Washington State in 1970 constituted a sizable market. Add in the rest of the Pacific Northwest and Alaska and the total exceeds 7,000,000. For many products California provides an added outlet.

Eighty years ago settlers depended almost entirely on other parts of the country for goods used in everyday life—shoes, clothing, lamps, paper, tools, paints, store fixtures, wagons, and sawmill machinery. But as fast as an enterprising individual could see sufficient market to support a new plant, manufacturing sprang up to meet local needs.

Early plants such as those for flour milling, furniture, and stove manufacturing were small, but as the population grew, larger plants with heavier investment were warranted. By the middle 1950's the first refineries producing gasoline and fuel oils were built on Puget Sound. Now there are four, and a fifth—the largest of all, costing over $100 million—was begun by Atlantic Richfield near Bellingham in 1969.

Growth feeds on growth at an accelerating rate. Beyond this, some manufacturers, notably in sportswear, luggage, specialized machinery and, of course, aircraft, have gone on to build far bigger volume elsewhere in the nation and overseas.

FARM PRODUCTS

The relentless soaring of population in America and throughout the world puts increasing demand on farmlands. Every year there are more mouths to feed, yet every year in America thousands of the most productive acres are lost to the spread of cities, factories, and freeways. In the West the loss of land is greatest in California, the nation's leading agricultural state.

Pressure for more food will mean long-term expansion in Washington's agriculture, a source in 1969 of $810 million in revenues to the state's farmers. For a number of years Japan, India, and other nations of Asia have taken four-fifths of all the wheat grown in Washington. In a good year wheat returns growers close to $140 million.

California, the nation's most populous state, by its very size and proximity becomes a bigger customer each year for the products of Washington's fields and orchards. Already California buys 20 per cent of Washington's apples, a crop that averages more than $75 million a year in value.

As one result of the greater demand for food, irrigation will expand, notably in the Columbia Basin. With water, dryland wheat farms and cattle ranges are converted to more intensive crops such as potatoes, corn, and beans. In turn, an increase in pro-

Columbia Basin Irrigation Project, near Quincy, Washington, when the irrigation system was being built in 1952. (Bureau of Reclamation photo.)

duction of food will bring parallel expansion in processing through canning, freezing, dehydration, and perhaps irradiation.

A CORNER OF HEAVEN

To the crowded millions in California, the Midwest, and the East, the magnificent outdoors of Washington represents a corner of heaven—whether for salt-water fishing off Westport, backpacking on a wilderness trail in the North Cascades, boating on the long stretch of the Columbia River above Coulee Dam, or leisurely driving through the pine-scented Blue Mountains in the corner of Washington that butts against Idaho and Oregon. The tourist trade is certain to loom bigger in Washington each year. Growth in recreation, incidentally, will also bring some difficult problems in regard to uses of forest lands, both public and private, and the sea shore.

Alaska, with its magnificent scenery and friendly people, continues to draw tourists north in ever-growing numbers. Beyond this the 1970's are certain to bring expansion in Alaska's industry, most spectacularly in oil but in forest and mineral resources as well. The impact will add to trade through business houses and ports on Puget Sound, long sensitive to the needs of the North. Today Alaska accounts for the greatest part of outbound tonnage moving through ports of Puget Sound.

Trade with southeast Asia continues to expand. It is not beyond reason to expect that some day China again may be open to trade with America, a trade which contributed to the development of rail and water transportation in Washington's early days.

As the region matures, it will attract types of business now centered primarily in older parts of the nation. Insurance is one. Already a score of companies that write life, fire, or casualty insurance have home offices in Washington. Some operate only statewide or regionwide, some throughout the nation. Together they handle millions of dollars of premiums each year. Their investments through purchase of bonds provide financing for municipal agencies such as school, water, sewer, and local improvement districts.

As one looks back to Washington's early days it is apparent that growth in population has come in three distinct waves. The first, which brought the early settlers, extended through the opening decade of the 1900's. The second came in the decade of World War II with the extraordinary activity in aircraft plants and shipyards.

The same scene five years later showing development of agriculture once water became available.

A third followed in the 1950's—not so large as that of the 1940's yet more sustained and founded on a broadening of the industrial base.

Now a new wave, more powerful than any yet experienced, is building up. In the years remaining until the state's centennial in 1989, this wave seems certain to bring the greatest growth in Washington's history, a growth solidly based on a maturing economy. Fortunately for posterity this expansion in homes and industry comes at a time when the people have never been more aware of the need to preserve as much as possible of the state's great natural setting.

BANKING IN THE YEARS AHEAD

Banking like any human endeavor undergoes continual change and evolution in response to new circumstances and new leadership. In the days of Robert Spencer and Manson Backus, banking concentrated on financing for industry and commerce—a specialty highly important, centuries old, and yet regarded today as narrow.

During the past thirty years banking has broken limitations imposed by habit and custom and has reached out with new services for consumers—in savings, in credit, and in the convenience of branch offices. Banks also have developed specialized services for industry and commerce that were unthinkable in the days of Spencer and Backus. The cumulative result has been growth not just in volume but also in ability to handle the changing financial needs of a greatly enlarged group of customers.

The transition to consumer or retail banking came slowly. Resistance was inevitable on the part of bankers and regulatory officials, who clung to the known and the conventional where risk-taking is a part of daily business and where the funds risked are those entrusted by customers. Above all, the transition was slowed by the memory of the hard, bitter depression, from which banking emerged battered and on the defensive. Under such circumstances it was an extraordinary man who could appraise tomorrow in terms other than the carnage of yesterday's depression and who was willing to drive ahead to new goals perhaps only dimly perceived.

Changes break rapidly now. Maxwell Carlson told associates early in the 1960's: "The wraps are coming off the banking business with the retirement or death of leaders in three groups—bankers,

Downtown Seattle, the waterfront, and the Space Needle, which was built for the 1962 World's Fair.

regulatory officials and lawmakers—men who had been conditioned by the depression."

As the depression fades into the past, a new attitude takes hold among bankers, an aggressiveness and a conviction that for vitality and growth banks must broaden the work they do in the nation's economy. With this attitude goes a new tool or facility—the computer. In large-scale manufacturing and distribution, use of the computer and data-processing systems built upon it have become routine. In banking the computer for the first time permits large-scale automation of a business which for centuries has been essentially hand-operated.

The result is not merely the elimination of an immense amount of drudgery and hence the ability to take on whole new areas of work. Beyond this is the ability to provide much faster, fuller information for decision-making, whether the need is for push-button information on a prospective borrower or on the New York money market. The impact of the computer on banking may well prove to be as great as the steam engine in the Industrial Revolution.

Of changes that even a decade may bring an NBofC officer in data-processing remarks: "What we'll be doing in ten years we don't know but it certainly won't be even close to what we are doing today."

Credit cards and computers will carry banking along toward what was once called the checkless society but more often is described now as the "less check" society. The trend clearly is toward use of fewer checks. Today an employer may give a bank a payroll report and request that the amounts indicated be credited directly to various employees' accounts. Soon an individual may authorize charges directly against his account when he buys at retail. But the day is not in sight when checks will be eliminated and the consumer will be able to get along without cash in his pocketbook.

Branch banking will continue to grow though not so fast as it has in the past twenty years. During the 1950's, two-thirds of all branches established by the National Bank of Commerce came through purchase of local banks whose owners preferred to become part of a larger system. During the 1960's, however, most branches were established *de novo*, that is, through the creation of a new office in an area not already served. From now on most new branches will be created *de novo* in areas of growing population.

The head office today, with one floor added to the original building and a new structure built to fill out the half-block.

Important branches also are likely to continue to go into retail shopping centers. Some major centers at the outset allowed only one branch, but shopping centers are finding it is better to have competitive banking offices and to make shopping centers into centers for finance as well as for retail trade.

It seems inevitable also that, at least in retail districts, banks will lengthen their hours of service beyond the schedule of 10:00 A.M. to 3:00 P.M. set decades ago. Then a bank had only a single office, the customer came in at the convenience of the banker, and the day's transactions had to be posted by hand and balanced after hours.

Consumer savings accounts will remain a basic source of funds for banks. Already at the National Bank of Commerce, as at most commercial banks, the total deposits held in savings accounts, investment certificates, and other time deposits exceed the total in checking accounts. This growth in time money comes not alone from consumers but from business accounts, too, as corporate treasurers seek to keep their temporarily excess funds constantly at work.

The place of residential mortgages in commercial banking should grow rather than diminish. Home mortgages provide the basic investment for consumer savings accounts. They are important to a bank for another reason. The biggest financial decision a young couple makes is the purchase of the first house. As a senior loan officer comments, "if you take care of the couple in the financing of the first house, you may have built a lifetime customer." There are also related services that a bank can provide the couple—perhaps a savings account, a safe deposit box, the financing of a car, a personal loan, and in time, the purchase of a larger house. In time also, some men who first walked into a bank to finance the purchase of a house become leaders in corporations that are customers of the bank.

The trust business continues one of the fast-developing aspects of commercial banking as individuals and corporations accumulate assets and as banks offer a wider range of special services in asset management—whether in pension and profit-sharing trusts, in custodial services, or a variety of investment funds.

The National Bank of Commerce is now more than eighty years old. Some of the thinking that guides it as it moves toward its cen-

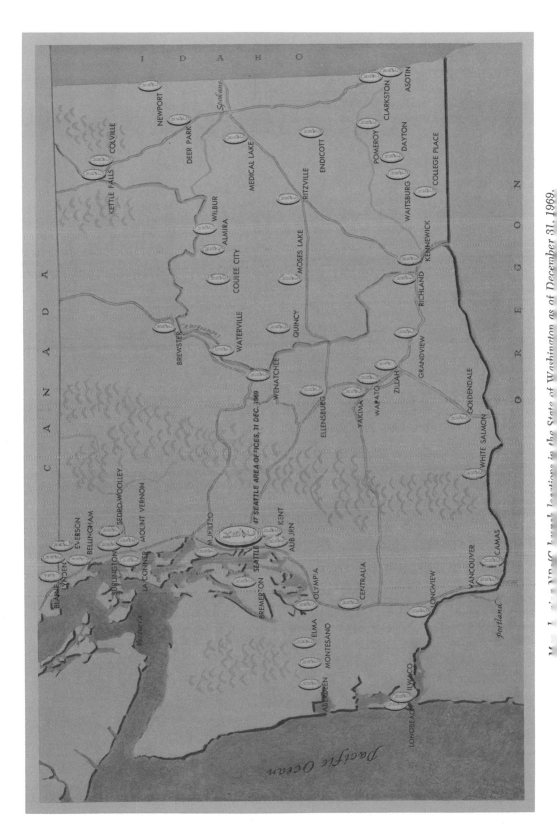

Map 1. — List of WPPSS Local locations in the State of Washington as of December 31, 1969.

tennial in 1989 was suggested in this comment of Maxwell Carlson to his associates:

Commercial banking is on the move. A new generation is coming along, free of the restraints from the depression, more aggressive, willing to innovate, and searching for opportunities.

Competition is stiffening, and not just from other banks. To be competitive the bank of the future must offer a greater variety of financial and related services. From these services can come additions to profits that build further growth.

Banks, in turn, have got to be more competitive for brain power. Our world, growing increasingly complex, calls for persons of greater expertise and, even more important, for leaders of ever broader education with an understanding of people—here and overseas.

Through the rapid changes in the years ahead, however, the fundamentals will hold constant. It is important that a bank maintain the quality of its assets so that in adversity it can provide its own liquidity for the protection of its depositors.

Our goal can be simply stated: We wish to run a competitive bank, a bank that is useful to its customers and its community, sound and safe for its depositors, and profitable for its stockholders.

PART V

APPENDIXES

THE NATIONAL BANK OF COMMERCE of Seattle

Directors (1889–1969)

Agen, John B.	1917–1920
Ainsworth, E. E.	1906–1914
Allison, Rex L.	1953–1963
Alvord, E. H.	1889–1890
Ambrose, Clarence M.	1967–
Anderson, Mrs. Agnes H.	1919–1930
Anderson, Fred A.	1928–1931
Backus, LeRoy M.	1906–1928
	1935–1948
Backus, Manson F.	1906–1935
Ballard, M. D.	1889–1899
Balmer, Thomas	1930–1959
Bedle, Ira W.	1928–1952
Bell, W. A.	1938–1951
Bishop, Edward K.	1938–1967
Black, Leo S.	1928–1951
Bloedel, Prentice	1956–
Bolger, Thomas E.	1969–
Boyd, Homer L.	1928–1965
Broughton, Charles J.	1957–
Brown, Winston D.	1966–
Brownell, F. H.	1910–1915
Buckner, C. E.	1928–1932
Butler, W. C.	1911–1919

Calvert, William, Jr.	1916–1928
Campbell, Edward S.	1962–
Campbell, John A.	1912–1921
Carlson, Maxwell	1947–
Carrington, Glenn	1943–
Clark, G. F.	1912–1916
Clarke, Caspar W.	1926–1930
Close, C. D.	1890–1890
Corbet, Darrah	1939–1967*
Corkery, William	1931–1934
Collins, W. G.	1911–1920
Colwell, J. Irving	1943–1958
Daub, Albert	1928–1935
Davies, T. A.	1911–1928
Deming, E. B.	1917–1928
DeSteiguer, George E.	1898–1911
Donworth, Judge George	1913–1928
Eastman, Dean H.	1961–
Eggert, C. F.	1898–1899
Elder, John H.	1889–1898
Faragher, A. W.	1947–1967*
Faragher, T. Robert	1969–
Farrell, J. D.	1909–1913
Fisken, Keith G.	1931–
Fox, Jonas H.	1917–1928
Fuller, Richard E.	1949–
Garretson, A. S.	1890–1893
Graves, E. O.	1906–1910
Gilman, D. H.	1890–1893
Green, Joshua A.	1906–1927
Greenough, T. L.	1906–1907
Gund, George F.	1894–1899
Hardenbergh, George E.	1928–1932
Hardy, Robert M.	1935–1960
Hatch, E. H.	1928–1942
Heckman, John R.	1928–1932
Hemphill, Wylie	1928–1949
Hemphill, Wylie M.	1962–
Henry, H. C.	1893–1917
Henry, Langdon C.	1921–1928

Hill, W. C.	1889–1890
Holyoke, Richard	1889–1897
Hughes, J. W.	1896–1906
Ingels, Lauren	1891–1892
Isaacson, Henry C.	1949–
Jerome, Timothy	1918–1928
Kilbourne, E. C.	1892–1896
Kirkwood, W. W.	1894–1895
	1905–1906
Larson, Peter	1893–1894
Leland, John D.	1952–1962
Lervick, Arne T.	1966–
Lewellyn, William H.	1889–1894
Lord, C. J.	1906–1937
Luce, F. H.	1917–1923
McChesney, J. T.	1915–1917
McCord, E. S.	1906–1931
McCord, Evan S.	1945–
MacDonald, Gregg C.	1960–1967
Maxwell, J. W.	1928–1951
Meadowcroft, A. H.	1957–
Merrill, R. D.	1913–1917
Miller, Alexander	1935–1941
Miller, Charles S.	1906–1944
Miller, Ralph H.	1928–1943
Mills, Blake D.	1928–1947
Moore, Louis H.	1920–1921
Morris, C. L.	1928–1938
Ostrander, H. F.	1917–1928
Patten, Charles E.	1906–1916
Pelly, Bernard B.	1957–
Pennington, W. J.	1967–
Phillips, Carl L.	1947–1952
Pigott, Paul	1934–1942
Prater, W. C.	1928–1950
Price, Andrew	1928–1955
Price, Andrew, Jr.	1955–
Price, John E.	1928–1929
Prosch, Thomas W.	1889–1898
Rabel, Otto R.	1945–1967*

Reed, Frank C.	1935–1942
Rhodes, Mrs. Harriet W.	1928–1929
Riley, J. D.	1892–1893
Rosenberg, S.	1896–1899
Sawyer, D. F.	1889–1890
Schafer, Edward P.	1951–1957
Schmitz, Dietrich G.	1927–1928
Scott, Gordon N.	1943–1964
Shawbut, B. F.	1890–1892
Shorrock, E.	1928–1929
Shorts, Bruce C.	1928–1945
Simpson, S. G.	1899–1900
Spencer, O. A.	1894–1895
Spencer, R. R.	1889–1896
	1897–1899
	1899–1916
Stacy, Robert S.	1906–1912
Stimson, C. W.	1928–1930
Stowell, Ralph J.	1965–
Swalwell, J. A.	1911–1918
Sweeney, E. F.	1891–1917
Tenneson, John T.	1947–1951
Thomsen, Charles M.	1930–1935
Thomsen, Moritz	1906–1928
Traphagen, D. H.	1928–1931
Trimble, George W.	1902–1915
Vance, George F.	1968–
Walker, R. S.	1918–1928
Wallace, Hugh C.	1900–1906
	1907–1921
Walsh, James A.	1968–
Waltz, Russell S.	1951–
White, C. F.	1906–1911
Wiley, Clifford	1928–1936
Witherspoon, Herbert	1928–1962
Wright, Bagley	1962–1969
Wright, Howard H.	1949–1966
Young, M. H.	1899–1913

* *Director Emeritus*

THE NATIONAL BANK OF COMMERCE of Seattle

Loans, Deposits, and Capital Accounts (1890–1969)

			CAPITAL					
DATE	LOANS	DEPOSITS	CAPITAL STOCK	SURPLUS	UNDIVIDED PROFITS	CAPITAL RESERVES	TOTAL CAPITAL	LOAN LOSS RESERVE
Oct. 2, 1890	$ 283,000	$ 224,000	$ 195,900	$ 7,000	$ –0–	$ –0–	$ 202,900	$ –0–
Dec. 2, 1891	353,000	195,000	259,600	18,000	—	—	277,600	—
Dec. 9, 1892	511,000	456,000	300,000	32,000	—	—	332,000	—
Dec. 19, 1893	473,000	218,000	300,000	37,000	—	—	337,000	—
Dec. 19, 1894	425,000	235,000	300,000	8,000	—	—	308,000	—
Dec. 13, 1895	478,000	399,000	300,000	6,000	—	—	306,000	—
Dec. 17, 1896	380,000	339,000	300,000	1,000	—	—	301,000	—
Dec. 15, 1897	335,000	541,000	150,000	9,000	—	—	159,000	—
Dec. 1, 1898	543,000	884,000	150,000	24,000	—	—	174,000	—
Dec. 2, 1899	682,000	1,558,000	150,000	43,000	—	—	193,000	—
Dec. 13, 1900	1,052,000	1,854,000	150,000	73,000	—	—	223,000	—
Dec. 10, 1901	1,329,000	2,273,000	150,000	110,000	—	—	260,000	—

DATE	LOANS	DEPOSITS	CAPITAL STOCK	SURPLUS	UNDIVIDED PROFITS	CAPITAL RESERVES	TOTAL CAPITAL	LOAN LOSS RESERVE
Nov. 25, 1902	$ 1,541,000	$ 2,930,000	$ 150,000	$ 172,000	$ —	$ —	$ 322,000	$ —
Nov. 17, 1903	1,599,000	2,786,000	150,000	199,000	—	—	349,000	—
Nov. 10, 1904	1,841,000	2,823,000	150,000	260,000	—	—	410,000	—
Nov. 9, 1905	2,056,000	3,212,000	300,000	163,000	—	—	463,000	—
Nov. 12, 1906	7,253,000	10,832,000	1,000,000	532,000	—	—	1,532,000	—
Dec. 3, 1907	7,106,000	10,644,000	1,000,000	785,000	—	—	1,785,000	—
Nov. 27, 1908	7,328,517	11,386,774	1,000,000	750,000	177,797	—	1,927,797	—
Nov. 16, 1909	8,991,227	13,006,195	1,000,000	750,000	296,052	—	2,046,052	—
Nov. 10, 1910	8,469,927	11,942,936	1,000,000	750,000	396,995	—	2,146,995	—
Dec. 5, 1911	8,141,539	12,044,488	1,000,000	750,000	423,736	—	2,173,736	—
Nov. 26, 1912	8,439,214	11,616,253	1,000,000	750,000	364,377	—	2,114,377	—
Oct. 21, 1913	8,508,878	11,060,039	1,000,000	750,000	417,565	—	2,167,565	—
Dec. 31, 1914	8,237,049	10,562,955	1,000,000	750,000	434,595	—	2,184,595	—
Dec. 31, 1915	8,198,806	12,406,701	1,000,000	750,000	352,287	—	2,102,287	—
Dec. 27, 1916	7,746,194	13,301,367	1,200,000	300,000	203,155	—	1,703,155	—
Nov. 20, 1917	10,073,612	17,032,763	1,000,000	500,000	176,954	—	1,676,954	—
Dec. 31, 1918	10,753,015	20,957,463	1,000,000	500,000	267,446	—	1,767,446	—
Dec. 31, 1919	13,116,602	22,185,666	1,000,000	500,000	199,929	—	1,699,929	—
Dec. 29, 1920	11,162,644	16,336,254	1,000,000	500,000	431,765	—	1,931,765	—
Dec. 31, 1921	10,225,349	17,000,653	1,000,000	500,000	409,341	—	1,909,341	—
Dec. 29, 1922	10,042,821	19,510,929	1,000,000	500,000	404,571	—	1,904,571	—
Dec. 31, 1923	10,210,276	20,422,229	1,000,000	500,000	237,621	100,000	1,837,621	—
Dec. 31, 1924	11,191,434	21,779,265	1,000,000	500,000	329,203	100,000	1,929,203	—
Dec. 31, 1925	12,834,746	22,536,232	1,000,000	500,000	432,643	100,000	2,032,643	—
Dec. 31, 1926	11,496,294	22,639,407	1,000,000	750,000	333,694	100,000	2,183,694	—

Dec. 31, 1927	$ 12,483,928	$ 22,942,583	$1,000,000	$1,000,000	$ 194,187	$ 100,000	$ 2,294,187	—
Dec. 31, 1928	13,673,333	24,222,667	1,000,000	1,000,000	320,423	100,000	2,420,423	—
Dec. 31, 1929	15,717,142	28,650,572	2,500,000	1,000,000	751,845	100,000	4,351,345	—
Dec. 31, 1930	14,575,459	28,074,488	2,500,000	1,000,000	870,710	100,000	4,470,710	—
Dec. 31, 1931	14,294,250	27,927,821	2,500,000	1,000,000	731,206	109,000	4,340,206	—
Dec. 31, 1932	9,835,123	26,121,858	2,500,000	1,000,000	520,641	50,706	4,071,347	—
Dec. 31, 1933	14,924,878	37,743,592	2,500,000	1,000,000	634,436	540,973	4,675,409	—
Dec. 31, 1934	15,323,165	42,244,939	2,500,000	1,000,000	1,053,103	202,983	4,756,086	—
Dec. 31, 1935	20,455,407	59,091,600	2,500,000	1,045,000	1,257,206	262,286	5,064,492	—
Dec. 31, 1936	21,618,754	69,427,815	2,500,000	1,127,000	1,694,437	430,273	5,751,710	—
Dec. 31, 1937	26,599,776	71,433,460	2,500,000	2,500,000	1,034,425	288,470	6,322,895	—
Dec. 31, 1938	25,710,275	73,889,140	2,500,000	2,500,000	1,233,174	704,422	6,937,596	—
Dec. 31, 1939	29,763,618	84,669,845	2,500,000	2,500,000	1,369,716	848,878	7,218,594	—
Dec. 31, 1940	37,913,489	102,641,178	2,600,000	2,535,900	1,629,376	1,142,573	7,771,949	—
Dec. 31, 1941	43,013,801	125,384,090	2,500,000	2,500,000	1,911,953	1,848,217	8,760,170	—
Dec. 31, 1942	39,206,470	181,120,708	2,500,000	2,500,000	2,260,434	2,090,250	9,350,684	—
Dec. 31, 1943	37,252,734	260,239,337	2,500,000	2,500,000	2,848,042	2,279,516	10,127,558	—
Dec. 31, 1944	39,461,362	340,079,289	3,000,000	3,000,000	3,443,656	2,844,619	12,288,275	—
Dec. 31, 1945	57,051,295	430,150,369	3,000,000	5,000,000	2,623,290	3,424,049	14,047,339	198,854
Dec. 31, 1946	84,521,741	371,300,592	3,000,000	5,000,000	4,624,839	4,760,041	17,384,880	493,857
Dec. 31, 1947	92,694,954	361,666,810	3,000,000	7,000,000	4,080,415	4,363,973	18,444,388	560,675
Dec. 31, 1948	101,149,583	343,549,590	3,000,000	7,000,000	5,428,588	4,738,702	20,167,290	1,224,316
Dec. 31, 1949	104,609,699	345,739,257	3,000,000	7,000,000	6,732,816	5,110,070	21,842,886	1,724,228
Dec. 31, 1950	125,312,703	367,510,969	4,000,000	10,000,000	3,661,675	6,014,023	23,675,698	1,957,990
Dec. 31, 1951	153,799,902	394,359,534	4,000,000	12,000,000	2,499,030	5,786,656	24,285,686	2,798,690
Dec. 31, 1952	168,660,539	415,042,177	4,000,000	12,000,000	3,381,611	6,530,192	25,911,803	2,843,859
Dec. 31, 1953	192,398,362	426,333,187	6,000,000	12,000,000	7,602,617	1,611,161	27,213,778	2,748,701
Dec. 31, 1954	191,263,540	430,957,379	6,000,000	14,000,000	6,889,944	2,969,204	29,859,148	2,957,644

CAPITAL

DATE	LOANS	DEPOSITS	CAPITAL STOCK	SURPLUS	UNDIVIDED PROFITS	CAPITAL RESERVES	TOTAL CAPITAL	LOAN LOSS RESERVE
Dec. 31, 1955	$222,108,218	$ 456,503,989	$ 6,000,000	$16,000,000	$ 6,517,618	$ 3,156,384	$31,674,002	$ 3,618,674
Dec. 31, 1956	247,215,236	489,454,559	6,000,000	16,000,000	7,609,694	3,111,943	32,721,637	4,888,645
Dec. 31, 1957	240,621,857	485,208,514	8,000,000	17,000,000	6,164,069	3,777,349	34,941,418	4,833,968
Dec. 31, 1958	231,574,474	510,478,517	8,000,000	17,000,000	8,039,672	4,816,502	37,856,174	4,771,247
Dec. 31, 1959	276,113,260	524,435,984	10,000,000	18,000,000	7,120,242	5,435,492	40,555,734	5,317,674
Dec. 31, 1960	288,773,182	538,607,833	10,000,000	20,000,000	7,628,056	6,231,418	43,859,474	5,641,484
Dec. 31, 1961	318,434,044	577,063,541	12,000,000	22,000,000	6,237,239	6,847,409	47,084,648	6,140,272
Dec. 31, 1962	344,565,942	629,163,132	12,000,000	23,000,000	7,809,713	7,691,696	50,501,409	6,514,146
Dec. 31, 1963	392,108,917	682,968,252	12,000,000	26,000,000	7,468,822	7,925,117	53,393,939	7,355,563
Dec. 31, 1964	408,384,641	684,206,307	14,000,000	26,000,000	8,171,607	9,067,481	57,239,088	7,696,524
Dec. 31, 1965	464,242,047	771,361,620	14,000,000	30,000,000	7,432,255	9,675,933	61,108,168	9,037,235
Dec. 31, 1966	513,432,149	843,925,510	15,000,000	30,000,000	9,815,682	10,080,826	64,896,508	10,153,959
Dec. 31, 1967	566,074,544	948,452,437	18,000,000	34,000,000	6,481,452	10,303,667	68,785,119	11,119,552
Dec. 31, 1968	660,558,073	1,083,024,292	20,000,000	37,000,000	10,039,585	5,617,491	72,657,086	13,030,845
Dec. 31, 1969	697,969,986	1,172,545,608	22,000,000	39,000,000	12,249,719	5,800,093	79,049,812	13,932,642

THE NATIONAL BANK OF COMMERCE of Seattle

*Loans, Deposits, and Capital of Unit Banks Acquired by NBofC
at the Time of Acquisition (Through December 31, 1969)*

BRANCH	DATE OPENED AS A BRANCH	LOANS	DEPOSITS	CAPITAL
Central	4–01–33	$ 385,088	$1,399,221	$291,544
University	4–01–33	173,922	871,544	137,553
Olympia	9–05–33	359,392	3,745,407	280,708
Grays Harbor	9–05–33	956,818	2,313,325	328,023
Bremerton	9–26–33	314,783	1,438,667	133,555
Montesano	12–01–33	431,810	852,728	137,973
Elma	12–01–33	165,424	487,989	55,099
Yakima	9–16–35	2,633,819	9,209,910	896,036
Wapato	9–16–36	120,148	638,338	47,048
Ellensburg	6–01–37	745,950	1,511,000	160,956
Vancouver	6–21–37	468,115	1,310,582	148,111
Columbia Valley	1–03–38	743,373	1,507,460	144,223
Longview	7–01–38	480,892	1,927,727	171,739
LaConner	9–01–38	138,810	198,231	55,740
Bellingham	3–01–39	464,419	1,707,151	177,042
Waterville	10–23–39	249,951	522,090	40,723
Kennewick	7–01–40	387,760	567,834	105,449
Camas	2–01–44	238,920	3,844,672	169,574

BRANCH	DATE OPENED AS A BRANCH	LOANS	DEPOSITS	CAPITAL
Coulee City	2–26–45	$ 65,392	$ 992,635	$ 62,871
Brewster	7–02–45	205,866	2,176,096	71,416
Ilwaco	1–28–46	99,972	2,540,896	122,807
Edmonds	7–22–46	274,064	2,734,875	143,019
Goldendale	6–01–48	1,059,441	3,318,831	251,311
Almira	7–10–48	129,038	1,904,982	85,300
Auburn	2–14–50	317,925	1,017,287	67,368
Quincy	1–30–50	226,612	718,530	53,452
White Salmon	10–30–50	700,260	2,752,943	124,902
Lynden	6–04–51	2,035,043	3,603,890	341,435
Colville	6–11–51	350,148	1,912,457	127,942
Burlington-Edison	3–17–52	1,159,686	2,506,645	215,656
Walla Walla County	5–12–52	488,020	1,582,522	112,596
Kirkland	9–28–53	4,348,119	8,218,545	654,264
Newport	2–22–54	899,098	2,765,904	141,312
Blaine	12–20–54	392,584	1,530,275	100,248
Waitsburg	4–25–55	688,274	2,909,388	214,807
Nooksack Valley	10–31–55	460,784	1,061,784	90,659
West Seattle	1–30–56	1,440,318	4,010,975	221,520
Clarkston	5–21–56	1,433,150	5,547,193	317,335
Sedro-Woolley	6–18–56	1,571,403	2,602,514	176,088
Mount Vernon	7–16–56	3,588,094	7,179,022	491,647
Pomeroy	1–21–57	766,328	2,150,572	172,878
Dayton	3–25–57	304,965	4,231,831	249,381
Deer Park	6–30–58	139,223	1,199,883	108,101
Ritzville	4–20–59	2,204,205	6,710,537	467,859
Endicott	6–22–64	853,937	1,821,222	226,779
Grandview	1–29–68	1,634,233	3,407,846	339,898
Wilbur	12 01 69	5,062,874	8,847,473	784,037

THE NATIONAL BANK OF COMMERCE of Seattle
Demand, Time, and Total Deposits (1928–1969)

DATE	DEMAND DEPOSITS	TIME DEPOSITS	TOTAL DEPOSITS	TIME DEPOSITS *as a percentage of total deposits*
Dec. 31, 1928	$ 17,761,406	$ 6,461,261	$ 24,222,667	26.7%
Dec. 31, 1929	22,144,785	6,505,787	28,650,572	22.7
Dec. 31, 1930	21,783,078	6,291,410	28,074,488	22.4
Dec. 31, 1931	19,440,970	8,486,851	27,927,821	30.4
Dec. 31, 1932	16,806,362	9,315,496	26,121,858	35.7
Dec. 31, 1933	27,315,415	10,428,177	37,743,592	27.6
Dec. 31, 1934	32,131,681	10,113,258	42,244,939	23.9
Dec. 31, 1935	44,464,276	14,627,324	59,091,600	24.8
Dec. 31, 1936	52,848,917	16,578,898	69,427,815	23.9
Dec. 31, 1937	52,266,696	19,166,764	71,433,460	26.8
Dec. 31, 1938	54,116,668	19,772,472	73,889,140	26.8
Dec. 31, 1939	61,871,198	22,798,647	84,669,845	26.9
Dec. 31, 1940	77,879,841	24,761,337	102,641,178	24.1
Dec. 31, 1941	98,968,636	26,415,454	125,384,090	21.1
Dec. 31, 1942	147,851,266	33,269,442	181,120,708	18.4
Dec. 31, 1943	220,174,955	40,064,382	260,239,337	17.7
Dec. 31, 1944	274,188,904	65,890,385	340,079,289	19.4
Dec. 31, 1945	342,301,673	87,848,696	430,150,369	20.4

DATE	DEMAND DEPOSITS	TIME DEPOSITS	TOTAL DEPOSITS	TIME DEPOSITS *as a percentage of total deposits*
Dec. 31, 1946	$275,813,429	$ 95,487,163	$ 371,300,592	25.7%
Dec. 31, 1947	269,262,225	92,404,585	361,666,810	25.5
Dec. 31, 1948	255,676,980	87,872,610	343,549,590	25.6
Dec. 31, 1949	262,188,844	83,550,413	345,739,257	24.1
Dec. 31, 1950	284,661,928	82,849,041	367,510,969	22.5
Dec. 31, 1951	308,003,036	86,356,498	394,359,534	21.9
Dec. 31, 1952	321,812,104	93,230,073	415,042,177	22.5
Dec. 31, 1953	318,543,353	107,789,834	426,333,187	25.3
Dec. 31, 1954	319,536,206	111,421,173	430,957,379	25.8
Dec. 31, 1955	335,601,453	120,902,536	456,503,989	26.5
Dec. 31, 1956	357,007,314	132,447,245	489,454,559	27.1
Dec. 31, 1957	344,276,356	140,932,158	485,208,514	29.0
Dec. 31, 1958	356,945,213	153,533,304	510,478,517	30.1
Dec. 31, 1959	357,990,966	166,445,018	524,435,984	31.7
Dec. 31, 1960	362,610,835	175,996,998	538,607,833	32.7
Dec. 31, 1961	382,626,491	194,437,050	577,063,541	33.7
Dec. 31, 1962	405,267,624	223,895,508	629,163,132	35.6
Dec. 31, 1963	385,137,617	247,830,635	632,968,252	39.2
Dec. 31, 1964	402,669,191	281,537,616	684,206,807	41.1
Dec. 31, 1965	423,678,592	347,683,028	771,361,620	45.1
Dec. 31, 1966	448,439,566	395,485,944	843,925,510	46.9
Dec. 31, 1967	477,139,644	471,312,793	948,452,437	49.7
Dec. 31, 1968	515,191,368	567,832,924	1,083,024,292	52.4
Dec. 31, 1969	487,943,209	684,602,399	1,172,545,608	58.4

NOTES

Chapter 1

1 Interview with Henry Broderick, May 6, 1964.
2 Interview with Mrs. George (Mary) de Steiguer, Jan. 2, 1964.
3 Robert Spencer letter to S. H. Branch, Marengo, Iowa, Sept. 22, 1888. Two volumes of copies of Spencer's letters remain, one covering 1888–1892, the other 1904–1907, in the files of the National Bank of Commerce.
4 Spencer letters, July 11, 1888.
5 Ibid., June 28, 1888.
6 Ibid., Nov. 29, 1888.
7 *Seattle Post-Intelligencer*, Oct. 28, 1888.
8 *Seattle Post-Intelligencer*, Oct. 30, 1888.
9 Spencer letters, Nov. 24, 1888.
10 Ibid., Nov. 17, 1888.

Chapter 2

1 W. H. Ruffner, *A Report on the Washington Territory* (New York: Seattle, Lake Shore and Eastern Railway, 1889), p. 10.
2 W. F. Prosser, *History of the Puget Sound Country* (New York: Lewis Historical Publishing Co., 1903), Vol. I, iii.
3 U.S. Treasury Department, *Report of the Internal Commerce of the United States for the year 1890,* p. 957.
4 Ibid., p. 969.

5 Ruffner, op. cit., p. 70.
6 U.S. Treasury Department, op. cit., p. 1,041.
7 Spencer letters, April 25, 1889.
8 *Seattle Post-Intelligencer,* April 25, 1889.
9 Ibid., Aug. 17, 1888.
10 Ibid., April 14, 1889.
11 Frederic James Grant (editor), *History of Seattle* (New York: American Publishing & Engraving Co., 1891), p. 376.
12 Spencer letters, Nov. 29, 1888.
13 Ibid., Dec. 3, 1888.
14 Ibid., Dec. 5, 1888.
15 Ibid., Dec. 9, 1888.
16 Ibid., Jan. 25, 1889.
17 Interview with Mrs. de Steiguer, Jan. 2, 1964.
18 Spencer letters, April 11, 1889.
19 Ibid., April 19, 1889.
20 Ibid., May 3, 1889.
21 See Note 17.
22 Spencer letters, June 29, 1889.
23 Grant, op. cit., p. 213.
24 Spencer letters, July 7, 1889.

Chapter 3

1 Spencer letters, Oct. 16, 1889.
2 Letters to the authors from the Northern Pacific Railway Company, St. Paul, Minn., Aug. 24 and Aug. 31, 1964.
3 Spencer letters, Sept. 21, 1889.
4 Spencer letters, Feb. 20, 1890.
5 Neil Roy Knight, *History of Banking in Washington,* unpublished doctoral thesis, 1935, University of Washington Library, two volumes; Vol. 1, p. 149.
6 Herbert Hunt, *Tacoma, Its History and Its Builders* (Chicago: S. J. Clarke Publishing Co., 1916), Vol. 1, p. 460.
7 *Report of Comptroller of Currency,* 1930, Table 460.
8 Hunt, op. cit., Vol. 2, p. 112.
9 Knight, op. cit., I, 103.
10 Ibid., p. 178–188.
11 Letter dated December 30, 1893, in Directors' Minutes, National Bank of Commerce.
12 Ralph W. Hidy, Frank Ernest Hill, and Allan Nevins, *Timber and Men, the Weyerhaeuser Story* (New York: Macmillan, 1963), p. 212.

Chapter 4

1 Directors' Minutes, National Bank of Commerce, Dec. 12 and 26, 1894.
2 Interview with Henry Broderick, May 6, 1964.
3 Washington National Bank, Minutes of stockholders' meeting, Jan. 4, 1905.

4   *Seattle Post-Intelligencer,* Oct. 29, 1904.
5   Directors' Minutes, National Bank of Commerce, Oct. 27, 1904, ff.
6   Spencer letters, Dec. 11, 1905.
7   *Seattle Post-Intelligencer,* March 22, 1906.
8   C. C. Conover, "Just Cogitating," *Seattle Times,* May 12, 1949.
9   Manson F. Backus letters, March 2, 1906, to E. O. Graves. The Backus letters are in the files of the National Bank of Commerce.

Chapter 5

1   Many details of Backus's life are set out in Neil Roy Knight, *Gold Horizon, the Life Story of Manson F. Backus* (Seattle: Dogwood Press, 1937). Some observations by Backus and Graves on their first trip west appear in the Seattle *Post-Intelligencer,* April 27, 1889.
2   Knight, op. cit., p. 64.
3   Backus letters, Nov. 16, 1903. Among illuminating sources for this period is a volume of personal letters of Manson F. Backus from Nov. 19, 1903, to Nov. 22, 1907. This volume, obviously one of a series, is the only one extant and apparently was not known to Knight in preparation of his biography of Backus.
4   Ibid., May 3, 1904.
5   Ibid., July 26 and Oct. 16, 1905.
6   Ibid., March 2, 1906.
7   Ibid., March 15, 1906.
8   Directors' Minutes, Washington National Bank, March 21, 1906.
9   Backus letters, March 28, 1906.

Chapter 6

1   Interview with J. A. Swalwell, October, 8, 1964.
2   Interview Nov. 10, 1964, with George Bringolf, who was on the staff of the National Bank of Commerce from 1906 to his retirement in 1948.
3   Interview with Joshua Green, July 1, 1964.
4   Spencer letters, March 27, 1906.
5   Ibid., Jan. 21, 1907.
6   Manson Backus letters, March 2, 1906.
7   Ibid., June 7, 1907.
8   Ibid., May 10, 1907.
9   *Seattle Post-Intelligencer,* Nov. 4, 1907.
10 Interview with Will France, Oct. 24, 1963.

Chapter 7

1   U.S. Department of Agriculture, Miscel. Publ. No. 669, *Lumber Production in the U.S., 1799–1946,* pp. 11–14.
2   U.S. Department of Commerce, Bureau of Corporations, *Special Report on Present and Past Conditions in the Lumber and Shingle Industry in the State of Washington,* Washington, D.C., pp. 9, 20, 1914.
3   Interviews July 31, 1964, with Virgil Peterson, manager, Red Cedar Shingle and Handsplit Shake Bureau, Seattle, and Donald H. Clark, an

early operator in shingles and shakes and later director of the Institute of Forest Products, University of Washington.

4 Stockholders' Minutes, National Bank of Commerce, Jan. 14, 1913.

5 Letter from E. K. Bishop, Sept. 20, 1963, and interview Sept. 27, 1963.

6 Interview with Will France, Oct. 24, 1963.

7 *Pacific Fisherman Yearbooks,* data from U.S. Bureau of Commercial Fisheries.

8 *Statistical Abstract of the U.S.,* 1910 and later years, data from *Reports of the Director of the Mint, U.S. Treasury.*

9 Obituary, Seattle *Post-Intelligencer,* Jan. 5, 1916.

10 *Projections of Apple Production in the U.S.,* prepared by the Economic Research Service, U.S. Department of Agriculture, for the Senate Committee on Commerce, Aug. 27, 1964.

11 Snokist Growers, letter July 22, 1968, and resumé of early history written by J. V. Ellis, Yakima County Horticultural Union, Dec. 6, 1923.

12 Neil Roy Knight, *Gold Horizon, the Life Story of Manson F. Backus* (Seattle: Dogwood Press, 1937), p. 88; Bringolf interview, Nov. 10, 1964.

Chapter 8

1 Price set out the details of this meeting in a letter April 22, 1928, to George Trimble, Denver, a large stockholder in the National Bank of Commerce.

2 *Fortune,* Vol. I, No. 1, Feb. 1930.

3 Letters found among papers in the Price home.

4 Letter marked "confidential" to Mrs. Herbert Lee, Santa Cruz, Calif., in December 1933, in reply to inquiry as to value of the shares of John E. Price & Co.

5 Interview Dec. 19, 1963 with Robert W. Sprague, retired trust officer, NBofC, who was earlier with Northwest Trust.

6 Price letter to Comptroller John Crissinger.

7 Minutes of Trustees, May 29, 1923.

8 Copy of letter in Andrew Price files.

9 Robert Sprague notation in checking research memorandum.

10 *Seattle Post-Intelligencer,* Jan. 14, 1926.

11 Draft of talk to Dexter Horton National Bank employees in 1928.

12 From general letter of solicitation in Price files.

13 *Fortune,* Vol. I, No. 1, Feb. 1930.

14 *Seattle Post-Intelligencer,* April 11, 1926.

Chapter 9

1 Investment Bankers' Association analysis of Marine Bancorporation.

2 Here, as was characteristic, Price jotted down the pros and cons for his own evaluation, then retained the sheet in his files.

3 Report on Marine Bancorporation isssued by Marine National Co., April 1930.

4 Memorandum to the authors from Hollis W. Fultz, Olympia, May 1964.

5 Price letter to Maxwell, March 10, 1928, to confirm oral understanding.

6   *Seattle Times,* March 21, 1928.
7   Comments of Lawrence M. Arnold, May 3, 1966.

Chapter 10

1   Interview with Joshua Green, July 1, 1964.
2   Letter to George Trimble, Denver, April 22, 1928.
3   Copy of letter, April 26, 1928, to Henry Broderick, in files of Burle Bramhall.
4   See Note 2.
5   Letter in Price files.
6   Price respected Lord's judgment, and when Lord was traveling they kept in touch by telegram.
7   W. H. Tucker saw the telegram and quoted it in an undated letter to Price.
8   Letter of Reed to De Steiguer, April 17, 1928, in Price files.
9   Interview with Bramhall, July 6, 1964.
10 Letter to all stockholders.
11 *The Washingtonian, a State Magazine of Progress,* Seattle, Sept. 1929.
12 Interviews with Merle Johnson Harp, Jan. 13, 1966, and March 26, 1966.
13 Marquis and Bessie R. James, *Biography of a Bank, the Story of the Bank of America* (New York: Harper & Bros., 1954), pp. 280–281.
14 *New York Times,* May 20, 1928.
15 Interview with Burle Bramhall, July 6, 1964.
16 Interview with Dietrich Schmitz, July 6, 1964.
17 Interview with Jay Larson, July 9, 1964.
18 Told to Ira Bedle and related in an interview with Mrs. Bedle, July 29, 1964.
19 Set out in a letter from Homer Boyd to Andrew Price, May 10, 1929.
20 Interview with Mrs. Merle Johnson Harp, January 13, 1966.
21 Notes in Price's hand.
22 Interview with Homer Boyd, July 2, 1964.
23 Interview with Mrs. Merle Johnson Harp, Jan. 13, 1966.
24 See Note 17.
25 Comment of Miss Katheryn Wilson, May 19, 1966.
26 Interviews with Homer Boyd.
27 Letter dated April 4, 1929.
28 Rough draft of letter to Boyd, which Price brought home with him from New York.
29 Interview with Joshua Green, July 1, 1964.
30 Another case where Price left a memorandum to himself.
31 Interview with Robert W. Sprague, Dec. 19, 1963.

Chapter 11

1   Ralph W. Hidy, Frank Ernest Hill, and Allan Nevins, *Timber and Men, the Weyerhaeuser Story* (New York: Macmillan, 1963), p. 434.
2   U.S. Department of Agriculture, Miscellaneous Publication No. 669, *Lumber Production in the United States, 1799–1946;* October 1948.
3   Ibid.

4 Records of Seattle Building Department.

5 Washington State Department of Agriculture, *Prices Received by Washington Farmers, 1910–1959;* Seattle, 1960.

6 U.S. Bureau of the Census, *Statistical Abstract,* 1929–34.

7 Washington Emergency Relief Administration, *Occupational Characteristics of Unemployed Persons,* Olympia, 1935.

8 Interview with Chester B. Starks, Seattle, March, 1965.

9 Ibid.

10 Ibid.

11 U.S. Bureau of the Census, *Historical Statistics, Colonial Times to 1957,* Series X97–118

12 Data on closing of state banks come from annual reports, Washington State Supervisor of Banking, 1929–1935; on closing of national banks from Comptroller of Currency, *Annual Reports,* 1929–34.

13 Neil Roy Knight, *History of Banking in Washington,* unpublished doctoral thesis, 1935, University of Washington Library, two volumes, Vol. II, p. 381.

14 *Yakima Republic,* Sept. 12, 1935.

Chapter 12

1 Employment data in this section are from the Washington State Employment Security Department, *Employment and Payrolls in Washington State, 1938–1942,* issued 1944, reissued 1948; and subsequent annual summaries.

2 Federal Reserve Bank of San Francisco, *The Aluminum Industry,* 1958.

3 Northwest Pulp & Paper Association, Seattle, *Economic Survey,* 1947–1968.

4 Statistical Reporting Service of U.S. Department of Agriculture and Washington State Department of Agriculture, *Annual Crop Report,* 1967.

Chapter 13

1 Interview with Ralph Stowell, Seattle, Aug. 19, 1965.

2 Interview with Maxwell Carlson, Seattle, Nov. 9, 1964. The picture of Andrew Price in these years comes from interviews with his associates—primarily Maxwell Carlson, Ralph Stowell, Barrett Green, Robert Sprague, and Homer Boyd.

3 Interview with Edgar Ruth, Seattle, Dec. 5, 1964.

4 C. Lowell Harriss, *History and Policies of the Home Owners' Loan Corp.* (New York: National Bureau of Economic Research, 1951), pp. 6, 22, 30–37.

5 Interview with Ross Williams, Seattle, April 21, 1965.

6 Interview with Barrett Green, Seattle, March 12, 1965.

7 Interviews with Robert W. Sprague, Dec. 19, 1963 and July 1, 1965; with John T. Glase, Seattle, Aug. 20, 1965.

8 Interview with Homer Boyd, Aug. 25, 1965.

9 Interview with Mrs. Merle Johnson Harp, Jan. 13, 1966.

10 See Note 6.

11   See Note 1.
12   Interview with Bert Sellin, NBofC vice-president, Aug. 25, 1965.
13   Interview with Kenneth Clark, NBofC cashier, Seattle, Aug. 1965.
14   Interviews with Herbert E. Vedder, Seattle, Sept. 28, 1965, formerly ad-
     vertising manager, NBofC, and William Sandiford, Cole & Weber, Seattle,
     the bank's advertising agency, September 1965.

Chapter 14

1   Annual meeting, Jan. 14, 1965.
2   Interview with Louis Delorie, Seattle, July 1, 1965.
3   Interview with Clarence L. Hulford, Seattle, July 1, 1965.
4   Interviews with Ralph Stowell in August 1965 and February-March 1966.
5   Interview with Walter J. Funk, March 10, 1965.
6   Interview with Edward S. Campbell, Seattle, Aug. 27, 1965.
7   Details on senior loan committee and current commercial loans are from
    Ralph Stowell.

Chapter 15

1   Some details on the holdings of Marine Bancorporation and its earnings
    appear in the annual reports. Starting in 1965 additional information has
    been filed in conformity with new regulations governing over-the-counter
    securities with the Securities and Exchange Commission at Washington,
    D.C. and Seattle.

Chapter 16

1   U.S. Forest Service, Forest Survey Report No. 101, *Production of Logs in
    Oregon and Washington 1925–1948,* supplemented by annual summaries
    by the U.S. Forest Service, Pacific Northwest and Range Experiment Sta-
    tion, Portland, for later years.

BIBLIOGRAPHY

Unpublished material

Much the largest and most important source of information for this history consists of unpublished materials and interviews. The early days leading up to the founding of the bank would have slipped away except for a volume of tissue copies of letters which Robert R. Spencer wrote and then preserved as a record for his own use. The letters were written between 1888 and 1892. The front cover and possibly some of the earliest letters are missing.

A second volume of tissue copies, marked "Personal, June 27 '04 to October 7 '07," is also among the bank's relics, but other volumes are lost. The second volume, while revealing as to Spencer's interests and attitudes and some of his personal investments, is less applicable to the bank.

A similar book of tissue copies includes letters written by Manson F. Backus, 1903–07. It reveals details of several bank mergers proposed and actual, but otherwise many of the letters would now be regarded as business routine. Other volumes in the series are missing.

Tissue copies of letters of Ralph S. Stacy, 1903–11, remain. They

267

include some letters about the bank written to Manson Backus when the latter was in San Francisco in January 1906.

Minutes of the National Bank of Commerce and Washington National Bank proved of help, though early entries were brief at best.

From the Andrew Price era there remain at the bank and at the home of Mrs. Andrew Price Patty voluminous files of correspondence, notes in Mr. Price's hand, and brochures, newspaper clippings, bank statements, and other materials on which Professor Olson spent the greater part of one summer working. Without this material the work of Andrew Price and the account of the formation of Marine Bancorporation could not have been reconstructed.

For the story of banking during the depression of the thirties, the unpublished doctoral thesis of Neil Roy Knight at the University of Washington Library proved extremely useful. Mr. Knight wrote the family-approved biography of Manson Backus, *Gold Horizon*. Another helpful doctoral thesis is that of Alexander N. MacDonald: *Seattle's Economic Development, 1880–1910,* also at the University of Washington Library.

Recollections about C. J. Lord and his start in banking in Olympia were prepared for the authors by Hollis W. Fultz, long a close friend of Lord. Correspondence with the Northern Pacific Railway Company, St. Paul, established the type of service available to western travelers in the nineteenth century.

Supplementing the unpublished materials were interviews with more than forty persons—men and women who played a part in the development of banking in Washington State, and not merely those associated with the National Bank of Commerce. Indeed, one of the purposes of this project was to capture the recollections of the dwindling number whose careers began in the distant early years of this century.

Those interviewed included such stalwarts of Seattle business as Henry Broderick, whose recollections go back to Robert Spencer when Spencer's bank was located where Broderick's office is today, and Joshua Green, Sr. They include also the late Homer Boyd, Andrew Price's closest associate, and Price's secretary, Mrs. Merle Johnson Harp.

Books and Monographs

Bagley, Clarence B. *History of Seattle.* 2 vols. Chicago: S. J. Clarke Publishing Co., 1916.

————. *History of King County, Washington.* 4 vols. Chicago: S. J. Clarke Publishing Co., 1929.

Grant, Frederic J. (Editor). *History of Seattle.* New York: New York American Publishing and Engraving Co., 1891.

Harriss, C. Lowell. *History and Policies of the Home Owners' Loan Corp.* New York: National Bureau of Economic Research, 1951.

Hidy, Ralph W., Hill, Frank Ernest, and Nevins, Allan. *Timber and Men, the Weyerhaeuser Story.* New York: Macmillan Co., 1963.

Hunt, Herbert. *Tacoma, Its History and Its Builders.* Vol. 1. Chicago: S. J. Clarke Publishing Co., 1916.

James, Marquis, and James, Bessie R. *Biography of a Bank, the Story of the Bank of America.* New York: Harper & Bros., 1954.

Knight, Neil Roy. *Gold Horizon.* Seattle: Frank McCaffrey, Dogwood Press, 1937.

Knight, Neil Roy. History of Banking in Washington; 2 vols. 1935. Unpublished doctoral thesis, University of Washington Library, Seattle, 1935.

Polk, R. L., & Co. *Seattle Directory,* Seattle, 1889 ff.

Preston, Howard H. *Trust Banking in Washington.* Seattle: University of Washington Press, 1953.

Price, John E., & Co., Seattle. Comparative Statement of the Banks of Seattle, 1903–1941. (Issued as leaflet after each bank call; bound volume at Seattle Public Library.)

Prosch, Thomas W. *A Chronological History of Seattle, from 1850 to 1897.* Prepared in 1900 and 1901; typed by W.P.A. Typing Project and donated to Seattle Public Library. No date.

Prosser, W. F. *History of the Puget Sound Country.* 2 vols. New York: Lewis Historical Publishing Co., 1903.

Ruffner, W. H. *A Report on the Washington Territory.* New York: Seattle, Lake Shore and Eastern Railway, 1889.

Spencer, Lloyd, and Pollard, Lancaster. *History of the State of Washington.* 4 vols. New York: American Historical Society, 1937.

Stewart, Edgar I. *Washington, Northwest Frontier.* 4 vols. New York: Lewis Historical Publishing Co., 1957.

Government Documents

Federal Reserve Bank of San Francisco. *The Aluminum Industry,* 1958.

U.S. Comptroller of the Currency. *Annual Reports,* 1890–98; 1929–34.

U.S. Department of Agriculture. Miscl. Pub. No. 669, *Lumber Production in the U.S., 1799–1946.*

U.S. Department of Commerce, Bureau of the Census. *Statistical Abtract,* 1910 ff. Also, *Historical Statistics, Colonial Times to 1957,* Series X97–118.

U.S. Department of Commerce, Bureau of Corporations. *Special Report on Present and Past Conditions in the Lumber and Shingle Industry in the State of Washington.* 1914.

U.S. Forest Service. Forest Survey Report No. 101, *Production of Logs in Oregon and Washington, 1925–48.*

U.S. Forest Service. Pacific Northwest Forest and Range Experiment Station, quarterly report: *Production, Prices, Employment and Trade in Pacific Northwest Forest Industries,* 1963 ff.

U.S. Treasury Department. *Report of the Internal Commerce of the United States for the year 1890.*

Washington State Department of Agriculture. *Prices Received by Washington Farmers, 1910–59,* Seattle, 1960.

Washington State Emergency Relief Administration. *Occupational Characteristics of Unemployed Persons.* Olympia, 1935.

Washington State Department of Agriculture and Statistical Reporting Service of U.S. Department of Agriculture. *Annual Crop Report,* 1947 ff.

Washington State Employment Security Department. *Employment and Payrolls in Washington State, 1938–42,* issued 1944, and subsequent annual summaries.

Washington State Supervisor of Banking. *Annual reports, 1929–35.*

INDEX